Student Study Guide

Steven Chermak

Criminal Justice
A Brief Introduction
7th Edition

Frank Schmalleger

Professor Emeritus
The University of North Carolina at Pembroke

PEARSON

Prentice
Hall

Upper Saddle River, New Jersey 07458

Executive Editor: Tim Peyton
Associate Editor: Sarah Holle
Marketing Manager: Adam Kloza
Managing Editor: Mary Carnis
Production Liaison: Barbara Marttine Cappuccio
Production Editor: Janet Bolton
Manufacturing Manager: Ilene Sanford
Manufacturing Buyer: Cathleen Petersen
Cover Image: Alan Schein, Photography/Corbis
Composition: Janet Bolton
Electronic Art: Carlisle Communications, Inc.
Printing and Binding: Bind-Rite Graphics
Proofreader: Maine Proofreading Services

Pearson Prentice Hall™ is a trademark of Pearson Education, Inc.
Pearson® is a registered trademark of Pearson plc
Prentice Hall® is a registered trademark of Pearson Education, Inc.

Pearson Education LTD.
Pearson Education Australia PTY, Limited
Pearson Education Singapore, Pte. Ltd.
Pearson Education North Asia Ltd.
Pearson Education Canada, Ltd.
Pearson Educacion de Mexico, S.A. de C.V.
Pearson Education—Japan
Pearson Education Malaysia, Pte. Ltd.
Pearson Education, Upper Saddle River, New Jersey

10 9 8 7 6 5 4 3 2
ISBN 0-13-225379-8

Contents

A Letter to Students

Dear Criminal Justice Student:

I hope you will take a few minutes to read this letter since it may be my only chance, as the author of your textbook, *Criminal Justice: A Brief Introduction*, to tell you the best way to use my book and the *Student Study Guide* that accompanies it. I'd also like to tell you why it's important to be successful in your introductory course.

When I wrote *Criminal Justice: A Brief Introduction*, I hoped to create a textbook that would accomplish the following goals:

1. Introduce beginning criminal justice students and others interested in the field to the basic concepts and terminology they would need to intelligently analyze the process of American criminal justice as it unfolds daily on street corners, in courtrooms, and in correctional settings across the country
2. Be the most current source to prepare students to work in the criminal justice system of the twenty-first century
3. Provide a realistic conceptual framework that students could feel comfortable adopting and that would guide their thinking about the American criminal justice system of today and of the future

There is, however, a "higher purpose" in studying criminal justice—and it has to do with why you should be especially attentive to your instructor, your textbook, this study guide, and the study of the subject matter of this course. Think of your course as a study in justice, and view your professor as a guide to justice issues in the modern world. Use your textbook, in combination with this study guide, other course materials, and the lectures your instructor provides, as a tool to evaluate the American criminal justice system relative to your understanding of fairness and right and wrong. If you do that, you will achieve the highest purpose I had in mind when I wrote *Criminal Justice: A Brief Introduction*: You will be firmer in your understanding of the fact that "Injustice anywhere is a threat to justice everywhere," and you will be a better citizen as a result.

To get the most out of *Criminal Justice: A Brief Introduction*, I urge you to give serious attention to the theme of my book (which is discussed in the first chapter). Use the theme as a tool for analyzing the concepts and ideas you encounter in the chapters that follow. Pay special attention to the lofty ideal of social justice that is discussed in Chapter 1, and think seriously about what *justice* means to you in specific situations in everyday life. Ask yourself, as you read the textbook, whether justice is being done in the day-to-day practice of American criminal justice—and if it is not, how the criminal justice system can be improved.

If you have suggestions about improving *Criminal Justice: A Brief Introduction* or any of our supplements, please don't hesitate to contact me. Likewise, if there are features you would like to see added to the next edition, I'd be happy to hear directly from you. Please write to me at:

The Justice Research Association
132 Lake Shore Drive, No. 317
North Palm Beach, FL 33408
e-mail: schmalleger@gmail.com

As you set out to study the American criminal justice system, my thoughts and best wishes for success go with you. Enjoy your course!

Sincerely,

Frank Schmalleger, Ph.D.
Professor Emeritus, The University of North Carolina at Pembroke

Introduction

This short introduction to the *Student Study Guide* discusses two important issues. First, I briefly provide some thoughts on why the study of criminal justice is important. Second, I share with you some basic tips on how to study.

Why Should You Study Criminal Justice?

I'm currently working on a research project with a colleague at Indiana University. We are members of a group called the Indianapolis Violence Reduction Partnership. Since 1997, individuals from local, state, and federal law enforcement agencies, local prosecutors, a U.S. attorney, and individuals working in the corrections field have been meeting biweekly to identify the causes of violent crime in Indianapolis, suggest solutions to respond to violent crime, and then implement these solutions. My role in the project is to bring a relevant theoretical and research understanding to the project. In addition, I have the opportunity to evaluate what works and what doesn't work in criminal justice. This project relates well to what you will be studying in this class. We have tried to develop better measurements to identify the crime picture, have implemented law enforcement strategies, have worked with court officials to change the way cases are processed, and have attempted to involve correctional agencies in the response to violence.

In addition, this project helps me show why the study of criminal justice is such an important topic. First, the study of criminal justice is important because crime and society's response to crime are among the greatest challenges facing every country. In Indianapolis, the Violence Reduction Partnership started meeting because we are concerned about the number of homicides. The homicide rate was increasing dramatically, and criminal justice practitioners believed that extraordinary steps had to be taken in order to respond to the problem. Indianapolis is like every other city in the United States—despite the good news that has been displayed prominently in the news media that crime and violent crime are going down, crime is still a major public concern. What can we do to reduce crime? How can we respond to violent crime? How can we eliminate gang and drug activities? In cities and towns, in suburban and rural areas, crime is a significant social problem, and the primary institution responsible for responding to it is the criminal justice system.

The second reason why criminal justice is such an interesting topic is that the successes and failures of the system affect everybody. The amount of crime and violence in a community affects its quality of life. For example, an incredible number of financial and personnel resources are expended to respond to crime. The components of the criminal justice system are primarily public-funded institutions. When money has to be spent on additional criminal justice resources to respond to crime, there is less money for other government and community programs. In addition, the existence of crime and feelings of insecurity melt the bonds that we have with other people in the community. When people don't feel safe, they prefer not to go out at night or to mingle with others in the community. They are less likely to trust and help each other. If the criminal justice system can respond more effectively to crime, it can strengthen community bonds.

Third, criminal justice is an exciting topic because you already know a great deal about it. You have probably had positive and negative experiences with the criminal justice system. Perhaps you have gotten a ticket or have been arrested for other reasons. It is also likely that you have asked for police assistance. One of the best three-digit numbers known to the public is 9-1-1. This is because people know that when they need assistance, this number is probably the best one to call to get a fast response. In addition, one of the things you will realize as you read the text-book is that you have already heard about many of the cases discussed. The Scott Peterson murder case, the Martha Stewart trial, and the September 11, 2001, terror-ist attacks (among many, many others) are discussed to illustrate specific criminal justice points. Moreover, you already have opinions about many of the topics dis-cussed: Should we have a death penalty? Should we build more prisons? Should we have long sentences for drug offenses? Should we loosen the procedural constraints on police when they are gathering evidence? You will be able to use your knowledge and opinions to react to the criminal justice issues presented and explored in the textbook.

How Can You Best Study?

Each chapter of the *Student Study Guide* includes two learning tips. The topics include taking tests, reading with comprehension, taking notes, utilizing study habits, and using strategies for active learning. Each tip is a short description of sim-ple steps you can take to improve your performance. It would be beneficial if you perused these tips frequently and used them as foundations to learning. In addition, the rest of this introductory section describes five general study strategies you can rely on for success in college:

    I. Effective Time Management
   II. Focused In-Class Performance
 III. Reading to Learn
 IV. Effective Test Preparation
   V. Use of University Resources

I. Effective Time Management

Most research on learning indicates that undergraduate students should spend 3 hours outside of class studying for every 1 hour in class. This means that if you are currently enrolled for 15 hours of course credit, you can expect to spend 45 hours outside of class completing the required coursework! I think you will appreciate the need for effective time management even more when you consider the outside activ-ities you participate in, the number of hours you work, and the other opportunities you have to enjoy your college experience. Don't worry; it is possible to balance study obligations with the activities that pull you away from studying. The key to finding this balance is effective time management. Here are four suggestions you can use to achieve study goals and to make good use of your time:

1. *Set long-term and short-term priorities.* Buy a calendar, if you haven't already, and put it in a prominent place in your room. Mark the dates of all tests, projects, or assignments due. Also, set priorities every day. Make a list of what you need to accomplish, and stick to it.
2. *Establish a daily routine.* It is important that you study every day. Pick a time when you are rested, energized, and focused, and make good use of it. Find a location that is quiet where you can work without interruptions.
3. *Plan well and be realistic.* If you work a lot of hours or if you have other obligations, then you may want to reduce the number of courses you enroll in. Also, rely on the "student grapevine" to discover information on the amount of work required for certain classes and specific professors. Take a few "easy" classes with a few "hard" classes.
4. *Review frequently.* Review your notes immediately after class or as soon after as possible. Review them again right before the next class session. These short (10- to 15-minute) sessions save a lot of time in the long run.

II. Focused In-Class Performance

It is very important that you attend class and concentrate while there. Do not fall into the trap of relying on a friend's set of notes. Even if your professor gives you the notes for the class, attend class and personalize them. Here are three more suggestions that will help:

1. *Learn to concentrate.* Try not to get distracted in class; stay focused on the materials being presented. Let me share an anecdote with you. I once had a student visit during my office hours very upset because she had received low C's on the first two tests. What was upsetting her was that she said she studied a lot, attended class, and did the reading. I asked to see her notes. She had gotten some of the main points from the lectures, but she also had multiple doodles on every page. Although her artwork was outstanding, I suggested that she needed to stop daydreaming and focus on the lecture materials. I asked her to sit in the front of the class, and I looked over her notes after every lecture for a couple of weeks. This simple solution resulted in a significant improvement in her performance.

2. *Be prepared for lecture.* Be physically and mentally alert when attending the lectures, and try not to be fatigued, hungry, or distracted. Complete the reading assignment before attending class; this will help you to identify important points made in the lectures. Review your notes from the prior class as a warm-up to the materials about to be presented.

3. *Take good notes.* Pay close attention to the professor's teaching style to identify how he or she highlights key points. Listen carefully and then select the key points of the lecture. Make sure your notes are well organized, and be sure to leave enough space to add information or study hints.

III. Reading to Learn

One of the best learning resources you have at your disposal is the textbook. It is nearly impossible for a professor to cover every important piece of information in the textbook. Professors pick and choose points of emphasis and expect students to take complete advantage of all of the information in the textbook. The following suggestions may help you do so:

1. *Overview and preview.* Spend some time looking over the materials contained in the entire textbook, and read the table of contents. Then preview each chapter prior to reading it. Also before reading each chapter, skim it; read sections, preview the headings and subheadings, and peruse the tables and graphs. Then read the introduction and summary before actually reading the chapter. This overview and preview will give you some perspective on the information in the book and the way it is organized.

2. *Select the main points.* One of the most difficult skills to develop is how to identify and highlight the most important information in a chapter. Try to prioritize the information in a section, and break it down into main points and supporting points. Underlining or highlighting the main points will help you remember them. Be an active reader; try to be engaged in the reading material by reacting to it and mentally challenging what was written. This will help streamline the material into your long-term memory.

3. *Use the* Student Study Guide. The *Student Study Guide* is a good reference that provides you with many opportunities to test whether you have really comprehended the material. The SSG is designed to help you learn terms, cases, and ideas presented in the textbook. In addition, it puts the issues discussed in the textbook in a broader perspective, allowing you to understand the application of these ideas to practical criminal justice situations.

The chapters of the study guide correspond directly with the chapters of the textbook, and each section of the SSG will help you learn the information presented in the textbook. For example, it might be helpful if you read the learning objectives and chapter summary in the SSG before reading the chapter in the textbook and then read them again after finishing the chapter. These two sections provide an overview of the key issues to be looking for when reading the textbook and to be reviewing when studying for exams. The SSG also has a section on key terms and key cases, giving you quick access to many of the main ideas of a chapter. The crossword puzzles and word search puzzles at the end of each chapter will test your understanding of the key terms and key cases. The SSG also includes a chapter outline and space for you to take notes on the readings or lectures. Try to answer the practice test questions without looking in the book. Remember that the textbook will be closed when you are taking an actual examination. Finally, when you complete the student activities and the additional practice questions, be sure to refer to issues that are addressed in the textbook.

IV. Effective Test Preparation

Taking tests is among the most stressful of all college activities. It is important that you recognize that the sources of test anxiety include society's heavy emphasis on grades, personal time pressures, and the mystery of not knowing how well you are going to do. The following three strategies can reduce this anxiety:

1. *Prepare*. Taking good notes, reading to learn the textbook, and staying on schedule are the first ingredients for test success. In addition, try to find out as much as possible about the test before taking it; read the syllabus closely for clues. Attend review sessions, if possible, but don't expect to be told what the questions are going to be. Use review sessions as opportunities to ask questions and to test how well you are prepared for the examination. You should always attend the class immediately prior to the examination date. Often there are opportunities to ask questions about the examination, and a professor might make slight adjustments on what will be covered because of lack of time. Going to review sessions, talking to former students, and attending the class right before the exam will help you predict what will be on the examination.

2. *Don't panic*. Patience is always a virtue, especially when you are taking an examination. Before you write anything, think about the question and think about the answers. When you are not sure which is the correct answer, eliminate as many answers as possible before you guess. Make sure to pace yourself so that you have enough time both to answer all the questions and to review the questions.

3. *Use study strategies that fit the instructor and the type of examination*. Multiple-choice, short-answer, and essay examinations are significantly different. Each type of examination tests your understanding and comprehension of the material but in slightly different ways. Multiple-choice and short-answer questions require considerably more memorization and identification of specific terms, cases, and key names. Essay questions require a large amount of information and facts as well as a more global understanding of the subject.

It is also important that you realize that all professors are slightly different in their expectations about what should be known. Try to learn as much as possible about a professor before taking an examination he or she prepared. If you are having difficulties finding out any information, it is best to be overprepared for the first examination. You can alter your study strategies as you learn more about his or her testing style. The best way to adapt your test preparation to match a professor's test style is to do a self-evaluation after each examination. Identify the questions that you answered incorrectly. Did most of your incorrect answers come on questions that were covered in lecture? In certain sections of the textbook? Or about specific terms or cases? Once you have completed this self-evaluation, you will be able to change your study strategies to improve your test performance.

V. Use of University Resources

Universities have an incredible number of resources that can enhance your class-room performance. For example, your university may have a writing center staffed by individuals trained to help with all stages of the writing process. Your library also has many resources and has many individuals willing and eager to help you succeed in college. Make an effort to learn about the resources as soon as possible, and then put them to use. Go back through orientation materials or surf your university's website for information, and note the services that might help you.

Your course instructor is also a valuable resource. Obviously he or she is the best person to provide you with assistance with your performance in his or her class. Don't be afraid to go to office hours or to schedule an appointment for assistance if you are having problems. Over time you can build a good relationship with an instructor and then rely on that person for information about potential majors, internship possibilities, and career opportunities.

1   What Is Criminal Justice?

Chapter Outline

- Introduction
- A Brief History of Crime in America
- The Theme of This Book
- American Criminal Justice: System and Functions

- American Criminal Justice: The Process
- Due Process and Individual Rights
- The Role of Research in Criminal Justice
- Multiculturalism and Diversity in Criminal Justice

Learning Objectives

After reading this chapter, you should be able to

- Identify the theme upon which this textbook builds.
- Highlight the differences between the individual-rights and public-order perspectives.
- Explain society's need for a system of order maintenance, and detail the role of law within that system.
- Describe the personal sacrifices necessitated by public order.
- Expound upon the relationship of criminal justice to social justice and other wider notions of equity and fairness.
- Explain the structure of the criminal justice system in terms of its major components.

- Describe the differences between the consensus and conflict models of the criminal justice system.
- Describe the process of American criminal justice, including the stages of criminal case processing.
- Explain the meaning of due process of law, and identify where due process guarantees can be found in the American legal system.
- Explain how multiculturalism and diversity present special challenges to, and opportunities for, the American system of criminal justice.

Chapter Summary

Chapter 1 begins with a brief history of crime in America. The civil rights movements of the 1960s and 1970s emphasized a new era for respect of individual rights. However, as crime rates increased dramatically through the 1970s and into the 1980s, the American public became fed up with crime and demanded tougher treatment of criminals. Thus, the theme of the book, individual rights versus public order, provides a framework for thinking about difficult criminal justice issues. This framework involves balancing the concern for individual rights (i.e., the right of individuals to be protected from overzealous and intrusive government actions) with the need for public order (i.e., the right of citizens to feel secure from criminal threats). Individual rights and community interests are a delicate balancing act for our **criminal justice system** to perform. This chapter discusses a series of high-profile cases, such as the Rodney King beating in Los Angeles; the fiery deaths of David Koresh and his followers in Waco, Texas; and the destruction of the World Trade Center in New York. Additionally, the **USA PATRIOT Act** is discussed as a new tool in combating terrorism. How can the criminal justice system be fair when dealing with such complex situations? Can the system be fair to the individual while ensuring public safety? Everyone—including victims, defendants, police officers, prosecutors, judges, correctional officers, and politicians—attempts to balance individual and community interests, which affects how justice is applied. Individuals who prefer to protect freedoms and liberties are called **individual-rights advocates**; individuals who believe that the interests of society should take precedence over liberties are called **public-order advocates**. Special concern is directed toward the concepts of **justice** and the wider form of equity called **social justice**.

The chapter also discusses how the criminal justice system subcomponents (i.e., police, criminal courts, and correctional agencies) function as a system. Supporters of a **consensus model** of justice believe there is a stable system, with a high level of cooperation among agencies in the system. The opposing view, known as the **conflict model**, sees these components as self-serving, with fragmented cooperation. Supporters of this model argue that the goals of criminal justice agencies and the individuals working within them differ and that the system's processes are additionally affected by outside influences such as political pressure, media coverage of high-profile cases, and discretion. Both models have some value in helping us understand the complexities facing the operations of the criminal justice system.

The author introduces the chronological stages for processing a criminal case, starting with the investigation and arrest. In some cases, the process starts with an arrest based on a **warrant**. During the arrest process, the suspect goes through **booking**. The court process begins when this suspect appears before a judge at the first appearance. Here the judge advises of the charges, sets **bail**, and might appoint counsel. A **grand jury** or **preliminary hearing** will then be conducted to determine whether the criminal justice process should continue. An **information** can result from a preliminary hearing, and an **indictment** can result from a grand jury hearing. The suspect then will be arraigned on the charges. A trial will be held, and if the person is found (or pleads) guilty, then sentencing occurs. Some defendants are ordered to prison, while others might receive probation.

Later in the chapter, the emergence of research in criminal justice is discussed as an outgrowth of **criminology**. This chapter concludes with a brief discussion of how **multiculturalism** and diversity present special challenges for the criminal justice system.

Key Concepts

Administration of Justice   The performance of any of the following activities: detection, apprehension, detention, pretrial release, post-trial release, prosecution, adjudication, correctional supervision, or rehabilitation of accused persons or criminal offenders.

Arraignment   Strictly, the hearing before a court having jurisdiction in a criminal case in which the identity of the defendant is established, the defendant is informed of the charge and of his or her rights, and the defendant is required to enter a plea. Also, in some usages, any appearance in criminal court prior to trial.

Bail   The money or property pledged to the court or actually deposited with the court to effect the release of a person from legal custody.

Booking   A law enforcement or correctional administrative process officially recording an entry into detention after arrest and identifying the person, the place, the time, the reason for the arrest, and the arresting authority.

Civil Justice   The civil law, the law of civil procedure, and the array of procedures and activities having to do with private rights and remedies sought by civil action. Civil justice cannot be separated from social justice because the kind of justice enacted in our nation's civil courts is a reflection of basic American understandings of right and wrong.

Concurrent Sentence   One of two or more sentences imposed at the same time, after conviction for more than one offense, and served at the same time. Also, a new sentence for a new conviction, imposed upon a person already under sentence for a previous offense, served at the same time as the previous sentence.

Conflict Model   A criminal justice perspective that assumes that the system's components function primarily to serve their own interests. According to this theoretical framework, justice is more a product of conflicts among agencies within the system than it is the result of cooperation among component agencies.

Consecutive Sentence   One of two or more sentences imposed at the same time, after conviction for more than one offense, and served in sequence with the other sentence. Also, a new sentence for a new conviction, imposed upon a person already under sentence for a previous offense, which is added to the previous sentence, thus increasing the maximum time the offender may be confined or under supervision.

Consensus Model   A criminal justice perspective that assumes that the system's components work together harmoniously to achieve the social product we call *justice*.

Crime   Conduct in violation of the criminal laws of a state, the federal government, or a local jurisdiction, for which there is no legally acceptable justification or excuse.

Crime-Control Model   A criminal justice perspective that emphasizes the efficient arrest and conviction of criminal offenders.

Criminal Justice   In the strictest sense, the criminal (penal) law, the law of criminal procedure, and the array of procedures and activities having to do with the enforcement of this body of law. Criminal justice cannot be separated from social justice because the kind of justice enacted in our nation's criminal courts is a reflection of basic American understandings of right and wrong.

Criminal Justice System   The aggregate of all operating and administrative or technical support agencies that perform criminal justice functions. The basic divisions of the operational aspects of criminal justice are law enforcement, courts, and corrections.

Criminology   The scientific study of the causes and prevention of crime and the rehabilitation and punishment of offenders.

Due Process   A right guaranteed by the Fifth, Sixth, and Fourteenth Amendments of the U.S. Constitution and generally understood, in legal contexts, to mean the due course of legal proceedings according to the rules and forms established for the protection of individual rights. In criminal proceedings, due process of law is generally understood to include the following basic elements: a law creating and defining the offense, an impartial tribunal having jurisdictional authority over the case, accusation in proper form, notice and opportunity to defend, trial according to established procedure, and discharge from all restraints or obligations unless convicted.

Due Process Model A criminal justice perspective that emphasizes individual rights at all stages of justice system processing.

Grand Jury A group of jurors who have been selected according to law and have been sworn to hear the evidence and to determine whether there is sufficient evidence to bring the accused person to trial, to investigate criminal activity generally, or to investigate the conduct of a public agency or official.

Indictment A formal, written accusation submitted to the court by a grand jury, alleging that a specified person has committed a specified offense, usually a felony.

Individual Rights The rights guaranteed to all members of American society by the U.S. Constitution (especially those found in the first ten amendments to the Constitution, known as the *Bill of Rights*). These rights are particularly important to criminal defendants facing formal processing by the criminal justice system.

Individual-Rights Advocate One who seeks to protect personal freedoms within the process of criminal justice.

Information A formal, written accusation submitted to a court by a prosecutor, alleging that a specified person has committed a specified offense.

Justice The principle of fairness; the ideal of moral equity.

Multiculturalism The existence within one society of diverse groups that maintain unique cultural identities while frequently accepting and participating in the larger society's legal and political system. *Multiculturalism* is usually used in conjunction with the term *diversity* to identify many distinctions of social significance. *Adapted from:* Robert M. Shusta et al., *Multicultural Law Enforcement*, 2d ed. (Upper Saddle River, NJ: Prentice Hall, 2002), p. 443.

Preliminary Hearing A proceeding before a judicial officer in which three matters must be decided: (1) whether a crime was committed, (2) whether the crime occurred within the territorial jurisdiction of the court, and (3) whether there are reasonable grounds to believe that the defendant committed the crime.

Probable Cause A set of facts and circumstances that would induce a reasonably intelligent and prudent person to believe that a particular other person has committed a specific crime. Also, reasonable grounds to make or believe an accusation. Probable cause refers to the necessary level of belief that would allow for police seizures (arrests) of individuals and full searches of dwellings, vehicles, and possessions.

Public-Order Advocate One who believes that under certain circumstances involving a criminal threat to public safety, the interests of society should take precedence over individual rights.

Social Control The use of sanctions and rewards within a group to influence and shape the behavior of individual members of that group. Social control is a primary concern of social groups and communities, and it is their interest in the exercise of social control that leads to the creation of both criminal and civil statutes.

Social Justice An ideal that embraces all aspects of civilized life and that is linked to fundamental notions of fairness and to cultural beliefs about right and wrong.

Trial In criminal proceedings, the examination in court of the issues of fact and relevant law in a case for the purpose of convicting or acquitting the defendant.

USA PATRIOT Act A federal law (Public Law 107-56) enacted in response to terrorist attacks on the World Trade Center and the Pentagon on September 11, 2001. The law, officially titled The Uniting and Strengthening America by Providing Appropriate Tools Required to Intercept and Obstruct Terrorism Acts, substantially broadened the investigative authority of law enforcement agencies throughout America and is applicable to many crimes other than terrorism.

Warrant In criminal proceedings, a writ issued by a judicial officer directing a law enforcement officer to perform a specified act and affording the officer protection from damages if he or she performs it.

Learning Tips

Taking Notes

Each chapter of this study guide includes a Chapter Outline. Enter appropriate comments from your instructor's lecture related to specific topics in the chapter. This feature will help you organize your notes for easy review and study.

The Syllabus

Students tend to look at a course's syllabus once or twice at the beginning of the semester and then disregard it. Try to use the syllabus as a guide to organizing your semester, preparing for each class, and gaining insight into what the instructor considers important in the class. Many instructors include a brief overview of the course that could provide the key for essay or short-answer questions, including definitions, later in the semester.

CJ Brief on the World Wide Web

A wealth of study help is available at your fingertips. Go online to cjbrief.com to access the dynamic CJ Brief website. You'll find links to study aids tailored to each chapter in the text, Web Extras and Library Extras, crime and justice news, and the Prentice Hall Criminal Justice Cybrary. In addition, there is a career center and message boards to discuss criminal justice issues with other students. Give it a try—go to the URL above to enter the home page for *Criminal Justice: A Brief Introduction*.

Other Web links to organizations and agencies related to the material in Chapter 1 include:

WEBSITE	URL
American Civil Liberties Union	http://www.aclu.org
Bureau of Justice Statistics	http://www.ojp.usdoj.gov/bjs
FBI's Counterterrorism Page	http://www.fbi.gov/aboutus /transformation/ct.htm
Justice for All	http://www.jfa.net
National Center for Victims of Crime	http://www.ncvc.org
National Criminal Justice Reference Service	http://www.ncjrs.org
National Memorial Institute for the Prevention of Terrorism	http://www.mipt.org
Office for Victims of Crime (OVC)	http://www.ojp.usdoj.gov/ovc
Preventing Crime: "What Works, What Doesn't"	http://cjcentral.com/sherman /sherman.htm
Terrorism Files	http://www.terrorismfiles.org
U.S. Department of Justice	http://www.usdoj.gov

Learner Activities

Activity 1

One of the most important issues faced by the criminal justice system is how best to respond to terrorism. Since the attacks of September 11, 2001, the public believes that terrorism is a significant threat in the United States. What do you think? Answer questions in the space provided below. You may want to look at the following websites for background information: The Prentice Hall Criminal Justice Cybrary at http://www.cybrary.info has an extensive collection of articles posted on terrorism; the National Criminal Justice Reference Service, at http://www.ncjrs.org, has information on terrorism; and the National Institute for the Prevention of Terrorism at http://www.mibt.org has data on terrorism.

1. Is terrorism a serious problem in this country? Why or why not?
2. What ten things can the criminal justice system do to respond to terrorism?
3. Of the ten items you cited, which one do you think might be most effective? Why?
4. Why is it so difficult to respond to terrorism?

_____

_____

_____

_____

_____

_____

Activity 2

How does the book define *justice*? Consider the facts of the following case:

Dale and Mike Parak were twin brothers and best friends. They spent their entire lives looking out for each other's interests. When growing up, the two were inseparable. They played sports together, double-dated frequently, and attended the same university. They grew closer as they aged, they got married at about the same time, and eventually both were divorced. After they retired from their jobs, they decided to live together to save money and because they still enjoyed each other's company.

When he was 70 years old, Mike was diagnosed with cancer. Doctors predicted that he had about six months to live. The brothers, however, agreed that Mike should not suffer. Mike and Dale wrote and signed a note stating that they decided to commit suicide. Dale broke 20 tranquilizers into Mike's evening meal and watched as he ate it. Yet when Dale checked on Mike one hour later, Mike was still alive. Dale panicked. He took a .38-caliber revolver from his desk and shot Mike, killing him instantly. Dale then went into the kitchen and took a handful of tranquilizers. He did not die. He awoke the next morning as somebody pounded on the front door. It was a neighbor who, seeing that Dale was dazed and confused, decided to call an ambulance and the police.

The responding police officer conducted an investigation, and Dale was arrested and charged with the murder of his brother, Mike. The prosecutor, although noting it to be a difficult case, pursued the case because she thought no citizen had the right to decide when someone should die. Dale Parak pled guilty to first-degree manslaughter and was sentenced to five years in a maximum-security prison. (Note that this was the lowest sentence that could be given to a defendant convicted of his crime.)

1. According to the definition of justice, was this sentence just? Why or why not?
2. If you were the prosecutor in this case, would you have charged Dale Parak? Why or why not?
3. If you were the judge in this case, how would you have sentenced Dale Parak? Why?
4. What would be an appropriate punishment in this case? Why?

_____

_____

_____

_____

_____

_____

Activity 3

An effective way for you to understand the conflict of goals that is characteristic of the different criminal justice components is to talk to criminal justice professionals about their priorities and expectations. This assignment requires you to interview at least one representative of law enforcement, one of the court, and one of a correctional agency. For example, you could interview a police officer, a prosecuting attorney, and a correctional officer. Or you could interview a sheriff's deputy, a judge, and a probation officer. Any combination of representatives would be fine. Prepare questions in advance to find out about the background characteristics of these individuals, why they chose their careers, and the types of activities they do in a typical day. Finally, ask them about the organization's goals. For example, you could ask: What would you say are the five most important goals of this organization?

When you complete your interviews, discuss what you discovered in the space below. Did the three people you interviewed have the same goals? If so, were these goals prioritized in the same manner?

_____

_____

_____

_____

_____

_____

Activity 4

Crime and justice are subjects that are frequently presented on television. Prime-time television shows, soap operas, music videos, and cartoons often portray images of crime and criminal justice.

In the space below, list at least three television shows that you have seen that depict the police, courts, and correctional components of the criminal justice system (three television shows for each component) and then answer the following questions. How do these shows present each component? Are the images positive or negative? What stages of the process are depicted? Do you think these images are fair representations of criminal justice? Why or why not?

_____

_____

_____

_____

_____

_____

Internet Activity

Visit Prentice Hall's Criminal Justice Cybrary at http://www.cybrary.info. Choose a topic that is relevant to the material provided in Chapter 1. Describe the types of resources available on that topic.

_____

_____

_____

_____

_____

_____

Distance Learning Activity

Visit the World Wide Web or Prentice Hall's Criminal Justice Cybrary at http://www.cybrary.info to collect information on the criminal justice system's response to terrorism after the World Trade Center and Pentagon attacks. Find at least one article that highlights individual-rights concerns and one that highlights public-order concerns. After you have completed the assignment, participate in a class discussion to compare and contrast the findings from the different essays if your instructor asks you to do so.

_____

_____

_____

_____

_____

_____

Student Study Guide Questions

True or False

_____ 1-1. A preliminary hearing involves a group of jurors selected from the community.

_____ 1-2. Expanding the rights of defendants to protect them from injustice would be most closely associated with a crime-control model of criminal justice.

_____ 1-3. The *Miranda* decision requires that during arrest and before questioning, police personnel advise a person of his or her rights at the time of the arrest.

_____ 1-4. Parole differs from probation in that paroled offenders serve a portion of their prison sentences before being released.

_____ 1-5. The reduction of crime is the ultimate goal of criminal justice.

_____ 1-6. The consensus model of the study of criminal justice assumes that the system's subcomponents function primarily to serve their own interests.

_____ 1-7. Bail is a mechanism that defendants use to avoid advancing to the later stages of the criminal justice process.

_____ 1-8. Indictments are filed on the basis of the outcome of a preliminary hearing.

_____ 1-9. A concurrent sentence is a sentence that requires an offender who has been found guilty of more than one charge to serve one sentence after another is completed.

_____ 1-10. Criminology is the application of scientific techniques to the investigation of a crime.

Multiple Choice

1-11. What decision(s) is (are) made at a suspect's arraignment?
    a. The suspect is required to enter a plea.
    b. The suspect is informed of the charges against him or her.
    c. The suspect is informed of his or her rights.
    d. All of the above are decisions made at arraignment.

1-12. Which of the following models assumes a systems model of criminal justice?
    a. due process model
    b. individual-rights model
    c. conflict model
    d. consensus model

1-13. Who would suggest that under certain circumstances involving criminal threats to public safety, the interests of society should take precedence over individual rights?
    a. a crime-control advocate
    b. a justice-ideal advocate
    c. an individual-rights advocate
    d. a public-order advocate

1-14. Who would support the full protection of personal freedoms and civil rights within the criminal justice process?
   a. a crime-control advocate
   b. a justice-ideal advocate
   c. an individual-rights advocate
   d. a public-order advocate

1-15. In the criminal justice process, a(n) _____ has to occur before a(n) _____.
   a. arraignment; preliminary hearing
   b. sentencing; trial
   c. arrest; first appearance
   d. booking; arrest

1-16. Upon being convicted of robbery and burglary, Jalen Arow is sentenced to seven years for the robbery and five years for the burglary. The sentence for burglary will be served right after the robbery sentence. This is an example of a(n) _____.
   a. unfair sentence
   b. discriminatory sentence
   c. consecutive sentence
   d. concurrent sentence

1-17. Who is credited with creating the crime-control model of criminal justice?
   a. Earl Warren
   b. Jerome Skolnick
   c. Colin Ferguson
   d. Herbert Packer

1-18. A _____ is a group of jurors selected to hear the evidence and to determine whether there is sufficient evidence to bring the accused person to trial.
   a. jury
   b. public forum
   c. grand jury
   d. preliminary hearing

1-19. The conflict model of criminal justice assumes that
   a. the efforts of the component parts of the system are fragmented, leading to a criminal justice nonsystem.
   b. the movement of cases and people through the system is smooth due to cooperation among components of the system.
   c. all parts of the system work together toward a common goal.
   d. police officers are the dominant actors in the criminal justice system.

1-20. A(n) _____ is a writ issued by a judicial officer directing a law enforcement officer to perform a specified act and affording him or her protection from damages if he or she performs it.
   a. indictment
   b. warrant
   c. pretrial release order
   d. information

Fill-In

1-21. Under certain circumstances involving criminal threats to public safety, a(n) _____ suggests that the interests of society should take precedence over individual rights.

1-22. The _____ is a perspective on the study of criminal justice that assumes that the system's subcomponents work together harmoniously to achieve that social product we call justice.

1-23. The crime-control model was first brought to the attention of the academic community by _____.

1-24. _____ are those who seek to protect personal freedoms within the process of criminal justice.

1-25. Jerome Skolnick's classic study of clearance rates provides support for the idea of a(n) _____.

1-26. _____ is the step of the criminal justice process that occurs immediately after arrest.

1-27. _____ is an ideal that embraces all aspects of civilized life and that is linked to fundamental notions of fairness and to cultural beliefs about right and wrong.

1-28. _____ is a legal criterion residing in a set of facts and circumstances that would cause a reasonable person to believe that another person has committed a specific crime.

1-29. The money or property pledged to the court to effect the release of a person from legal custody is called _____.

1-30. The _____ assumes that the criminal justice system's components function primarily to serve their own interests.

Crossword Puzzle

Across

3. Usually used in conjunction with diversity.
4. Principle of fairness.
5. Scholar responsible for creating the crime-control and due process models.
8. Type of advocate who stresses the interests of society.
9. Federal law enacted in response to the terrorist attacks on the World Trade Center and the Pentagon on September 11, 2001.
11. Also called the preliminary examination.
12. Provides the legal basis for an apprehension by the police.
13. Type of sentence that runs at the same time.
15. Constitutional requirement of fairness and equity.
16. A grand jury returns a(n) _____.

Down

1. Scientific study of the causes and prevention of crime and the rehabilitation and punishment of offenders.
2. Money or property pledged to the court to effect the release of a person from legal custody.
6. When a law enforcement official records an entry into detention after arrest.
7. Type of sentence where offenders are ordered to serve one sentence after another.
10. "The first appearance of the defendant before the court that has the authority to conduct a trial."
14. Model emphasizing a systems perspective.

Word Search Puzzle

```
D Y T C D Y E P N U X L N B D T G E U B G P H J F D F O M J
P Q R W Y X L T A K O T O I L N A E Q O P S A H W E D H Q X
R C I Y O O Y K A E K T Y Q N D W J K O E Z N T P V Y J H M
O R A M R V P S I W O R V M J F X U M K A T T A D D G R Y U
B I L C N A D H T D U G W D E S O S R I P X H L I A G F C L
A M Q P G T Q C Y J E W G A I D T R D N T D W N N J N O O T
B E T F S I U V D H N T C K P D D L M G A T Z D D W D I N I
L C T G W M W N E G T U V V R U T E P A I C U C I O U H S C
E O C H O T A W L M T A J V I Z A P H C T B A M V B L U E U
C N D A W R L I H K S M N T E G C E C W B I S Q I W C C C L
A T U X G Q B M M Z T G A V I J D F G A N C O C D E Q P U T
U R P V C O N S E N S U S M O D E L T I H C H N U D E L T U
S O U C O N C U R R E N T S E N T E N C E J U L A B Z O I R
E L B K C X P T A R R A I G N M E N T S Y O G Q L S A V V A
H M L M Q Z H Y S U P R E L I M I N A R Y H E A R I N G E L
R O I Y J H E U Z L S E F J Z Z F T J C F X X W I J Y B S I
A D C D W U T J F E L A M Z P S M B T R B A V Y G Q D E E S
X E O I R J S O V I S K P R U C Z E J I O N D Y H R A J N M
V L R G W U L T V B U Y E A B L T X G M M L S T T C J Y T S
D Q D L V N V X I U J I T I T G F A F E W N F P S T W X E X
K Q E O Z K Y Z U C U Y J Z J R N D U W R U V F A M T K N F
A Z R W Q V C S X E E J J W F E I X V J U K M S D S T Z C X
G V A H C O N F L I C T M O D E L O X Y X G E G V S Y R E M
J Y D E V R B C R I M I N A L J U S T I C E Y Z O X B Z W V
B E V J H I A K N F V Q H K M J J A M A D E N T C D I P J X
X B O O W Z J R Y I N D I C T M E N T A C K M Z A U H U M D
S S C O I T I F C R I M I N O L O G Y T I T J N T B X M U C
G P A A D T B U F J A H Q S J U Y D C P N Y O W E J W C Y A
G L T Q U K A B J L R X R E I N M D B A I L U N L A U H I P
P R E L T E U T X H R W P L Z B Q C H M K D O A W N V H Y Y
```

Arraignment
Bail
Booking
Concurrent Sentence
Conflict Model
Consecutive Sentence
Consensus Model
Crime
Crime-Control Model
Criminal Justice
Criminology

Grand Jury
Indictment
Individual-Rights Advocate
Information
Justice
Multiculturalism
Preliminary Hearing
Probable Cause
Public-Order Advocate
Trial
USA PATRIOT Act

2 The Crime Picture

Chapter Outline

- Introduction
- The Uniform Crime Reports
- The National Crime Victimization Survey
- Comparisons of the UCR and NCVS
- Special Categories of Crime

Learning Objectives

After reading this chapter, you should be able to

- Name and compare the two major national crime data–gathering programs in the United States today.
- Explain what crime statistics can tell us about crime in America.
- Discuss some of the limitations inherent in statistical reports of crime.
- Describe the FBI's Crime Index, and list the eight major crimes that make up the index.
- Explain why crime statistics are generally expressed as rates instead of simple numerical tabulations.

- Describe the two major categories of Part I offenses in the Uniform Crime Reports.
- Explain the hierarchy rule, and discuss how it affects crime reporting.
- Discuss the meaning of the term *clearance rate*.
- Explain how the National Incident-Based Reporting System operates, and describe how it differs from the traditional Uniform Crime Reporting Program.
- Identify the special categories of crime discussed in this chapter.

Chapter Summary

Justin Stellar was standing at a bus stop when four teenagers approached him and asked for his wallet. Although he said he didn't want any trouble and gave them his wallet without resistance, one of the teenagers hit Justin in the head with a baseball bat. He was knocked unconscious and was rushed to the hospital for his injuries.

How would these crimes be classified by the criminal justice system? Chapter 2 in the text describes various crime classification instruments. For example, if Justin or the hospital reported this incident to the police, it could eventually be part of that department's annual uniform crime statistics submitted to the FBI. Or if Justin's household was one of the households selected for the National Crime Victimization Survey (NCVS), then his victimization could be included as part of these victimization statistics (if he reported it to interviewers). If the teenagers were arrested, a prosecutor might charge the youths with aggravated assault and robbery. If the reported facts were more detailed and included the information that Justin was an African-American male and the teenagers spray painted a racial epithet on his back while he was unconscious, this crime might be classified as a hate crime.

The two primary sources of data used to understand the crime picture in America are official statistics and victimization statistics. The most-cited and well-known official source of data is the **Uniform Crime Reports (UCR)**, compiled annually by the FBI. There are approximately 16,000 police departments throughout the United States that voluntarily submit statistics on crimes reported to them. The FBI compiles these statistics and then reports the figures as either **Part I offenses** or **Part II offenses**.

The best-known source of victimization statistics is the **National Crime Victimization Survey (NCVS)**. This survey asks citizens directly about their victimization experiences, including characteristics of the perpetrator, the crime, and the incident. This survey includes information on six crimes: rape, robbery, assault, burglary, larceny, and motor vehicle theft.

Although both of these sources provide some general understanding of the crime problem, they have limitations. In developing the UCR, the FBI relies on the willingness of police departments to report and assumes that the information is accurately represented. But citizens do not report all crimes because, for a variety of reasons, they do not want to involve the police. Fear of retaliation, embarrassment, and belief that the police cannot do anything about it anyway are cited as reasons for not reporting crimes. These factors reduce the accuracy of UCR data. Victimization statistics might present a more accurate portrait of crimes not reported to the police, but this source of data has other limitations. Respondents, for example, might lie or exaggerate the circumstances of their victimization.

The text also provides general descriptions of the eight index offenses and interesting descriptive information about each offense category. **Murder, forcible rape, aggravated assault, robbery, larceny-theft, burglary, motor vehicle theft**, and **arson** are discussed in detail. Murder, for example, does not occur frequently (compared to the other index offenses), but when murders do take place, the police are able to clear a large percentage of them (approximately 62%). When a murder does occur, young males (18 to 24 years old) are most likely to have committed this type of crime. The Uniform Crime Report is being enhanced by a broader reporting system called the **National Incident-Based Reporting System (NIBRS)**.

This chapter also has a section on women and crime, discussing women as victims. Although women are not as likely as men to be victimized, they are more likely to be injured by crime and to be in fear of crime. When women are victimized by crime, however, they are more likely to be injured compared to men.

The text also introduces other ways of understanding the crime picture. It examines the criminal justice system's interest in **hate crime**, crime against the elderly, **white-collar crime, organized crime**, drug crime, and **computer crime**. It discusses gun violence in the United States, highlighting major pieces of federal legislation enacted to regulate gun ownership.

This chapter also discusses **terrorism** and distinguishes between **domestic and international terrorism**. The basic distinction between the two is that domestic terrorism describes the violence committed by groups operating entirely within the United States, and international terrorism focuses on violence committed by a group or an individual with a connection to a foreign power or whose activities transcend national boundaries. For example, the bombing of the Murrah Building in Oklahoma City by Timothy McVeigh is an example of domestic terrorism, and the September 11, 2001, attacks are an example of international terrorism. **Cyberterrorism**, in contrast, focuses on the use of computers and the Internet to plan and carry out terrorist attacks.

Although statistics are important to a general understanding of crime, their value is tempered by their inability to indicate clearly how crime affects individuals. Was Justin Stellar able to recover from his crimes physically? Psychologically? Emotionally? Was the criminal justice system responsive to his personal needs?

Key Concepts

Aggravated Assault (UCR)   The unlawful intentional inflicting, or attempted or threatened inflicting, of serious injury upon the person of another. While *aggravated assault* and *simple assault* are standard terms for reporting purposes, most state penal codes use labels like *first-degree* and *second-degree* to make such distinctions.

Arson (UCR)   The burning or attempted burning of property, with or without the intent to defraud.

Assault (UCR)   An unlawful attack by one person upon another. Historically, *assault* meant only the attempt to inflict injury on another person; a completed act constituted the separate offense of battery. Under modern statistical usage, however, attempted and completed acts are grouped together under the generic term *assault*.

Bureau of Justice Statistics (BJS)   A U.S. Department of Justice agency responsible for the collection of criminal justice data, including the annual National Crime Victimization Survey.

Burglary (UCR)   The unlawful entry of a structure to commit a felony or a theft (excludes tents, trailers, and other mobile units used for recreational purposes). For the UCR, the crime of burglary can be reported if (1) an unlawful entry of an unlocked structure has occurred, (2) a breaking and entering (of a secured structure) has taken place, or (3) a burglary has been attempted.

Clearance Rate   A traditional measure of investigative effectiveness that compares the number of crimes reported or discovered to the number of crimes solved through arrest or other means (such as the death of the suspect).

Computer Crime   Any crime perpetrated through the use of computer technology. Also, any violation of a federal or state computer-crime statute. Also called *cybercrime*.

Computer Virus   A computer program designed to secretly invade systems and either modify the way in which they operate or alter the information they store. Viruses are destructive software programs that may effectively vandalize computers of all types and sizes.

Corporate Crime   A violation of a criminal statute by a corporate entity or by its executives, employees, or agents acting on behalf of and for the benefit of the corporation, partnership, or other form of business entity. *Source*: Michael L. Benson, Francis T. Cullen, and William J. Maakestad, *Local Prosecutors and Corporate Crime* (Washington, DC: National Institute of Justice, 1992), p. 1.

Crime Index (UCR)   An inclusive measure of the violent and property crime categories, or Part I offenses, of the Uniform Crime Reports. The Crime Index has been a useful tool for geographic (state-to-state) and historical (year-to-year) comparisons because it employs the concept of a crime rate (the number of crimes per unit of population). However, the addition of arson as an eighth index offense and the new requirements with regard to the gathering of hate-crime statistics could result in new Crime Index measurements that provide less-than-ideal comparisons.

Crime Typology   A classification of crimes along a particular dimension, such as legal categories, offender motivations, victim behavior, or the characteristics of individual offenders.

Cyberstalking   The use of the Internet, e-mail, and other electronic communication technologies to stalk another person. *Source*: Violence Against Women Officers, *Stalking and Domestic Violence: Report to Congress* (Washington, DC: U.S. Department of Justice, 2001).

Cyberterrorism   A form of terrorism that makes use of high technology, especially computers and the Internet, in the planning and carrying out of terrorist attacks.

Dark Figure of Crime   Crime that is not reported to the police and that remains unknown to officials.

Date Rape   Unlawful forced sexual intercourse with a female against her will that occurs within the context of a dating relationship. Date rape, or acquaintance rape, is a subcategory of rape that is of special concern today.

Domestic Terrorism   The unlawful use of force or violence by a group or an individual who is based and operates entirely within the United States and its territories without foreign direction and whose acts are directed at elements of the U.S. government or population. *Source*: Adapted from Federal Bureau of Investigation, *FBI Policy and Guidelines: Counterterrorism*. Web posted at http://www.fbi.gov/contact/fo/jackson/cntrterr.htm. Accessed March 4, 2002.

Forcible Rape (UCR)   The carnal knowledge of a female forcibly and against her will. For statistical reporting purposes, the FBI defines *forcible rape* as "unlawful sexual intercourse with a female, by force and against her will, or without legal or factual consent." Statutory rape differs from forcible rape in that it generally involves nonforcible sexual intercourse with a minor.

Hate Crime   A criminal offense in which the motive is hatred, bias, or prejudice based on the actual or perceived race, color, religion, national origin, ethnicity, gender, or sexual orientation of another individual or group of individuals. Also called *bias crime*.

Identity Theft   A crime in which an imposter obtains key pieces of information, such as Social Security and driver's license numbers, to obtain credit, merchandise, and services in the name of the victim. The victim is often left with a ruined credit history and the time-consuming and complicated task of repairing the financial damages. *Source*: Identity Theft Resource Center website at http://www.idtheftcenter.org. Accessed April 4, 2002.

International Terrorism   The unlawful use of force or violence by a group or an individual who has some connection to a foreign power, or whose activities transcend national boundaries, against people or property in order to intimidate or coerce a government, the civilian population, or any segment thereof, in furtherance of political or social objectives. *Source*: Adapted from Federal Bureau of Investigation, *FBI Policy and Guidelines: Counterterrorism*. Web posted at http://www.fbi.gov/contact/fo/jackson/cntrterr.htm. Accessed March 4, 2002.

Larceny-Theft (UCR)   The unlawful taking or attempted taking, carrying, leading, or riding away of property, from the possession or constructive possession of another. Motor vehicles are excluded. Larceny is the most common of the eight major offenses, although probably only a small percentage of all larcenies are actually reported to the police because of the small dollar amounts involved.

Malware   Malicious computer programs such as viruses, worms, and Trojan horses.

Motor Vehicle Theft (UCR)   The theft or attempted theft of a motor vehicle. *Motor vehicle* is defined as a self-propelled road vehicle that runs on land surface and not on rails. The stealing of trains, planes, boats, construction equipment, and most farm machinery is classified as larceny under the UCR Program, not as motor vehicle theft.

Murder   The unlawful killing of a human being. Murder is a generic term that in common usage may include first- and second-degree murder, manslaughter, involuntary manslaughter, and other similar offenses.

National Crime Victimization Survey (NCVS)   An annual survey of selected American households conducted by the Bureau of Justice Statistics to determine the extent of criminal victimization—especially unreported victimization—in the United States.

National Incident-Based Reporting System (NIBRS)   An incident-based reporting system that collects data on every single crime occurrence. NIBRS data will soon supersede the kind of traditional data provided by the FBI's Uniform Crime Reports.

Organized Crime   The unlawful activities of the members of a highly organized, disciplined association engaged in supplying illegal goods and services, including gambling, prostitution, loan-sharking, narcotics, and labor racketeering, and in other unlawful activities. *Source*: The Organized Crime Control Act of 1970.

Part I Offenses   A set of UCR categories used to report murder, rape, robbery, aggravated assault, burglary, larceny, and motor vehicle theft, as defined under the FBI's Uniform Crime Reporting Program. Also called *major crimes*.

Part II Offenses   A set of UCR categories used to report data concerning arrests for less serious offenses.

Property Crime   A UCR offense category that includes burglary, larceny, auto theft, and arson.

Rape   Unlawful sexual intercourse, achieved through force and without consent. Broadly speaking, the term *rape* has been applied to a wide variety of sexual attacks and may include same-sex rape and the rape of a male by a female. Some jurisdictions refer to same-sex rape as *sexual battery*.

Robbery (UCR)   The unlawful taking or attempted taking of property that is in the immediate possession of another by force or violence and/or by putting the victim in fear. Armed robbery differs from unarmed, or strong-arm, robbery with regard to the presence of a weapon. Contrary to popular conceptions, highway robbery does not necessarily occur on a street—and rarely in a vehicle. The term *highway robbery* applies to any form of robbery that occurs outdoors in a public place.

Sexual Battery   Intentional and wrongful physical contact with a person, without his or her consent, that entails a sexual component or purpose.

Software Piracy   The unauthorized duplication of software or the illegal transfer of data from one storage medium to another. Software piracy is one of the most prevalent computer crimes in the world.

Spam   Unsolicited commercial bulk e-mail (UCBE), whose primary purpose is the commercial advertisement or promotion of a commercial product or service.

Stalking   Repeated harassing and threatening behavior by one individual against another, aspects of which may be planned or carried out in secret. Stalking might involve following a person, appearing at a person's home or place of business, making harassing phone calls, leaving written messages or objects, or vandalizing a person's property. Most stalking laws require that the perpetrator make a credible threat of violence against the victim or members of the victim's immediate family.

Terrorism   A violent act or an act dangerous to human life in violation of the criminal laws of the United States or of any state committed to intimidate or coerce a government, the civilian population, or any segment thereof, in furtherance of political or social objectives. *Source*: Federal Bureau of Intelligence, Counterterrorism Section, *Terrorism in the United States, 1987* (Washington, DC: FBI, 1987).

Transnational Organized Crime   Unlawful activity undertaken and supported by organized criminal groups operating across national boundaries.

Uniform Crime Reports (UCR)   An annual FBI publication that summarizes the incidence and rate of reported crimes throughout the United States.

Violent Crime   A UCR offense category that includes murder, rape, robbery, and aggravated assault.

White-Collar Crime   Violations of the criminal law committed by a person of respectability and high social status in the course of his or her occupation. Also, nonviolent crime for financial gain utilizing deception and committed by anyone who has special technical and professional knowledge of business and government, irrespective of the person's occupation.

Learning Tips

Preclass Review

One way to give yourself a head start is to arrive at class early. Review the notes from the preceding class meeting, and review sections that were assigned. This will help you recall the focus of the previous class and get your mind prepared for the present class, and it may point out questions you intend to ask.

Office Hours

Very few students take advantage of posted office hours. As a consequence, very few students develop a relationship with the instructor, and most students are then hard-pressed to find a faculty member to write a recommendation letter or help with career advice as their college years draw to a close. Faculty members enjoy talking to students about specific courses and career opportunities in criminal justice. If you do go to an instructor's office during office hours, make sure you spend some time preparing in advance, creating a few questions on concepts from the class that might be unclear to you or exploring some facet of the class that interests you.

CJ Brief on the World Wide Web

Web links to organizations and agencies related to the material in Chapter 2 include:

WEBSITE	URL
Bureau of Justice Assistance	http://www.ojp.usdoj.gov/BJA
Bureau of Justice Statistics	http://www.ojp.usdoj.gov/bjs
FBI Hate Crime Statistics	http://www.fbi.gov/ucr/ hatecm.htm
Fedstats	http://www.fedstats.gov
Sourcebook of Criminal Justice Statistics	http://www.albany.edu/ sourcebook

WEBSITE	URL
Uniform Crime Reports	http://www.fbi.gov
Violence Policy Center	http://www.vpc.org

Learner Activities

Activity 1

Pick a newspaper that interests you. You could use your campus newspaper, a local city newspaper, or a national newspaper such as *USA Today*. In addition, most newspapers post articles on the Web.

Collect 30 crime articles from your newspaper. Read the articles you have collected, and then answer the following questions:

1. What types of crime are presented in the news?
2. What characteristics of crime victims are presented in the news? What characteristics of defendants are presented in the news?
3. Compare what you have discovered with the statistical information discussed in Chapter 2. Do the news media provide an accurate picture of crime in society?

_____

_____

_____

_____

_____

_____

Activity 2

Determine the number of index crimes reported to your university police department for each of the last five years. This information should be readily available to you from the police department, and it probably is posted on its website. Universities have been required to publish annual security reports since 1992. If you are having difficulties finding this information, check the Security on Campus website at http://www.campussafety.org. Click on the College and University Campus Crime Statistics link. Include in your statistics the number of murders, forcible rapes, aggravated assaults, robberies, burglaries, motor vehicle thefts, larcenies, and arson cases that have been reported for each of the last five years. Answer the following questions, using these data, in the space provided below. Is your campus safe? Do the data show increases, decreases, or no change in the number of crimes committed on your campus? What types of things does your university do to make the campus safe for students?

_____

_____

_____

_____

_____

_____

Activity 3

Create a victimization questionnaire that you can use to determine the amount and types of victimization that occur on campus. Be sure to ask about the types of victimization experienced, the circumstances of each incident (Where did the incident occur? What time?), and whether the student reported the incident to the police. In addition, collect demographic data so that you will be able to classify the responses by sex, age, and race. After you have completed the questionnaire, administer it to at least 50 students and then tabulate the results. What did you learn about victimization from the surveys? What types of victimization were reported? Were there differences by sex? Race? Age?

_____

_____

_____

_____

_____

_____

Activity 4

Read the materials posted at **Library Extra 2–7** and **Library Extra 2–8** at cjbrief.com, and then answer the following questions. What did you learn about the use of self-report surveys in the measurement of crime? What are the strengths and weaknesses of using self-report data?

Library
EXTRA

_____

_____

_____

_____

_____

_____

Activity 5

Visit Prentice Hall's Criminal Justice Cybrary at http://www.cybrary.info. Click on Statistics. This section provides helpful information and interesting links to a variety of statistical data sources. Included here is a variety of crime statistics from throughout the world. For example, there are data from the British Crime Survey and the World Crime Survey. For this assignment, you are to collect crime data for any country of your choice other than the United States. In the space below, first discuss the amount and types of crimes in that country. Second, compare the crime picture of that country to what we have learned in this chapter about the United

States according to Uniform Crime Report statistics and National Crime Victimization Survey data.

_____

_____

_____

_____

_____

_____

Internet Activity

Visit Prentice Hall's Criminal Justice Cybrary (http://www.cybrary.info), and use its search feature to find links to both the Uniform Crime Reports and the _Sourcebook of Criminal Justice Statistics_. Visit both sites in order to gather information about murder. How much information is available at these sites? What does it consist of? What are the similarities and the differences in the availability of information on the crime of murder between these two sites? Generally speaking, how do the two sites compare? Which one did you find more useful? Why?

_____

_____

_____

_____

_____

_____

Distance Learning Activity

Read some of the following materials about new and promising strategies implemented to respond to juvenile homicide: (1) Blueprints for Violence Prevention (see section on model program descriptions) at http://www.ncjrs.org/html/ojjdp/jjbul2001_7_3/contents.html; (2) Gun Use by Male Juveniles (see section on promising gun strategies) at http://www.ncjrs.org/html/ojjdp/jjbul2001_7_2/contents.html; (3) Homicides of Children and Youth at http://www.ncjrs.org/pdffiles1/ojjdp/187239.pdf; (4) Youth Gang Homicides in the 1990s at http://www.ncjrs.org/txtfiles1/ojjdp/fs200103.txt; and (5) Office of Juvenile Justice and Delinquency Prevention page at http://ojjdp.ncjrs.org/ojstatbb/index.html. After reading these materials, answer the following questions. What data about the juvenile homicide problem exist? What are the major trends in the incidence of juvenile violence over the last ten years? What innovative strategies have been used to respond more effectively to the juvenile homicide problem?

_____

_____

_____

_____
_____
_____

Student Study Guide Questions

True or False

_____ 2-1. Rapes are significantly more likely than motor vehicle thefts to be reported to the police.

_____ 2-2. Robbery is a crime against property; burglary is a personal crime.

_____ 2-3. Violent crimes are generally more serious than property offenses.

_____ 2-4. The NIBRS eliminates the need for the UCR hierarchy rule.

_____ 2-5. The elderly are generally less likely to be victimized by violent and property crimes.

_____ 2-6. Although women are far less frequently victimized by crime than men are, they are more likely to be injured by crime.

_____ 2-7. Drug-related and other "victimless" crimes are all considered Part I offenses by the Federal Bureau of Investigation.

_____ 2-8. Clearance rates refer to the proportion of crimes reported to the police.

_____ 2-9. The National Crime Victimization Survey is compiled annually by the Bureau of Justice Statistics.

_____ 2-10. Murder and aggravated assault are both considered Part I violent crime offenses.

Multiple Choice

2-11. Which of the following offense categories includes crimes such as larceny and arson?
   a. hate crime
   b. organized crime
   c. violent crime
   d. property crime

2-12. Which of the following agencies is responsible for compiling the Uniform Crime Reports?
   a. U.S. Marshals Service
   b. Office of Juvenile Justice and Delinquency
   c. Bureau of Justice Statistics
   d. Federal Bureau of Investigation

2-13. Which of the following is *not* one of the Uniform Crime Reports Part I offenses?
   a. drug possession
   b. motor vehicle theft
   c. murder
   d. rape

2-14. What is the reason rape victims give most often for not reporting the crime to the police?
   a. not worth the victim's time
   b. fear of reprisal
   c. fear of embarrassment
   d. police cannot do anything about it

2-15. Which of the following is *not* a problem with traditional Uniform Crime Report statistics?
   a. Certain crimes are rarely reported to the police.
   b. When a number of crimes are committed in the same incident, only the most serious crime will be included in UCR data.
   c. Victims may believe that the police cannot do anything about a crime, so they do not report it to them.
   d. Certain crimes, such as victimless crimes, are not included in the UCR.
   e. All of the above are problems.

2-16. Which Part I offense is most likely to be reported to the police by the victim?
   a. robbery
   b. motor vehicle theft
   c. larceny
   d. rape

2-17. The National Crime Victimization Survey does *not* include information about which crime?
   a. robbery
   b. murder
   c. household larceny
   d. motor vehicle theft

2-18. The stealing of farm machinery would be classified under what category of the UCR?
   a. burglary
   b. robbery
   c. larceny
   d. motor vehicle theft

2-19. Megan Anderson unlawfully entered a computer services building and stole a laser printer. What crime did she commit?
   a. aggravated assault
   b. forcible rape
   c. robbery
   d. burglary

2-20. Which of the following is *not* a victimless crime?
   a. gambling
   b. motor vehicle theft
   c. drug use
   d. prostitution

Fill-In

2-21. _____ is the least reported of all violent index crimes.

2-22. _____ is intentional and wrongful physical contact with a person, without his or her consent, that entails a sexual component or purpose.

2-23. _____ is unlawful forced sexual intercourse with a female against her will that occurs in the context of a dating relationship.

2-24. The type of assault that includes the use of a weapon or the need for medical assistance for the victim is called _____.

2-25. _____ are criminal offenses in which there is evidence of the perpetrator's prejudice based on the race, religion, sexual orientation, or ethnicity of the victim(s).

2-26. The most common of the eight major index offenses is _____.

2-27. _____ is the use of the Internet, e-mail, and other electronic communication technologies to stalk another person.

2-28. The unlawful use of force or violence by a group or individual based entirely in the United States is called _____.

2-29. The index offense that is most likely to be reported to the police by a victim is _____.

2-30. The type of assault that is usually limited to pushing or shoving is _____.

Crossword Puzzle

Across

2. Type of crime first defined by Edwin Sutherland in 1939.
3. Burglary, larceny, auto theft, and arson.
6. Crime most likely to ruin a victim's credit history.
7. Classification scheme used in the study and description of criminal behavior.
8. Type of rape within the context of a relationship.
9. _____ organized crime.
11. Also called cybercrime.
14. Burning or attempted burning of property, with or without the intent to defraud.
15. The FBI's national source of crime data.

16. Crimes not reported to police and remain unknown to officials are part of the _____.
17. Unlawful killing of a human being.

Down

1. New Uniform Crime Reports.
4. Use of the Internet to stalk a person.
5. Agency responsible for collecting the National Crime Victimization Survey.
10. Murder, rape, robbery, and aggravated assault.
12. Number of crimes reported divided by the number of crimes solved.
13. Another name for the Part I offenses of the UCR.

Word Search Puzzle

```
T A H Z K G S I D E N T I T Y T H E F T S Z I D J Q S C T L
D U I C I N M J T T M S L K Q D K R V P D W A Z U L A J D E
Q J O W E L T U U X Q R Z N S E C W M N C G L Y E L S Q C G
Q K Y A D U R S R A D C Y B E R S T A L K I N G Q F O W R A
N C H D S A H P F D S V R K O K L T J F R P H B L W F U I T
A P A S F S F A K P E S Q L D E G C X S Y A K B D Q T U M H
F B T F Z I A M H A X R K K A C B Y F J N V Q U W S W O E T
I T E B D D L U G R O I L V D R J J S M C C J P S U A E I C
B X C W N J M Y L N T S D C O M C J T C V Z O A T S R I N I
U A R D F V D U M T B A D O M O Q E G L S C E G K L E P D E
K G I P Z U R L E J R W N M E T H Q N Q P P E I W E P P E Q
Q G M H B W I P G X V D S J S O W Y D Y O V Q R V E I E X L
S R E U Y R I U N A Y X F N T R E A B N T A K X B L R Z A A
F A D P G O W J X P F V B P I V P S T I U H Q S M D A F R Z
P V M C V B U R G L A R Y Z C E X R W L Q I E U P D C E M R
V A G B O V S J J N J W D F T H V B A P D I O F D C Y Z E V
L T U B T R X R I B C S A N E I F A I P P Y X R T V S M Q E
F E V J X I O T Y S R E B W R C F J G U E P C D B H I N C S
M D I M F H B D T U J D K U R L Q G A T R L P L P R X A T Q
P A Q M M Q A R S O N M B D O E E J A I L L L D C N T S J I
W S P I X A T V Y I F S I S R T U K Y M B C J R H E I V R X
E S T L R N L J A A E H X N I H I N T L Z W E A J R Z P N Q
V A Q W O R L W K U S T K D S E R D C V G T T M Y A H Q Z Z
I U J L B G O O A C K N H Z M F W F B P U W U Z F T S Q I I
A L D I B N W G I R S M Q U N T I T D P C Y H N S Z H P Y T
K T O K E O C S Y N E D Y Z D L H B M V Q E B R Y E E P F K
C J K K R Q A O A E X D J Z G G E O Y A Z O B Y K X O Q G C
U I S G Y J C A K V M S F H S R C B V P L I S C U L I M Y K
R W M M V X B S U X W M B X N F N F M U N A D O O T A M U W
T E L X R K M Y U U V N L C L E A R A N C E R A T E A V D Z
```

Aggravated Assault

Arson

Assault

Burglary

Clearance Rate

Computer Crime

Crime Index

Cyberstalking

Domestic Terrorism

Hate Crime

Identity Theft

Larceny-Theft

Malware

Motor Vehicle Theft

Murder

NCVS

NIBRS

Rape

Robbery

Software Piracy

Spam

3 Criminal Law

Chapter Outline

- Introduction
- The Nature and Purpose of Law
- The Rule of Law
- Types of Law

- General Categories of Crime
- General Features of Crime
- Elements of a Specific Criminal Offense
- Types of Defenses to a Criminal Charge

Learning Objectives

After reading this chapter, you should be able to

- Explain the impact of common law on contemporary American criminal justice.
- Discuss the nature of the rule of law, and describe its purpose in Western democratic societies.
- Identify the various categories or types of law, and explain the purpose of each.
- List the five categories of criminal law violations.

- List the eight general features of crime.
- Explain the concept of *corpus delicti*.
- Discuss the four broad categories of criminal defenses that our legal system recognizes.
- Explain the legal concept of insanity, and distinguish it from psychiatric explanations of mental illness.

Chapter Summary

Imagine our society without laws. How would order be maintained? How would individuals be protected from harm? How would society be protected? Law provides these protections, insulating society from mass chaos. Chapter 3 discusses many areas of law—including the historical sources of modern law, the purposes of law, the types of law, and the elements of a criminal law violation.

Chapter 3 explains why we have laws. One of the primary purposes of laws is to preserve and maintain social order. Laws can also promote change in society or help society adapt to change. For example, new laws have been created in response to the computer revolution, and many criminal laws were created to adapt to rapid social and technological changes.

The text discusses different types of law. **Common law** is the traditional body of unwritten legal precedents created by judges in their everyday practices. **Criminal law**, which is the focus of this chapter, is concerned with offenses against society. The criminal justice processing machinery operates according to criminal law. Chapter 3 also distinguishes criminal law from civil law. **Civil law** provides legal guidance regulating the relationships between individuals. Sometimes criminal and civil cases overlap; for example, an individual could be charged under criminal law but also be sued in civil court by the victim. **Case law** involves the decisions of courts that provide guiding principles to future decisions.

Chapter 3 also provides a discussion of general categories of crime. Specifically, the text discusses five categories of violations: **misdemeanors, felonies, offenses, treason**, and **inchoate offenses**. Finally, Chapter 3 discusses the general features of crime. Let's walk through a situation in view of the features discussed.

Facts: Joan killed her husband by stabbing him with a kitchen knife. Joan had been frequently subjected to beatings, some resulting in hospitalization, from her husband. Moreover, her husband had threatened to kill Joan on at least four prior occasions.

1. *Actus reus*. The first general feature of crime is that there has to be an act in violation of the law. Here the act is murder. If Joan stabbed her husband and he survived, she could be charged with attempted murder. If Joan took steps to complete the murder but was unable to carry out her attempt, she could be charged with conspiracy to commit murder. If she approached an undercover police officer and asked him to commit a murder, she could be charged with solicitation to commit a murder.

2. *Mens rea*. A guilty mind is the second general feature that has to be established and is probably the most complex because it involves subjective evaluation of the mind. Should Joan be held at blame for this crime? Did Joan intend the consequences of her action?

3. **Concurrence**. The third element is the concurrence of the act and the intent. Joan's actions have to be linked with her intent.

4. **Harm**. The harm in this case, the death of another human being, is easily identified.

5. **Causation**. There has to be a link between the act and the harm. If Joan shot her husband and he survived for a month but then died of complications related to a cancerous brain tumor, it would be difficult to convict Joan of murder because the act (the shooting) would not be linked to the harm (the death).

6. **Legality**. There has to be a law on the books to punish someone for his or her behavior. Murder is well defined in our law books.

7. **Punishment**. Not only must there be a law on the books, but that law must provide a punishment for the crime. Statutory punishments for murder are among the severest punishments available to judges.

Even if each of the statutory elements can be established, a defendant has the opportunity to raise defenses that could excuse his or her actions. For example, Joan might argue that she committed the act in self-defense as a battered woman who thought her life was in danger.

The last part of Chapter 3 discusses several types of defenses, including alibi, justification, excuse, procedural, and innovative. The **alibi defense** is very straightforward in that the defendant argues that he or she was nowhere near the crime when it happened. **Justification defenses** are when the defendant admits to committing the act but claims it was necessary to avoid a greater evil. Examples include self-defense, necessity, and defense of home. **Excuse defenses** are when a defendant claims that some personal condition or circumstance was such that he or she should not be held accountable. Examples include age, insanity, involuntary intoxication, and unconsciousness. **Procedural defenses** are defenses based on procedure, such as entrapment, double jeopardy, collateral estoppel, selective prosecution, denial of speedy trial, and prosecutorial misconduct.

Key Concepts

Actus Reus   An act in violation of the law. Also, a guilty act.

Alibi   A statement or contention by an individual charged with a crime that he or she was so distant when the crime was committed, or so engaged in other provable activities, that his or her participation in the commission of that crime was impossible.

Alter Ego Rule   In some jurisdictions, a rule of law that holds that a person can only defend a third party under circumstances and only to the degree that the third party could act on his or her own behalf.

Attendant Circumstances   The facts surrounding an event.

Case Law   The body of judicial precedent, historically built on legal reasoning and past interpretations of statutory laws, that serves as a guide to decision making, especially in the courts.

Civil Law   The branch of modern law that governs relationships between parties.

Common Law   Law originating from usage and custom rather than from written statutes. The term refers to an unwritten body of judicial opinion, originally developed by English courts, that is based upon nonstatutory customs, traditions, and precedents that help guide judicial decision making.

Concurrence   The coexistence of (1) an act in violation of the law and (2) a culpable mental state.

Corpus Delicti   The facts that show that a crime has occurred. The term literally means the "body of the crime."

Criminal Law   The branch of modern law that concerns itself with offenses committed against society, its members, their property, and the social order.

Criminal Negligence   Behavior in which a person fails to reasonably perceive substantial and unjustifiable risks of dangerous consequences.

Defense (to a criminal charge)   Evidence and arguments offered by a defendant and his or her attorney to show why that person should not be held liable for a criminal charge.

Diminished Capacity   A defense based upon claims of a mental condition that may be insufficient to exonerate the defendant of guilt but that may be relevant to specific mental elements of certain crimes or degrees of crime. Also called *diminished responsibility*.

Double Jeopardy   A common law and constitutional prohibition against a second trial for the same offense.

Element (of a crime)   In a specific crime, one of the essential features of that crime, as specified by law or statute.

Entrapment   An improper or illegal inducement to crime by agents of enforcement. Also, a defense that may be raised when such inducements have occurred.

Espionage   The "gathering, transmitting, or losing" of information related to the national defense in such a manner that the information becomes available to enemies of the United States and may be used to their advantage. *Source*: Henry Campbell Black, Joseph R. Nolan, and Jacqueline M. Nolan-Haley, *Black's Law Dictionary*, 6th ed. (St. Paul, MN: West, 1990), p. 24.

Excuse   A legal defense in which the defendant claims that some personal condition or circumstance at the time of the act was such that he or she should not be held accountable under the criminal law.

Felony   A criminal offense punishable by death or by incarceration in a prison facility for at least one year.

Guilty But Mentally Ill (GBMI)   A verdict, equivalent to a finding of "guilty," that establishes that the defendant, although mentally ill, was in sufficient possession of his or her faculties to be morally blameworthy for his or her acts.

Hudud Crime   A serious violation of Islamic law regarded as an offense against God. Hudud crimes include such behavior as theft, adultery, sodomy, alcohol consumption, and robbery.

Inchoate Offense   An offense not yet completed. Also, an offense that consists of an action or conduct that is a step toward the intended commission of another offense.

Incompetent to Stand Trial   In criminal proceedings, a finding by a court that, as a result of mental illness, defect, or disability, a defendant is incapable of understanding the nature of the charges and proceedings against him or her, of consulting with an attorney, or of aiding in his or her own defense.

Infraction   A minor violation of state statute or local ordinance punishable by a fine or other penalty or by a specified, usually limited, term of incarceration.

Insanity Defense   A legal defense based on claims of mental illness or mental incapacity.

Islamic Law   A system of laws, operative in some Arab countries, based on the Muslim religion and especially the holy book of Islam, the Koran.

Jurisprudence   The philosophy of law. Also, the science and study of the law.

Justification   A legal defense in which the defendant admits to committing the act in question but claims it was necessary in order to avoid some greater evil.

Law   A rule of conduct, generally found enacted in the form of a statute, that proscribes or mandates certain forms of behavior. Statutory law is often the result of moral enterprise by interest groups that, through the exercise of political power, are successful in seeing their valued perspectives enacted into law.

Legal Cause   A legally recognizable cause. A legal cause must be demonstrated in court in order to hold an individual criminally liable for causing harm.

Mens Rea   The state of mind that accompanies a criminal act. Also, a guilty mind.

Misdemeanor   An offense punishable by incarceration, usually in a local confinement facility, for a period whose upper limit is prescribed by statute in a given jurisdiction, typically one year or less.

M'Naghten Rule   A rule for determining insanity which asks whether the defendant knew what he or she was doing or whether the defendant knew that what he or she was doing was wrong.

Motive   A person's reason for committing a crime.

Offense   A violation of the criminal law. Also, in some jurisdictions, a minor crime, such as jaywalking, that is sometimes described as *ticketable*.

Penal Code   The written, organized, and compiled form of the criminal laws of a jurisdiction.

Precedent   A legal principle that ensures that previous judicial decisions are authoritatively considered and incorporated into future cases.

Procedural Defense   A defense that claims that the defendant was in some significant way discriminated against in the justice process or that some important aspect of official procedure was not properly followed in the investigation or prosecution of the crime charged.

Procedural Law   The part of the law that specifies the methods to be used in enforcing substantive law.

Reasonable Force   A degree of force that is appropriate in a given situation and is not excessive. Also, the minimum degree of force necessary to protect oneself, one's property, a third party, or the property of another in the face of a substantial threat.

Reckless Behavior   Activity that increases the risk of harm.

Rule of Law   The maxim that an orderly society must be governed by established principles and known codes that are applied uniformly and fairly to all of its members.

Self-Defense   The protection of oneself or of one's property from unlawful injury or from the immediate risk of unlawful injury. Also, the justification that the person who committed an act that would otherwise constitute an offense reasonably believed that the act was necessary to protect self or property from immediate danger.

Stare Decisis   The legal principle that requires that in subsequent cases on similar issues of law and fact courts be bound by their own earlier decisions and by those of higher courts having jurisdiction over them. The term literally means "standing by decided matters."

Statutory Law   Written or codified law; the "law on the books," as enacted by a government body or agency having the power to make laws.

Strict Liability   Liability without fault or intention. Strict liability offenses do not require *mens rea*.

Substantive Criminal Law   The part of the law that defines crimes and specifies punishments.

Tazir Crime   A minor violation of Islamic law that is regarded as an offense against society, not God.

Tort   A wrongful act, damage, or injury not involving a breach of contract. Also, a private or civil wrong or injury.

Treason   "A U.S. citizen's actions to help a foreign government overthrow, make war against, or seriously injure the United States." Also, the attempt to overthrow the government of the society of which one is a member. *Source*: Daniel Oran, *Oran's Dictionary of the Law* (St. Paul, MN: West, 1983), p. 306.

Key Cases

Ake v. *Oklahoma.*   In this case, the U.S. Supreme Court held that the government must ensure access to a competent psychiatrist whenever a defendant indicates that insanity will be an issue at trial (*Ake* v. *Oklahoma*, 470 U.S. 68 [1985]).

The Crown v. *Dudly & Stephens.*   This famous case illustrated the necessity defense (*The Crown* v. *Dudley & Stephens*, 14 Q.B.D. 273 [1884]).

Durham v. *United States.*   This case provides the Durham rule for gauging insanity. This rule states that a person is not criminally responsible for his or her behavior if the person's illegal actions were the result of some mental disease or defect (*Durham* v. *United States*, 214 F.2d 862 [1954]).

Ford v. *Wainwright.*   In this case, the U.S. Supreme Court decided that prisoners who become insane while incarcerated cannot be executed (*Ford* v. *Wainwright*, 477 U.S. 399 [1986]).

Foucha v. *Louisiana.*   The U.S. Supreme Court held that a defendant found not guilty by reason of insanity in a criminal trial could not be institutionalized indefinitely without showing that he or she was either dangerous or mentally ill (*Foucha* v. *Louisiana*, 540 U.S. 71 [1992]).

U.S. v. *Brawner.*   This case provides the Brawner rule for gauging insanity. This rule places responsibility for deciding insanity with the jury. Juries are primarily guided by their own sense of fairness (*U.S.* v. *Brawner*, 471 F.2d 969 [1972]).

U.S. v. *Felix.*   In this case, the U.S. Supreme Court ruled that the double jeopardy clause applies only to the prosecution of the same offense. Another offense or involvement in a conspiracy to commit that offense is not considered the same offense and thus would not be in violation of the double jeopardy clause (*U.S.* v. *Felix*, 190 F.3d 540 [1999]).

Learning Tips

Binders

Use binders to take notes. They allow you to insert and remove pages, so you can easily add handouts, chapter notes, or notes from classmates and remove unnecessary information. Additionally, to review material, you can organize pages in a manner that allows you to easily recognize the overall strategy of lectures.

Memory Techniques

You can enhance your memory by creating associations. Your memory stores information in patterns that make sense to you. When you gather additional information, you will recall it more effectively if it is stored near similar information in your brain. For example, an important term in Chapter 3 is *tort*. A good way to remember this term is to associate it with civil law. Tort is a private or civil wrong; civil law regulates activity involving personal interests.

CJ Brief on the World Wide Web

Web links to organizations and agencies related to the material in Chapter 3 include:

WEBSITE	URL
American Bar Association	http://www.abanet.org/crimjust/home.html
American Prosecutor's Research	http://www.ndaa-apri.org
Dumb Laws	http://www.dumblaws.com
International Center for Criminal Law	http://www.icclr.law.ubc.ca
Legal Law Help	http://www.legallawhelp.com
The Rule of Law	http://www.users.bigpond.com/smartboard/btof/index18.htm
United Nations Human Rights Website	http://www.ohchr.org/english
United States Attorney General's Office	http://www.usdoj.gov/ag
WashLaw Web	http://www.washlaw.edu

Learner Activities

Activity 1

Visit the link at **Library Extra 3–3**. Read an article posted in an online law review journal, and summarize the content of the article. Be sure to provide the citation.

_____

_____

_____

_____

_____

_____

Activity 2

It would be helpful to refer to the text's discussion of the insanity defense before tackling this activity.

The insanity defense is one of the more controversial and complex defenses available to defendants. It is controversial because the public thinks that defendants are excused from punishment when found not guilty as the result of this defense. The complexity lies in the link it makes between the medical and legal professions.

Consider the legal implications of the following case. Tom Smith had recently escaped from a mental hospital when he was picked up by a concerned motorist. At a highway rest area, Tom killed the motorist by strangulation. He was charged with murder. On two prior occasions, Tom had been found not guilty by reason of insanity.

The medical implications are that Tom has the IQ of about a ten-year-old child. He has a 35-year history of mental illness, dating back to his return from the Vietnam War. Tom suffers from posttraumatic stress disorder, unable to recover from the horrors he experienced in the war. He is delusional, and he strangled the motorist because he listened to Grateful Dead rock music, which caused Tom to think he was the Antichrist.

The prosecution had no trouble establishing the elements of the crime. The defense attorneys used an insanity defense (irresistible-impulse test), claiming that Tom belongs in a mental hospital, not a maximum-security prison. If you were the judge in this case, what would you decide? Should Tom be punished as a criminal or treated as a person with a mental illness? Be sure to explain your answer.

_____

_____

_____

_____

_____

Activity 3

An effective way for you to understand domestic violence and battered women's syndrome is to interview a domestic-violence expert or a provider of victims' services. This activity requires you to contact such a professional in your community to discuss domestic violence and battered women's defense. Look in the telephone book for a shelter for abused or battered women, or contact the prosecutor's office for information on how to contact a provider of victims' services. A mental health facility is also a good resource. Complete an informational interview with this person to learn about domestic violence in your community. Ask about the extent of the problem and the types of resources available to domestic-violence victims, and ask the person to comment on battered women's syndrome.

When you complete this interview, discuss what you discovered in the space below.

_____

_____

_____

_____

_____

Activity 4

Presented below are several case descriptions. If you were a defense attorney asked to take each of these cases, what would you recommend as the best defense? (Refer to Table 3-2 in the textbook for assistance.)

1. Art Kapser and John Gelbor were good friends and coworkers. After work, Art and John went bowling. After John picked up a spare in the seventh frame, the two got into an argument on proper scoring of a spare. John punched Art in the face, knocking him to the floor, and screamed, "If you don't shut up, I will kill you." Art left the bowling alley but returned with a .38-caliber revolver and shot John in the back, killing him instantly. Art was charged with murder. What could Art use as a defense?

2. Kellie Koser attended a college party. One of the partygoers handed her a beer. She drank it, although she did not know that the beer contained a sedative. She got tired quickly and decided to drive home. She fell asleep at the wheel and killed a bicyclist. She was charged with manslaughter. What could Kellie use as a defense?

3. Shelly Morrison and Todd Rutlow both drive the same model of pickup truck. Both trucks are black with white pinstripes, both have red fuzzy dice hanging from the rearview mirror, and both have a bumper sticker with the slogan "Peace Is Possible." Moreover, both leave their keys in the ignition when it is parked. Shelly, after completing a long day of Christmas shopping, got into a black truck and drove away. She did not know it was Todd's truck. Police quickly apprehended Shelly and charged her with motor vehicle theft. What would you recommend as a defense?

4. Charles Shuter was charged with raping his 14-year-old daughter. The prosecutor also charged the mother with conspiracy to commit rape because she knew about the rape and bought condoms for her husband to use when committing the crime. The mother claims she did not contact the police because her husband threatened to kill her. What would you recommend as a defense for the mother?

5. When Marnee Diaz lost her job, she couldn't keep up with her bills. In order to put food on the table, she began robbing banks. What would you recommend as a defense?

6. Carol Smith is addicted to crack but enrolled herself in a drug-treatment program to control her addiction. An undercover police officer joined the same program to get information about drug suppliers. He got friendly with Ms. Smith and asked her to buy him some crack. She refused on four occasions. On the fifth occasion, however, she brought him one rock of crack cocaine. She was arrested for drug possession. What defense would you recommend?

7. Jason Jenser was a heavy drinker. Whenever he drank, he beat his lover, Bill Boone. He frequently put a gun to Bill's head, threatened to kill him, and caused him numerous physical injuries. Bill wanted to leave, but Jason threatened him with physical violence, so he stayed. That same evening, while Jason was sleeping, Bill picked up a shotgun and killed him. What defense would you recommend?

_____

_____

_____

_____

_____

_____

Internet Activity

Visit law.com (http://www.law.com) and find the law dictionary that the site provides. (*Hint*: Click on Look Up Legal Terms.) Enter each of the key terms (one at a time) at the start of Chapter 3 into the dictionary, and compare the definitions there with the definitions in the textbook (see the glossary). Write the definitions from the two sources side by side and compare them. What differences exist? What terms are in the textbook that are not in the online dictionary?

_____

_____

_____

_____

_____

_____

Distance Learning Activity

Visit the website for the *National Law Journal* or some other major industry legal publication. (National Law Journal page is at http://www.nlj.com, and Court TV On-Line is at http://www.courttv.com.) Submit a summary of one of the articles or cases posted on the website. If your instructor asks you to do so, share your summary with the other students in your class, and participate in an online discussion about the issues that students wrote about.

_____

_____

_____

_____

_____

_____

Student Study Guide Questions

True or False

_____ 3-1. A basic distinction between criminal and civil law is that criminal acts injure individuals and society as a whole.

_____ 3-2. Misdemeanors are generally less serious than felonies.

_____ 3-3. Procedural law defines behaviors as criminal and specifies punishment.

_____ 3-4. The rule of law is also referred to as the supremacy of law.

_____ 3-5. Civil law is primarily concerned with assessing intent.

_____ 3-6. The Durham insanity rule states that a person is not guilty of a crime if, at the time of the crime, he or she didn't know what he or she was doing or didn't know that it was wrong.

_____ 3-7. Treason is the act of a U.S. citizen who helps a foreign government overthrow, make war against, or seriously injure the United States.

_____ 3-8. Procedural defense is based on discrimination by the justice system.

_____ 3-9. Contract law is the body of regulations created by governments to control the economic activities of industry, business, and individuals.

_____ 3-10. Insanity is a legal definition and not a psychiatric one.

Multiple Choice

3-11. Which of the following is generally considered the most serious?
   a. felonies
   b. misdemeanors
   c. offenses
   d. infractions

3-12. Which of the following is a procedural defense?
   a. duress
   b. mistake of fact
   c. double jeopardy
   d. infancy

3-13. Which type of law refers to a traditional body of unwritten legal precedents created through everyday practice and supported by court decisions?
   a. civil
   b. conflict
   c. common
   d. administrative

3-14. Murder, robbery, and drug offenses would all be defined as crimes under _____ law.
   a. civil
   b. criminal
   c. common
   d. administrative

3-15. What type of law results from legislative action and is thought of as the "law on the books"?
   a. procedural
   b. administrative
   c. statutory
   d. substantive

3-16. Tax laws, health codes, and restrictions on pollution are examples of _____ law.
   a. administrative
   b. procedural
   c. civil
   d. criminal

3-17. What is the Latin term that means "the body of the crime"?
   a. _actus reus_
   b. _mens rea_
   c. _stare decisis_
   d. _corpus delicti_

3-18. Which of the following is _not_ an excuse defense?
   a. involuntary intoxication
   b. self-defense
   c. infancy
   d. insanity

3-19. Which of the following elements of crime means "guilty mind"?
   a. concurrence
   b. harm
   c. *actus reus*
   d. *mens rea*

3-20. A woman breaks into a home and, once inside, is cornered by the family Rottweiler, Spike. When the homeowner gets home and sees what Spike has in his possession, she calls the police, who arrest the suspect. Based on these facts, the woman who broke into the home could be charged with _____.
   a. conspiracy to commit burglary
   b. nothing (she did not commit a crime)
   c. burglary
   d. attempted burglary

Fill-In

3-21. _____ governs relationships between parties.

3-22. A(n) _____ is an offense punishable by incarceration, usually in a local confinement facility, for a period of time whose upper limit is prescribed by statute in a given jurisdiction, typically limited to a year or less.

3-23. The _____ holds that a person is not guilty of a crime if, at the time of the crime, he or she either didn't know what he or she was doing or didn't know that it was wrong.

3-24. A(n) _____ consists of an action or conduct which is a step toward the intended commission of another crime.

3-25. The _____ states that person is not criminally responsible for his or her behavior if his or her illegal actions were the result of some mental disease or defect.

3-26. _____ is a procedural defense similar to double jeopardy.

3-27. _____ is the science and study of law.

3-28. A(n) _____ is an offense punishable by death, or by incarceration for at least a year.

3-29. _____ literally means "guilty mind."

3-30. _____ is the part of the law that defines crimes and specifies punishments.

Crossword Puzzle

Across

2. Offense punishable by incarceration in a prison facility for at least one year.
3. _____ criminal law describes what constitutes particular crimes and specifics appropriate punishment for each offense.
4. Science and study of the law.
5. Improper or illegal inducement to crime by agents of enforcement.
6. Law originating from custom.
7. _____ criminal law specifies the rules that determine how those who are accused of a crime are dealt with in the judicial system.
8. "Body of the crime."
10. Supremacy of the law is also called _____.
12. Judicial precedent.
13. Guilty act.
15. Less serious than a felony; more serious than an infraction.
16. Facts surrounding an event.

Down

1. Prohibition against a second trial for the same offense.
6. Branch of modern law that governs relationships between parties.
9. Coexistence of an act in violation of the law and a culpable mental state.
11. Guilty mind.
14. Private or civil wrong or injury.

Word Search Puzzle

```
J H H X T H I B S C G R M U A Z Z P H N A X Y Z B B V A V Z
G D I E X Y G C K K X C E X O I W G N H Z A C Z U C R U P C
V H I I Z N I O B L I D V A E V N X H C S M U Y T N I A C F
U U D M T M Z U S V M T D K S S T S Y B I O V O F Z W O R A
Q I L B I Q O X Z G C V A N S O G Z U A R V Z L B Z L B K L
N U E P R N J X L H E L Y Q M S N U E P M I I O L I L R M N
P L G O V E I I U P N P N F A V V A B O I R B L X Y R M O N
E U Q E F P L S L G U V D P R W O A B B S K F E L X B W I K
N D Q X N S P L H Y E S P I O N A G E L D M L V U A T Q J H
A W W V O D R A K E V J K A M Z J F B E E U G L I S W U W T
L X K N E O E M G Z D U A B L T X W X B M F Y S P C T J N X
C H A D G U C I M D T C J L L C G K G A E W O T J Y W G K V
O N Y B S B E C J C R G A I T U L P B Y A I U R D S W F B G
D W P L V L D L J B E A S P E E S U T W N B V J C I W J E X
E J I A X E E A O J A S G Y A R R D M N O P B L U E K S P O
F K J R L J N W I G S D M P D C R E X H R L Q Z J U N H J C
S M H N Z E T Q I S O M G F R I I H G S Y H C Y T E Z J U U
I W E Z T O F N T V N F L H U K C T U O Z M C T F V P K R L
N T V N P P L U S I W L E J L P O D Y L R L U F I W D F I T
F O K O T A U A Y E N I H L E M H L Z D A U O T O R T V S U
R W V G X R R S W T O G S H O L O P Z U B E L E C C R W P R
A E U Y P D A B Y M X P J U F N Z T K V T V B E I V G P R A
C C O V U Y W P Q L I O N D L D Y J I A Y B A J J N O A U L
T A R Q C E Q B M O M L X U A E E O O V E V Z C S S V Y D D
I S G Q Q S A P N E N R Q D W Z X H Y U E F V H Q C L N E E
O E Q H N V S T O C N I C C Z H C C N I H T M A P H M R N F
N L B T O L T P K P Y T B R O N C X U X P U V K L Y E B C E
L A V V N U L A U G V V J I I H B S A S J K X X U I T L E N
K W J H B M F V A Z C F E M Y S D D R V E L P E J X B K V S
D W O X O W A A Z U P V O E N T C O N C U R R E N C E I P E
```

Alibi	Inchoate Offense
Alter Ego Rule	Infraction
Case Law	Islamic Law
Civil Law	Jurisprudence
Concurrence	Law
Cultural Defense	Misdemeanor
Diminished Capacity	Motive
Double Jeopardy	Penal Code
Entrapment	Precedent
Espionage	Reasonable Force
Excuse	Rule of Law
Felony	Tort
Hudud Crime	Treason

4 Policing: Purpose and Organization

Chapter Outline

- Introduction
- The Police Mission
- American Policing Today: From the Federal to the Local Level
- Police Administration

- Policing Epochs
- Police–Community Relations
- Scientific Police Management and Evidence-Based Policing
- Discretion and the Individual Officer

Learning Objectives

After reading this chapter, you should be able to

- Explain the basic purposes of policing in democratic societies.
- List and describe the three major levels of public law enforcement in the United States today.
- Identify the three styles of policing, and discuss differences in these approaches.

- Describe community policing, and explain how it is different from traditional policing.
- Describe the changed role of American police in the post-9/11 environment.
- Explain police discretion, and identify factors that influence a police officer's use of discretion.

Chapter Summary

Chapter 4 begins by defining the basic purposes of policing in a democratic society. These purposes include enforcing the law, apprehending offenders, preventing crime, and preserving the peace. Next, the chapter explains the major levels of American policing jurisdictions. First are the federal law enforcement agencies. Although there are dozens of federal law enforcement agencies, the text describes in detail the best known: the Federal Bureau of Investigation. The importance of the FBI's counterterrorism division is emphasized. Second, the role of state-level agencies is examined. State police agencies are organized under one of two models, either centralized or decentralized, depending upon the type of state-sponsored activities they perform. Third, local agencies, including municipal departments and sheriffs' departments, are discussed. The text notes there are approximately 13,580 municipal police departments and 3,100 sheriff's departments. The New York City Police Department is mentioned as the nation's largest local agency, with 39,000 full-time sworn officers.

Chapter 4 covers issues related to police administration. For example, police departments have unique policing styles formed in response to community and organizational factors. Three types of policing styles, developed by James Q. Wilson, are discussed in Chapter 4. First, police officers employed in **watchman-style** departments are most concerned with maintaining order. Some authors have been critical of this policing style for its use of threats or brutal practices. Second, police officers in **legalistic-style** departments are expected to enforce the letter of the law, meaning that their discretion to use a nonenforcement response is limited. Moreover, these officers are likely to ignore violations of social norms that do not violate the law. Third, officers in a **service-style** department are most concerned with helping citizens rather than strictly applying the letter of the law. These officers would work closely with social services and other resource groups to help solve community and individual problems.

As more police departments today are moving toward the more modern service-oriented policing style, an outgrowth of this effort has been **police–community relations (PCR)** programs. The current movement toward community policing has its roots in the police–community relations (PCR) programs advocated in the 1960s as well as in the **team policing** ideas of the 1970s. More recently, modern police departments have sought to forge a partnership between the police and the community. Thus, **community policing** is the newest police strategy that calls for police departments to develop community relationships and to solicit citizen assistance in solving problems. This chapter discusses several examples of community policing programs, such as the Chicago Police Department's comprehensive community-policing program called Chicago's Alternative Policing Strategy (CAPS).

Chapter 4 also describes important research studies, such as the **Kansas City Experiment**, that have had a tremendous impact on the current structure and philosophy of police departments. This experiment, conducted in the mid-1970s, tested (among other things) the effectiveness of preventive patrol in deterring crime and making citizens feel safe. The results from this study indicate that the number of officers on preventive patrol does not have a deterrent effect on preventable crimes and does not make citizens feel safe. These findings have forced police departments to alter how they use police officers on patrol, employing such innovative police strategies as **directed patrol**.

The final section of Chapter 4 introduces the concept of **police discretion** and the individual officer. Separate from the "official" policing style of a department, individual officers retain considerable discretion in making choices when enforcing the law. When "working the streets," police officers are not under constant supervision; hence they have board authority to resolve matters both formally and informally. The text describes potential factors that might influence the ways officers use discretion, such as background of the officer, characteristics of the suspect, department policy, community interest, and pressures from victims.

Key Concepts

Chain of Command   The unbroken line of authority that extends through all levels of an organization, from the highest to the lowest.

Community Policing   A collaborative effort between the police and the community that identifies problems of crime and disorder and involves all elements of the community in the search for solutions to these problems." *Source*: Community Policing Consortium, *What Is Community Policing?* (Washington, DC: The Consortium, 1995).

CompStat   A crime-analysis and police-management process built on crime mapping that was developed by the New York City Police Department in the mid-1990s.

Crime Prevention   The anticipation, recognition, and appraisal of a crime risk and the initiation of action to eliminate or reduce it.

Directed Patrol   A police management strategy designed to increase the productivity of patrol officers through the scientific analysis and evaluation of patrol techniques.

Evidence-Based Policing   The use of best available research on the outcomes of police work to implement guidelines and evaluate agencies, units, and officers.

Exemplary Projects Program   An initiative, sponsored by the Law Enforcement Assistance Administration, designed to recognize outstanding innovative efforts to combat crime and to provide assistance to crime victims.

Kansas City Experiment   The first large-scale scientific study of law enforcement practices. Sponsored by the Police Foundation, it focused on the practice of preventive patrol.

Law Enforcement Assistance Administration (LEAA)   A now-defunct federal agency established under Title I of the Omnibus Crime Control and Safe Streets Act of 1968 to funnel federal funding to state and local law enforcement agencies.

Legalistic Style   A style of policing marked by a strict concern with enforcing the precise letter of the law. Legalistic departments may take a hands-off approach to otherwise disruptive or problematic behavior that does not violate the criminal law.

Line Operations   In police organizations, the field activities or supervisory activities directly related to day-to-day police work.

Police-Community Relations (PCR)   An area of police activity that recognizes the need for the community and the police to work together effectively and that is based on the notion that the police derive their legitimacy from the community they serve. Many police agencies began to explore PCR in the 1960s and 1970s.

Police Discretion   The opportunity of law enforcement officers to exercise choice in their daily activities.

Police Management   The administrative activities of controlling, directing, and coordinating police personnel, resources, and activities in the service of preventing crime, apprehending criminals, recovering stolen property, and performing regulatory and helping services.

Police Subculture   A particular set of values, beliefs, and acceptable forms of behavior characteristic of American police with which the police profession strives to imbue new recruits. Socialization into the police subculture commences with recruit training and continues thereafter.

Problem-Solving Policing   A type of policing that assumes that many crimes are caused by existing social conditions within the community and that crimes can be controlled by uncovering and effectively addressing underlying social problems. Problem-solving policing makes use of community resources, such as counseling centers, welfare programs, and job-training facilities. It also attempts to involve citizens in crime prevention through education, negotiation, and conflict management.

Quality-of-Life Offense   A minor violation of the law (sometimes called a *petty crime*) that demoralizes community residents and businesspeople. Quality-of-life offenses involve acts that create physical disorder (for example, excessive noise or vandalism) or that reflect social decay (for example, panhandling and prostitution).

Scientific Police Management   The application of social scientific techniques to the study of police administration for the purpose of increasing effectiveness, reducing the frequency of citizen complaints, and enhancing the efficient use of available resources.

Service Style   A style of policing marked by a concern with helping rather than strict enforcement. Service-oriented police agencies are more likely to take advantage of community resources, such as drug-treatment programs, than are other types of agencies.

Sheriff   The elected chief officer of a county law enforcement agency. The sheriff is usually responsible for law enforcement in unincorporated areas and for the operation of the county jail.

Span of Control   The number of police personnel or the number of units supervised by a particular officer.

Staff Operations   In police organizations, activities (such as administration and training) that provide support for line operations.

Strategic Policing   A type of policing that retains the traditional police goal of professional crime fighting but enlarges the enforcement target to include nontraditional kinds of criminals, such as serial offenders, gangs and criminal associations, drug-distribution networks, and sophisticated white-collar and computer criminals. Strategic policing generally makes use of innovative enforcement techniques, including intelligence operations, undercover stings, electronic surveillance, and sophisticated forensic methods.

Team Policing   The reorganization of conventional patrol strategies into "an integrated and versatile police team assigned to a fixed district." *Source*: Sam S. Souryal, *Police Administration and Management* (St. Paul, MN: West Publishing Co., 1977), p. 261.

Watchman Style   A style of policing marked by a concern for order maintenance. Watchman policing is characteristic of lower-class communities where informal police intervention into the lives of residents is employed in the service of keeping the peace.

Learning Tips

Acronyms

To learn a series of facts, especially a lengthy series, use mnemonic acronyms. Acronyms are words that are formed through the first letters of a list of words. For example, ROR is an acronym for Released on Recognizance. Mnemonic devices can enhance the memorization of almost anything, from simple lists to a variety of criminal justice definitions.

Flash Cards

Flash cards are extremely beneficial for memorizing case names and definitions. Write key words, vocabulary, phrases, names, or theories on one side of the card, and write their meanings on the other. This is especially helpful for the numerous legal cases that are included in the text. Study with the flash cards when you study at home, ride on the bus, wait for classes to begin, or have spare time.

CJ Brief on the World Wide Web

Web links to organizations and agencies related to the material in Chapter 4 include:

WEBSITE	URL
Alcohol, Tobacco, Firearms, and Explosives	http://www.atf.treas.gov
The CIA	http://www.odci.gov
Drug Enforcement Administration	http://www.usdoj.gov/dea
Immigration and Naturalization Service	http://www.ins.usdoj.gov
Law Enforcement Links	http://www.leolinks.com
U.S. Coast Guard	http://www.uscg.mil
U.S. Customs Service	http://www.customs.ustreas.gov
U.S. Marshals Service	http://www.usdoj.gov/marshals
U.S. Postal Inspection Service	http://www.usps.gov/websites/depart/inspect
U.S. Secret Service	http://www.treas.gov/usss

Learner Activities

Activity 1

The text describes the Chicago Police Department's community policing program. Before beginning this assignment, read that section of the text again. This activity requires you to find information about one other police department's community policing program. There are several ways to do this. First, you could interview officers from the department you select. Second, you can visit the department's website. Most police departments have websites, and if they have a community policing program, information should be posted on it. Third, there is a large body of research on community policing. You should be able to retrieve books or articles describing various community policing programs from the library. A good book describing a few different approaches to community policing is *The New Blue Line* by David Bayley and Jerome Skolnick. Finally, you can learn from the community policing studies posted on the National Criminal Justice Reference Service page at http://www.ncjrs.org.

In the space provided below, compare and contrast what you found with the textbook's discussion of community policing in Chicago.

_____

_____

_____

_____

Activity 2

Answer the following questions on police discretion in the space provided below. Should police officers enforce the law equally in all situations? In what types of situations should police officers be allowed to not enforce the law? In what types of situations should they be required to fully enforce the law? Why does police discretion exist? What are its strengths and weaknesses?

_____

_____

_____

_____

_____

_____

Activity 3

In Chapter 4, the text describes individual police officer discretion as an important aspect of policing but also notes the dangers of having limited oversight of officers in most situations. Below are a number of examples, not uncommon in police work, in which police officers have had to exercise discretion. After each example, discuss how you, as a police officer, would respond to the situation. There are no right answers, but be certain to justify your response with an explanation.

1. You are dispatched to a low-income apartment complex. A man (his name is Arnold), who is homeless and addicted to crack, refuses to leave the entrance area to the building. He allows those living in the building to enter and does not bother most of them; however, a tenant has called to complain and would like him removed. It is midwinter and the temperature is below freezing. As the responding officer, how would you use your discretion to respond to this situation? Why?

2. While on random preventive patrol in a high-crime neighborhood, you notice two young children (you think they are about eight or nine years old) hanging around outside a drugstore. When you approach them, they start acting very nervous (it is about eight o'clock at night). As you talk to them, a third kid, the same age, comes out of the store followed by the cashier, who tells you that the kid has just tried to steal three candy bars. How would you respond to this situation? Justify your action.

3. While randomly patrolling a neighborhood, you observe a vehicle run a red light. While in pursuit, you also notice that the person is driving in a haphazard manner. After the person stops his vehicle, you discover that he is drunk. The person driving the car, however, is also your favorite uncle. How would you respond to this situation? How does your response differ from your responses to the two previous situations?

4. Your department has received a call from a citizen complaining that his next-door neighbors have been fighting for the last two hours (it is 3:30 A.M.). When you knock on the door and announce that you are the police, the fighting abruptly stops. A male, about 24 years old, opens the door and apologizes

for the disturbance and promises that they will be quiet. However, he will not allow you into the home to talk with the person whom he was fighting with. How would you resolve this situation?

_____

_____

_____

_____

_____

Activity 4

In Chapter 4, the text discusses the important role that federal agencies play in law enforcement. The text highlights the activities of the Federal Bureau of Investigation but mentions that there are dozens of federal law enforcement agencies. This activity requires that you learn about the activities of a federal law enforcement agency other than the FBI. You can do this by visiting the website of a federal agency. Choose an agency. In the space provided below, compare and contrast the activities of the Federal Bureau of Investigation and the agency that you selected. In what ways are the law enforcement activities of that agency similar to the activities of the FBI? In what ways are they different?

_____

_____

_____

_____

_____

_____

Internet Activity

Use the Prentice Hall Criminal Justice Cybrary (http://www.cybrary.info) to find descriptions of patrol studies on the Web. What kinds of studies did you find? What do they deal with? What were the findings or results of each of these studies? (_Hint_: You might want to first check the National Criminal Justice Reference Service at http://www.ncjrs.org.)

_____

_____

_____

_____

_____

_____

Distance Learning Activity

In the space below, highlight the pros and cons of community policing. Some of the strengths and weaknesses are discussed in the textbook, but you should also visit websites containing community policing information. For example, see **Library Extras 4–6** and **4–7** and **Web Extra 4–12** at cjbrief.com.

Library
EXTRA

Web
EXTRA

_____

_____

_____

_____

_____

_____

Student Study Guide Questions

True or False

_____   4-1. Legalistic police agencies are more likely to take advantage of community resources, such as drug-treatment programs, than are other types of departments.

_____   4-2. A centralized state law enforcement agency combines the tasks of major criminal investigations with highway patrol.

_____   4-3. Congress created the Federal Bureau of Investigation in 1980 because crime rates had increased dramatically in the previous decade.

_____   4-4. A watchman style of policing is characteristic of lower-class communities where informal police intervention in the lives of residents is used to help keep the peace.

_____   4-5. The idea of team policing is thought to have originated in Aberdeen, Scotland.

_____   4-6. Police subculture generally refers to a group of corrupt officers working to undermine the goals of a police organization.

_____   4-7. Quality-of-life offenses are general minor law violations that demoralize citizens by creating disorder.

_____   4-8. Results from the Kansas City Preventive Patrol Experiment indicate that officers on preventive patrol deter crimes, such as burglary and robbery; therefore, citizens feel safe.

_____   4-9. Directed patrol is a police management strategy designed to increase the productivity of patrol officers through the application of scientific analysis and evaluation of patrol techniques.

_____   4-10. CompStat is a process that originally was developed by the New York City Police Department.

Multiple Choice

4-11. Which of the following aspects of the police mission focuses on responding to quality-of-life offenses?
   a. providing services
   b. apprehending offenders
   c. preventing crime
   d. preserving the peace

4-12. Which federal law enforcement agency has responsibility for maintaining the Uniform Crime Reports?
   a. U.S. Marshals Service
   b. U.S. Customs Service
   c. Federal Bureau of Investigation
   d. Drug Enforcement Administration

4-13. Which of the following is *not* a criticism of community policing strategies *except*:
   a. Efforts to promote community policing can demoralize a department.
   b. All public officials are not ready to accept community policing.
   c. Not all police officers accept this new image of police work.
   d. Goals of community policing are too narrowly defined.

4-14. Which of Wilson's policing styles is becoming increasingly popular today?
   a. service
   b. paternalistic
   c. watchman
   d. legalistic

4-15. Of the three corporate strategies that guide American policing, which emphasizes an increased capacity to deal with crimes that are not well controlled by traditional methods?
   a. community policing
   b. corporation policing
   c. strategic policing
   d. problem-solving policing

4-16. Which factor does *not* influence the discretionary decisions of individual officers?
   a. background of the officer
   b. pressures from crime victims
   c. departmental policy
   d. all of the above

4-17. Officer Sally Kainer works in a department she describes as being concerned with community problems. She has been encouraged by the department to develop ties with other community agencies, such as the local chapter of Big Brothers/Big Sisters, and to rely on them for assistance. Which of Wilson's policing styles does Sally's department represent?
   a. service style
   b. paternalistic style
   c. watchman style
   d. legalistic style

4-18. A _____ is responsible for the operation of a county jail.
   a. sheriff
   b. uniformed patrol officer
   c. U.S. marshal
   d. state highway patrol officer

4-19. Neighborhood Watch and drug-awareness workshops are examples of
   a. police–community relations programs.
   b. team policing programs.
   c. police crime-fighting activities.
   d. innovative police strategies.

4-20. Enforcing the strict letter of the law characterizes the _____ style of policing.
   a. service
   b. paternalistic
   c. legalistic
   d. watchman

Fill-In

4-21. The _____ style of policing is marked by a concern for order maintenance.

4-22. The _____ was the study credited with beginning the tradition of scientific police evaluation.

4-23. _____ retains the traditional police goal of professional crime fighting but enlarges the enforcement target to include nontraditional types of criminals.

4-24. A department using the _____ style of policing may take a hands-off approach to otherwise disruptive or problematic forms of behavior that are not violations of the criminal law.

4-25. _____ is a police management strategy designed to increase the productivity of patrol officers through the application of scientific analysis and evaluation of patrol techniques.

4-26. _____ assumes that many crimes are caused by existing social conditions and that crimes can be controlled by uncovering and effectively addressing underlying social problems.

4-27. The _____ is responsible for operating the Combined DNA Index System.

4-28. _____ is a collaborative effort between the police and the community that identifies problems of crime and disorder and that involves all elements of the community in the search for solutions to these problems.

4-29. The _____ style of policing is marked by a concern with helping rather than strictly enforcing the law.

4-30. A(n) _____ is a minor violation of the law that demoralizes community residents and businesspeople.

Crossword Puzzle

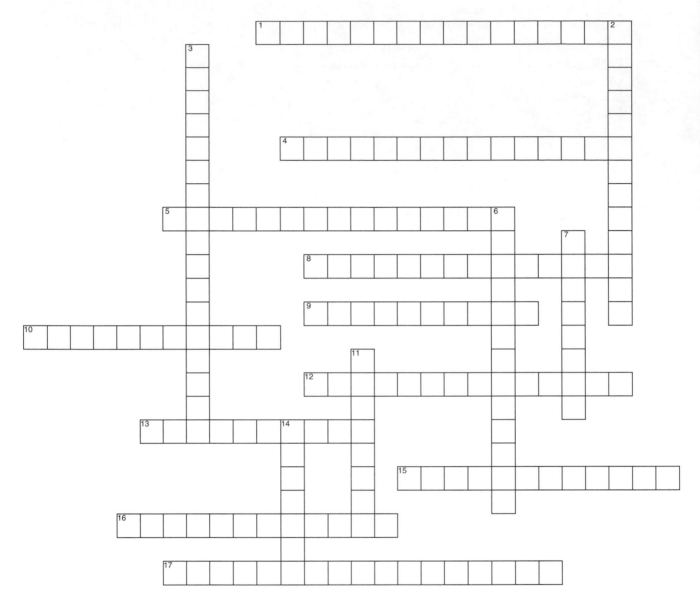

Across

1. Also called police culture.
4. Term that represents a proactive approach to the problem of crime.
5. Support police line operations.
8. Field or supervisory activities directly related to daily police work.
9. Exercise in choice.
10. Another name for quality-of-life offenses.
12. Unbroken line of authority.
13. Department in Wilson's typology concerned with strict enforcement of the law.
15. Time it takes to respond to a call for service.
16. Versatile police team assigned to a fixed district.
17. Corporate police strategy that is a holdover from the reform era.

Down

2. Using research to guide police decision making.
3. Newest corporate police strategy.
6. Number of units supervised by a particular commander.
7. Crime-analysis process developed by the NYPD in the 1990s.
11. Department in Wilson's typology concerned with order maintenance.
14. Style of police department likely to use community policing.

Word Search Puzzle

```
U T Q Q C D N V D U J D G F U P I I N R B D D R M K O S K C
B P A P O X T B O M K T W F I J P S E S R F D H Y T X P W D
D N L O M E M D B H Z F Q T E B T D N F U T H T Y S N V S T
H J E L M N X I P W L V D K V H R O U I Y H N E A Q M G E E
P S V I U J M E S H Q J A E K N I C Y J W I W A I Y O X O E
A K I C N H A I M E Z P K J U T N B U Q L U R M W V I C E J
B P D E I S S U P P S C F O A W A G H I K Y P P R B E G M G
I O E C T X T P T B L D R R O Z Z Q D Y P L N O S P M U V D
P L N O Y N Z R A A O A E D I S C R E T I O N L A X X S S B
K I C M P P U D A N G P R X X S E I R B H Y W I E M K Y C U
C C E M O L Z F S T O U O Y L Z I X J L R S D C E W L J O I
V E B U L G W J E F E F G M P K Z Z C W P I I I H G J N M G
D S A N I C L M F A I G C T G R U Y S S C U N N N F L O P C
N U S I C I D A O W C E I O E I O X S O B V E G X E X D S R
D B E T I T T G A R I O C N E H J Q H F T H W E E N T T I
L C D Y N S J N A T L E B P P T E E E O E J B L O A S N A M
Y U P R G J X L Y C D E T X X O R U R C U R Y I M G I W T E
Z L O E H N R W O H Z I G U Z N L O Z I T T I M F Z J F C P
Y T L L T F H Q F M B L I A G D I I L X S S O F T W O K F R
B U I A O J P Q W A D D M S L E Q C C E R C P K F J B B G E
R R C T C L O J Z N G P W H E I L Z C I F E K R M E L J N V
C E I I L Q K I A S F C Y E X Y S I Z O N X U G O W T T K E
T V N O E B J Y J T Q Y H N T N V T N H A G Z M J G O H E N
M B G N K Q N Y K Y V B H X M R G I I M X B I D V C R N I T
F N N S H A U G I L E W T O E V A F E C T S R Q P V O A U I
X M E T O D M D V E S Y Z S H H O B U M S E R P I H A I M O
B A M V X A Y T D S K F G E C F X R C B Z T X Q I Q K J M N
X D W U L I N E O P E R A T I O N S Z C L X Y O T M H J D D
Q W R E S P O N S E T I M E D L E N G P J V K L Z H B C X T
A E Q F Y I Y M S Z Z P H Z V K V Z X A T N B A E U P S F N
```

Chain of Command

Community Policing

CompStat

Crime Prevention

Discretion

Evidence-Based Policing

Exemplary Projects Program

Legalistic Style

Line Operations

Police–Community Relations

Police Subculture

Response Time

Service Style

Sheriff

Span of Control

Staff Operations

Strategic Policing

Team Policing

Watchman Style

5 Policing: Legal Aspects

Chapter Outline

- Introduction
- The Abuse of Police Power
- Individual Rights
- Search and Seizure
- Arrest
- The Intelligence Function

Learning Objectives

After reading this chapter, you should be able to

- Explain how the Bill of Rights and democratically inspired legal restraints on the police ensure personal freedoms in our society.
- Describe the nature of due process and specific constitutional amendments on which due process guarantees are based.
- Explain the importance of the exclusionary rule and the fruit of the poisoned tree doctrine.
- Define arrest, and describe how popular depictions of arrest by the police may not be consistent with legal understandings of the term.

- Describe the circumstances under which police officers may search vehicles and the extent to which such searches are permissible.
- Explain how the need to ensure public safety may justifies certain suspicionless searches.
- Recite the *Miranda* warnings, and describe in detail recent U.S. Supreme Court cases that have affected *Miranda* warning requirements.
- Describe the nature of electronic evidence, and explain how first-on-the-scene law enforcement personnel should handle it.

Chapter Summary

Chapter 5 examines the legal constraints on police behavior. It discusses how law enforcement agents are constrained by procedural law, highlighting the legal rules that affect the search and seizure of evidence, arrest, and interrogation.

When conducting investigations, law enforcement officers rely heavily on physical evidence to substantiate criminal charges. The legal constraints on evidence collection are found in the Fourth Amendment. In general, law enforcement agents get a warrant to search and seize evidence when they can demonstrate **probable cause** to a neutral magistrate (a judge). If probable cause were later found to have been lacking, any items seized would be excluded as evidence. *Weeks* v. *United States* established the **exclusionary rule** for federal cases; *Mapp* v. *Ohio* made this rule applicable to the states.

There are many exceptions to the requirement that law enforcement agents obtain a warrant before collecting evidence, although most of them require that the agents establish probable cause. For example, if a police officer is in a place where he or she is legally allowed to be, then that officer can seize as evidence any contraband **in plain view** (*Harris* v. *U.S.*), although he or she could not move an object to put it in plain view (*Arizona* v. *Hicks*; *U.S.* v. *Irizarry*). Another exception is a search incident to an arrest. When arresting a suspect, law enforcement agents can search the person and the area in the immediate control of that person without a warrant (*Chimel* v. *California*; *U.S.* v. *Rabinowitz*). Other exceptions include emergencies, stop-and-frisk situations, concern for public safety, vehicle searches, and consent searches.

The probable cause standard also applies to the law of **arrest**. Law enforcement agents arrest, or obtain a warrant to arrest, a suspect when the facts cause a reasonable person to believe that a specific individual has committed a crime. There are, however, instances when police officers might question someone they suspect of committing a crime but may not arrest. For example, a police officer might stop to question a suspicious-looking individual and do a quick pat-down search for weapons (*Terry* v. *Ohio*). If the citizen is able to dispel the concerns of the officer, then that person is free to leave.

Chapter 5 concludes with a discussion of **interrogation**. Law enforcement agents can, and do, question citizens suspected of committing a crime, but they cannot conduct an interrogation before ensuring that the suspect is protected against self-incrimination. Courts have prohibited physically coercive techniques when questioning suspects (*Brown* v. *Mississippi*). The privilege against self-incrimination does not preclude officers from using psychologically coercive techniques to elicit confessions as long as the suspect is informed of his or her rights prior to custodial interrogation (*Miranda* v. *Arizona*).

The Fourth and Fifth Amendments mandate the two most significant and controversial procedural constraints on police behavior. These constraints have evolved considerably over the last 40 years because of changes in the ideological makeup of the Supreme Court. For example, evidence obtained based on an invalid warrant can still be used when the officer was acting in "**good faith**" (*United States* v. *Leon*). Also, law enforcement agents can question suspects without reading them their *Miranda* rights when public safety is at risk (*New York* v. *Quarles*).

Key Concepts

Anticipatory warrant   A search warrant issued on the basis of probable cause to believe that evidence of a crime, while not currently at the place described, will likely be there when the warrant is executed.

Arrest   The act of taking an adult or juvenile into physical custody by authority of law for the purpose of charging the person with a criminal offense, a delinquent act, or a status offense, terminating with the recording of a specific offense. Technically, an arrest occurs whenever a law enforcement officer curtails a person's freedom to leave.

Bill of Rights The popular name given to the first ten amendments to the U.S. Constitution, which are considered especially important in the processing of criminal defendants.

Compelling Interest A legal concept that provides a basis for suspicionless searches when public safety is at issue (urinalysis tests of train engineers are an example). It is the concept on which the Supreme Court cases of *National Treasury Employees Union* v. *Von Raab* (1989) and *Skinner* v. *Railway Labor Executives' Association* (1989) turned. In those cases, the Court held that public safety may sometimes provide a sufficiently compelling interest to justify limiting an individual's right to privacy.

Digital Criminal Forensics The lawful seizure, acquisition, analysis, reporting, and safeguarding of data from digital devices that may contain information of evidentiary value to the trier of fact in criminal events.

Electronic Communications Privacy Act (ECPA) A law passed by Congress in 1986 establishing the due process requirements that law enforcement officers must meet in order to legally intercept wire communications.

Electronic Evidence The information and data of investigative value that are stored in or transmitted by an electronic device. *Source*: Adapted from Technical Working Group for Electronic Crime Scene Investigation, *Electronic Crime Scene Investigation: A Guide for First Responders* (Washington, DC: National Institute of Justice, 2001), p. 2.

Emergency Search A search conducted by the police without a warrant that is justified on the basis of some immediate and overriding need, such as public safety, the likely escape of a dangerous suspect, or the removal or destruction of evidence.

Exclusionary Rule The understanding, based on Supreme Court precedent, that incriminating information must be seized according to constitutional specifications of due process or it will not be allowed as evidence in a criminal trial.

Fleeting Targets Exception An exception to the exclusionary rule that permits law enforcement officers to search a motor vehicle when they have probable cause but do not have a warrant. The fleeting targets exception is predicated on the fact that vehicles can quickly leave the jurisdiction of a law enforcement agency.

Fruit of the Poisoned Tree Doctrine A legal principle that excludes from introduction at trial any evidence later developed as a result of an illegal search or seizure.

Good-Faith Exception An exception to the exclusionary rule. Law enforcement officers who conduct a search or seize evidence on the basis of good faith (that is, when they believe they are operating according to the dictates of the law) and who later discover that a mistake was made (perhaps in the format of the application for a search warrant) may still use the seized evidence in court.

Illegally Seized Evidence Any evidence seized without regard to the principles of due process as described by the Bill of Rights. Most illegally seized evidence is the result of either police searches conducted without a proper warrant or improperly conducted interrogations.

Inherent Coercion The tactics used by police interviewers that fall short of physical abuse but that nonetheless pressure suspects to divulge information.

Interrogation The information-gathering activities of police officers that involve the direct questioning of suspects.

Landmark Case   A precedent-setting court decision that produces substantial changes in both the understanding of the requirements of due process and the practical day-to-day operations of the justice system.

Latent Evidence   Any evidence of relevance to a criminal investigation that is not readily seen by the unaided eye.

***Miranda* Triggers**   The dual principles of custody and interrogation, both of which are necessary before an advisement of rights is required.

***Miranda* Warnings**   The advisement of rights due criminal suspects by the police before questioning begins. *Miranda* warnings were first set forth by the Supreme Court in the 1966 case of *Miranda* v. *Arizona*.

Plain View   A legal term describing the ready visibility of objects that might be seized as evidence during a search by police in the absence of a search warrant specifying the seizure of those objects. To lawfully seize evidence in plain view, officers must have a legal right to be in the viewing area and must have cause to believe that the evidence is somehow associated with criminal activity.

Probable Cause   A set of facts and circumstances that would induce a reasonably intelligent and prudent person to believe that a particular other person has committed a specific crime. Also, reasonable grounds to make or believe an accusation. Probable cause refers to the necessary level of belief that would allow for police seizures (arrests) of individuals and full searches of dwellings, vehicles, and possessions.

Psychological Manipulation   Any manipulative action by police interviewers designed to pressure suspects to divulge information that is based on subtle forms of intimidation and control.

Reasonable Suspicion   The level of suspicion that would justify an officer making further inquiry or conducting further investigation. Reasonable suspicion may permit stopping a person for questioning or for a simple pat-down search. It is also a belief, based on a consideration of the facts at hand and on reasonable inferences drawn from those facts, that would induce an ordinarily prudent and cautious person under the same circumstances to conclude that criminal activity is taking place or that criminal activity has recently occurred. Reasonable suspicion is a *general* and reasonable belief that a crime is in progress or has occurred, whereas probable cause is a reasonable belief that a *particular* person has committed a *specific* crime.

Search Incident to an Arrest   A warrantless search of an arrested individual conducted to ensure the safety of the arresting officers. Because individuals placed under arrest may be in possession of weapons, courts have recognized the need for arresting officers to protect themselves by conducting an immediate search of arrestees without obtaining a warrant.

"Sneak and Peek" Search   A search that occurs in the suspect's absence and without his or her prior knowledge. Also known as a delayed notification search.

Suspicionless Search   A search conducted by law enforcement personnel without a warrant and without suspicion. Suspicionless searches are permissible only if based on an overriding concern for public safety.

Writ of *Certiorari*   A writ issued from an appellate court for the purpose of obtaining from a lower court the record of its proceedings in a particular case. In some states, this writ is the mechanism for discretionary review. A request for review is made by petitioning for a writ of *certiorari*, and the granting of review is indicated by the issuance of the writ.

Key Cases

Alabama v. *White*.   The Court ruled that an anonymous tip could form the basis for a stop when the informant accurately predicts the behavior of the suspect (*Alabama* v. *White*, 110 S.Ct. 2412 [1990]).

Arizona v. *Fulminante*.   The Court ruled that a confession was coerced in this specific case but also found that a coerced confession can be a harmless trial error if other evidence still proves guilt (*Arizona* v. *Fulminante*, 111 S.Ct. 1246 [1991]).

Brecht v. *Abrahamson*.   The Court held that prosecutorial efforts to use a defendant's silence against him or her will not invalidate a finding of guilt by a jury unless the "error had substantial and injurious effect or influence in determining the jury's verdict" (*Brecht* v. *Abrahamson*, 113 S.Ct. 1710, 123 L.Ed.2d 353 [1993]).

Brown v. *Mississippi*.   Law enforcement agents cannot use physically coercive interrogation techniques to elicit confessions (*Brown* v. *Mississippi*, 297 U.S. 278 [1936]).

California v. *Hodari D.*   The Court held that if a suspect runs from the police and discards incriminating evidence, the suspect can be arrested based on that evidence (*California* v. *Hodari D.*, 111 S.Ct. 1547 [1991]).

Carroll v. *United States*.   A warrantless search of an automobile or other vehicle is valid if based on probable cause that contraband is present (*Carroll* v. *United States*, 267 U.S. 132 [1925]).

Chimel v. *California*.   A search, incident to a lawful arrest, is limited to the area in the immediate control or grabbing area of the suspect (*Chimel* v. *California*, 395 U.S. 752 [1969]).

Dickerson v. *U.S.*   It upheld the 1966 U.S. Supreme Court decision of *Miranda* v. *Arizona* (*Dickerson* v. *U.S.*, 530 U.S. 428 [2000]).

Escobedo v. *Illinois*.   This case recognized the suspect's right to have legal counsel present during police interrogation (*Escobedo* v. *Illinois*, 378 U.S. 478 [1964]).

Florida v. *Bostick*.   This case is the basis for permitting warrantless "sweeps" of intercity buses (*Florida* v. *Bostick*, 111 S.Ct. 2382 [1991]).

Horton v. *California*.   The courts declared that inadvertance is not a necessary condition to justify a plain-view search (*Horton* v. *California*, 110 S.Ct. 2301, 47 Cr.L. 2135 [1990]).

Illinois v. *Perkins*.   *Miranda* warnings are not required when a suspect does not believe that he or she is speaking to a law enforcement officer (*Illinois* v. *Perkins*, 495 U.S. 292 [1990]).

Indianapolis v. *Edmond*.   In this case, the Supreme Court decided to strike down a narcotics checkpoint, stating that the Fourth Amendment prohibits even a brief "seizure" of a motorist under a program whose purpose is indistinguishable from a general interest in crime control (*Indianapolis* v. *Edmond*, 531 U.S. 32 [2000]).

Kyllo v. *U.S.*   The U.S. Supreme Court held that the use of a device not in general public use to explore details of a private home is surveillance, which is a Fourth Amendment search (*Kyllo* v. *U.S.*, 533 U.S. 27 [2001]).

Mapp v. *Ohio*.   The Fourth Amendment's exclusionary rule is applicable to the states through the due process clause of the Fourteenth Amendment (*Mapp* v. *Ohio*, 367 U.S. 643 [1961]).

Minnick v. *Mississippi*.   The court held that interrogation may not resume after the suspect has had an opportunity to consult his or her lawyer when the lawyer is no longer present (*Minnick* v. *Mississippi*, 498 U.S. 146 [1990]).

Miranda v. *Arizona.*   A person in custody must be advised of various warnings and his or her legal rights prior to being subjected to custodial interrogation (*Miranda* v. *Arizona*, 384 U.S. 436 [1966]).

Nix v. *Williams.*   This case created the "inevitable discovery exception" to the *Miranda* requirements (*Nix* v. *Williams*, 104 S.Ct. 2501 [1984]).

Richards v. *Wisconsin.*   The U.S. Supreme Court ruled that police can make "no-knock" entries if announcing their presence might inhibit the investigation of the crime (*Richards* v. *Wisconsin*, 117 S.Ct. 1416 [1997]).

Silverthorne Lumber Co. v. *U.S.*   This case established the fruit of the poisoned tree doctrine (*Silverthorne Lumber Co.* v. *U.S.*, 251 U.S. 385 [1920]).

Smith v. *Ohio.*   The Court held that an individual has the right to protect his or her belongings from unwarranted police inspection (*Smith* v. *Ohio*, 110 S.Ct. 1288 [1990]).

Terry v. *Ohio.*   This case established the stop-and-frisk exception. A citizen can be briefly detained by law enforcement agents without probable cause when the agents have reasonable suspicion to believe the person has committed or is about to commit a crime. An agent can conduct a limited pat-down search of the suspect (*Terry* v. *Ohio*, 392 U.S. 1 [1968]).

U.S. Department of Justice v. *Landano.*   The U.S. Supreme Court required that an informant's identity be revealed through a federal Freedom of Information Act request (*U.S. Department of Justice* v. *Landano*, 113 S.Ct. 2014, 124 L.Ed.2d 84 [1993]).

U.S. v. *Drayton.*   The Supreme Court decided that police officers are not required to advise bus passengers of their right to refuse to cooperate with officers conducting searches (*U.S.* v. *Drayton*, 122 S.Ct. 2105 [2002]).

U.S. v. *Patane.*   The Supreme Court found that a mere failure to give *Miranda* warnings does not violate a suspect's constitutional rights or even the *Miranda* rule (*U.S.* v. *Patane*, 542 U.S. 630 [2004]).

U.S. v. *Robinson.*   This case establishes that a search incident to a lawful arrest does not violate Fourth Amendment protections (*U.S.* v. *Robinson*, 414 U.S. 218 [1973]).

Weeks v. *United States.*   Evidence obtained by federal officers in violation of the Fourth Amendment will be excluded from admission in federal prosecutions (the exclusionary rule) (*Weeks* v. *United States*, 232 U.S. 383 [1914]).

Wilson v. *Arkansas.*   The U.S. Supreme Court ruled that police officers must knock and announce their identity before entering a dwelling even when they have a search warrant (*Wilson* v. *Arkansas*, 115 S.Ct. 1914 [1995]).

Learning Tips

On Exams, Go with Your First Instinct

It is usually best to stick with your first choice on the objective questions (true-or-false and multiple-choice questions). Avoid going against your first instinct unless, through reflection or deduction, you are convinced that your second answer is correct.

Study with a Friend

It is difficult to remember the holdings of the cases cited in Chapter 5 because there are so many of them. Have a friend or classmate quiz you on holdings of the various cases. This will help ensure that you can identify the specifics of the cases when you are taking the examination.

CJ Brief on the World Wide Web

Web links to organizations and agencies related to the material in Chapter 5 include:

WEBSITE	URL
American Bar Association	http://www.abanet.org
American Civil Liberties Union (ACLU)	http://www.aclu.org
American Prosecutors Research Institute	http://www.ndaa-apri.org
Justice Denied	http://www.justicedenied.org
Kuglick's Forensic Resource and Criminal Law	http://www.kruglaw.com
Law Enforcement Links	http://www.leolinks.com
Police Guide	http://www.policeguide.com
Stanford Law and Policy Review	http://www.stanford.edu/group/SLPR
U.S. Evidence Law	http://www.law.cornell.edu/topics/evidence.html

Learner Activities

Activity 1

Recall from the discussion in Chapter 1 that justice requires a fair balance between individual and community interests. The Supreme Court's interpretation of the Fourth Amendment provides an effective illustration of the difficulties in finding a fair balance. A public-order advocate might argue that the exclusionary rule has handcuffed the abilities of the police to effectively protect the community. An individual-rights advocate, however, might argue that such changes have resulted in positive reform of the police and that such rights need to be expanded. What is your opinion? If the president appointed you to the Supreme Court, would you be willing to overturn *Mapp* v. *Ohio* and eliminate the exclusionary rule? Why or why not?

_____

_____

_____

_____

_____

_____

Activity 2

In the following search-and-seizure situations, note whether you think the evidence seized would be excluded in a court of law. In addition, try to note cases that apply to each circumstance.

1. Police Officer Adams observed an automobile driving the wrong way on a one-way street. When the officer tried to stop the automobile, the driver fled, resulting in a high-speed chase. The chase ended when the driver's car crashed into a telephone pole. Concerned that the car might ignite from a gas leak, Officer Adams pulled the unconscious woman from the car. After he had

pulled the woman a safe distance from the car, he went back into the car to locate her purse for identification, at which time he found a knife covered in blood on the front seat. It was later discovered that the knife was used in the murder of another police officer. Should the knife be excluded? What court case(s) justify your decision?

2. While off duty and at a party, Officer Boone was asked by the home owner to get some ice from his basement. Since the ice machine was not immediately apparent, Officer Boone opened two doors, and behind door two were six marijuana plants. Officer Boone arrested the home owner. Would you exclude the marijuana plants? What court case(s) justify your decision?

3. Defendant Chase was suspected of selling stolen property from his dorm room. An undercover campus police officer knocked on Chase's door, and when Chase answered, the officer asked for an affordable radar detector. In response, Defendant Chase said that he just got two new ones last night. While in the room, the officer noticed various other items that she suspected were stolen. She bought one of the radar detectors and then used it to convince a judge to issue a search warrant of the room. Among the items confiscated in the search with the warrant were four radar detectors, three television sets, two air-conditioning units, and 1,500 compact discs. Should this evidence be excluded? What court case(s) justify your decision?

4. Police Officer Doe and Police Officer Evans were observing a street corner for drug activity and noticed Defendant Ford selling drugs to Defendant Gillis. The officers quickly got to the corner but were able to arrest only Defendant Gillis. Before they could handcuff him, Gillis swallowed what appeared to them to be one balloon of heroin. Police Officer Evans forced his finger down Defendant Gillis's throat, causing him to vomit. Among the extracted material was one balloon of heroin. Would this evidence be excluded? What court case(s) justify your decision?

5. When executing a valid arrest warrant for an assault charge in Defendant Hood's home, Officer Ivers seized a handgun in the search incident to the arrest. Alarmed that her life was in danger, Officer Ivers made Defendant Hood lie with his face down to the floor and quickly perused three adjoining rooms. While walking through the kitchen, Officer Ivers noticed a pile of semiautomatic weapons on the table and seized them as evidence. Should these weapons be excluded? What case(s) justify your decision?

_____

_____

_____

_____

_____

_____

Activity 3

One of the important policy issues being debated in courts and among politicians is whether the *Miranda* decision should be overturned. Visit the Prentice Hall Criminal Justice Cybrary at http://www.cybrary.info. Use the search function to find websites about the application of the *Miranda* rule. After you peruse several sites, answer the following question in the space provided below. Should police officers be required to read a *Miranda*-type warning prior to custodial interrogation, or should *Miranda* be overturned? Explain your answer.

_____

_____

_____

_____

_____

_____

Activity 4

Chapter 5 provides an analysis of many landmark cases. The full texts of several of these Supreme Court decisions are posted as Library Extras. For example, included are the full texts of the _Brown_ v. _Mississippi, Harris_ v. _U.S., Mapp_ v. _Ohio, Miranda_ v. _Arizona, Silverthorne Lumber Company_ v. _U.S., Terry_ v. _Ohio,_ and _Weeks_ v. _U.S._ decisions. Read the full text of one of these cases. Then, in the space provided below, provide a complete summary of the case. Be sure to discuss the facts of the case and the Court's decision, and then provide the reason(s) for the Court's decision in the case.

_____

_____

_____

_____

_____

_____

Internet Activity

Use the Cybrary (http://www.cybrary.info) to find information about legal issues and policing. Use the search function available to locate information about the exclusionary rule. What kinds of information did you find?

_____

_____

_____

_____

_____

_____

Distance Learning Activity

Write a case scenario that raises a Fourth Amendment concern. Submit the case or cases relevant to resolving this concern. Here is an example of what this exercise asks you to do. Defendant Sally Smith was watching television when a police officer knocked at her door. Sally opened the door and said, "What do you want?" The officer responded, "I just wanted to talk to you about a robbery that occurred over on 8th and Vine." Sally answered, "Sure, come on into my home. I don't have anything to hide." While sitting at the kitchen table, the officer noticed a marijuana plant on a window ledge. The officer then placed Sally in handcuffs, arresting her for possession of a controlled substance. The officer then searched Sally and found a small bag of cocaine in her right front pocket. The relevant cases are tied to consent issues, plain view, and search incident to arrest. If your instructor asks you to do so, submit your scenario to the other students in your class and see whether they can identify the key procedural issues and cases.

_____

_____

_____

_____

_____

_____

Student Study Guide Questions

True or False

_____ 5-1. Most jurisdictions allow arrest for a felony without a warrant as long as probable cause is established.

_____ 5-2. Officers may not stop and question an unwilling citizen when they have no reason to suspect him or her of a crime.

_____ 5-3. Hidden evidence is considered any evidence not readily seen by the unaided eye.

_____ 5-4. Public safety may provide a sufficiently compelling interest such that an individual's right to privacy can be limited under certain circumstances.

_____ 5-5. If the police initiate an arrest in a person's home, because of the law regarding search incident to arrest, they could search the entire residence, including drawers, closets, and trunks.

_____ 5-6. A writ of certiorari is the warrant federal agents need to make an arrest.

_____ 5-7. Probable cause must be satisfactorily demonstrated by police officers in a written affidavit to a magistrate before a search warrant can be issued.

_____ 5-8. Certain emergencies permit police to search premises without a warrant.

_____ 5-9. Nontestimonial evidence, such as blood, cannot be seized as evidence.

_____ 5-10. The Electronic Communications Privacy Act prohibits law enforcement officers from seizing electronic communications under any circumstances.

Multiple Choice

5-11. Which of these statements about the search and seizure of evidence is false?
    a. A warrantless search of an automobile is valid if it is based on probable cause that contraband is present.
    b. Evidence in plain view seen by an officer, when the evidence is in a place where the officer is legally allowed to be, will not be excluded.
    c. Evidence illegally seized by the police cannot be used in a trial under most circumstances.
    d. In all circumstances, police officers must get a warrant in order to seize evidence.

5-12. Which constitutional amendment establishes legal boundaries for the search and seizure of evidence?
    a. Fourth
    b. Fifth
    c. First
    d. Second

5-13. Which constitutional amendment establishes legal boundaries for the interrogation of suspects?
    a. Fourth
    b. Fifth
    c. First
    d. Second

5-14. Which of the following legal principles excludes from introduction at trial any evidence obtained as a result of an originally illegal search or seizure?
    a. plain-view doctrine
    b. public-safety exception
    c. good-faith exception
    d. fruit of the poisoned tree doctrine

5-15. Which U.S. Supreme Court case established the public-safety exception to the *Miranda* rule?
    a. *Brown* v. *Mississippi*
    b. *New York* v. *Quarles*
    c. *Mapp* v. *Ohio*
    d. *Weeks* v. *United States*

5-16. Which of the following U.S. Supreme Court cases does *not* involve police interrogation of suspects?
    a. *Brown* v. *Mississippi*
    b. *Chimel* v. *California*
    c. *Miranda* v. *Arizona*
    d. *Escobedo* v. *Illinois*

5-17. Which U.S. Supreme Court case made the exclusionary rule applicable to the states?
    a. *Brown* v. *Mississippi*
    b. *New York* v. *Quarles*
    c. *Mapp* v. *Ohio*
    d. *Weeks* v. *United States*

5-18. Which of the following U.S. Supreme Court cases does *not* involve the search of a vehicle?
    a. *United States* v. *Ross*
    b. *United States* v. *Leon*
    c. *Carroll* v. *U.S.*
    d. *South Dakota* v. *Opperman*

5-19. In which of the following situations would a law enforcement agent *not* be required to read a suspect the *Miranda* warnings?
   a. A suspect makes a spontaneous statement, stating "I just killed my wife," to officers arriving at the scene.
   b. A police officer arrests a person for robbery and assault. When traveling to the police station for booking purposes, she asks the suspect, "What do you know about this robbery?"
   c. An off-duty police officer apprehends a purse snatcher. As the officer waits for a police car to transport the suspect, he asks, "How many purses have you stolen in the last month?"
   d. Jason Melo, convicted of rape and burglary, was serving time in a maximum-security prison; he was also a suspect in a murder investigation. In the visiting room of the prison, the detective asked Jason, "Did you murder your brother-in-law?"

5-20. In which of the following situations would a law enforcement officer be able to conduct a search if he or she did not have probable cause to do so?
   a. vehicle search
   b. search incident to an arrest
   c. suspicionless search
   d. none of the above

Fill-In

5-21. The case that established the good-faith exception to the exclusionary rule is _____.

5-22. The case that articulated the fruit of the poisoned tree doctrine is _____.

5-23. The case that established a two-pronged test to the effect that informant information could establish probable cause if both criteria were met is _____.

5-24. The case that established the famous requirement of police to advise a suspect of his or her rights is _____.

5-25. The case that first recognized the need for emergency searches is _____.

5-26. The case that held a search incident to an arrest invalid when it goes beyond the person arrested and the area subject to that person's "immediate control" is _____.

5-27. The case that established the stop-and-frisk exception to the exclusionary rule is _____.

5-28. The case that placed limits on an officer's ability to seize evidence discovered during a pat-down search is _____.

5-29. The case that made the exclusionary rule applicable to the states is _____.

5-30. The case that established the exclusionary rule in federal cases is _____.

Crossword Puzzle

Across

4. Required standard for a search warrant.
7. Police activity regulated by *Brown* v. *Mississippi*.
8. Amendment concerned with unreasonable searches and seizures.
10. Exception predicated on the fact that vehicles can quickly leave the jurisdiction.
11. Rule that means evidence illegally seized by the police cannot be used in a trial.
13. Concept central to *National Treasury Employees Union* v. *Von Raab*.
14. Amendment providing protection against self-incrimination.
15. Case establishing the famous requirement of a police rights advisement of suspects.
16. First landmark case on search and seizure.
17. _____ of the poisoned tree doctrine.

Down

1. ECPA.
2. Cases that produce substantial changes in the understanding of the requirements of due process.
3. Writ of _____.
5. Evidence of relevance to a criminal investigation that is not readily seen by the unaided eye.
6. Exception established in *U.S.* v. *Leon*.
9. *Arizona* v. *Hicks* focuses on this exclusionary rule exception.
12. Tactics used by police interviewers that fall short of physical abuse but that nonetheless pressure suspects to divulge information.

Word Search Puzzle

```
M S I F I H L G N F M G Z F E S N W L Y U V B A R L G I M N
M D C L A T E N T E V I D E N C E O R U M C Y F J P A E T T
C O F L E E T I N G T A R G E T S E X C E P T I O N R F X X
X T X E J K H D G L V M Q A E D F C U D P Q V Q W F F L K Q
F F J N C A E N F I Z V W F N R X V K E H A U E V D G Y Y R
T G K I L S W P Z W F D M E I D Z U X P Z F A W I S N R A S
B O S R J U D D G V H Y G S O A A Y Q H T U Y G E O U P T W
T O F A B Z C J G G P K V L H H X T S F S D T F I T J D Z A
N D J D C O M P E L L I N G I N T E R E S T W C P D M Z P N
V F F A H L C U F U Y V H G B G M D Q I W S I V K Q H Z O C
S A P Q S U E H U O X T D B S P X O L J G P V Q Q B Q I I F
U I W R I T O F C E R T I O R A R I X Q S G R L B Y T H N E
S T H Z U E M L H P E C R R P K C V M U F Z E B X A R Z H L
P H C I P L X I T G Z J U J G W O Y S G Q J B R G Y Q M E E
I E M Q I F R E R M P F T F W K G E G A C W O O S B J U R C
C X I K T V U M I A I C R Y R Y L L I F E B R J O N P Z E T
I C B X H C R E Z H N W S B O B B Y H K O R Q O P R H T N R
O E J O U S P R G K O D M I A J G N J K E H H U R C D L T O
N P I V K V I G K X O F A N J V Y T M T C J S V O V P A C N
L T U U S A H E Q D R W O W C I Z J N V G J K L B T D N O I
E I T L W F V N P W E S X A A X Q I D L E G B Y A N A D E C
S O V K U U A C R S A M Q C E R P G Y T O Z B M B B W M R E
S N N Y L U Q Y R E N T A Z Q W N L C N E C P A L F P A C V
S E T X A Y C S R T W D S B O M M I A R A O G Y E F G R I I
E A J N P B W E A R R E S T C K E T N I B J G W C D H K O D
A K P Y F P K A N C R M F H D A I N J G N P B N A E E C N E
R G Y N C W F R A K V S D X C P T J S X S V D H U U M A D N
C D N G F M M C X F Y T D J J F J X I D J S I C S D U S U C
H T L O Z Q M H E X C L U S I O N A R Y R U L E E S Z E A E
T S N E A K A N D P E E K E O O P G Y N E Y P H W R V K U O
```

Arrest

Compelling Interest

ECPA

Electronic Evidence

Emergency Search

Exclusionary Rule

Fleeting Targets Exception

Good-Faith Exception

Inherent Coercion

Interrogation

Landmark Case

Latent Evidence

Miranda Triggers

Miranda Warnings

Plain View

Probable Cause

Reasonable Suspicion

Sneak and Peek

Suspicionless Search

Writ of *Certiorari*

6 Policing: Issues and Challenges

Chapter Outline

- Introduction
- Police Personality and Culture
- Corruption and Integrity
- The Dangers of Police Work
- Terrorism's Impact on Policing
- Police Civil Liability

- Racial Profiling and Biased Policing
- Police Use of Force
- Professionalism and Ethics
- Ethnic and Gender Diversity in Policing
- Private Protective Services

Learning Objectives

After reading this chapter, you should be able to

- Describe the police working personality, and relate it to police culture.
- List and describe different types of police corruption, and discuss methods for building police integrity.
- Explain the dangers of police work, and discuss what can be done to reduce those dangers.
- Describe terrorism's impact on police agencies in America today.
- Describe the civil liability issues associated with policing, including racially biased policing.

- Describe efforts to enhance police professionalism.
- Discuss ethnic and gender diversity in policing today.
- Describe the nature and extent of private protective services in the United States today, and describe the role these services might play in the future.
- Explain the relationship between private security and public policing in America.

Chapter Summary

Chapter 6 discusses several important police issues, including police personality and culture, corruption, dangers of police work, terrorism and policing, police civil liability, professionalism and ethics, and private security. One powerful influence on law enforcement officers is the police culture. New recruits are molded by the police culture as supervisors and other officers teach rookie officers the informal policies of the department. Thus, there are two sets of rules that new police officers must learn and follow. The first set of rules includes those formal departmental policies and legal constraints that the officers learn in the training academy. The second set of rules involves the informal socialization that takes place as officers interact with older experienced officers who teach how formal rules are interpreted. For example, experienced officers might explain to a new recruit that accepting free meals or bribes is expected, despite departmental policy clearly forbidding such behavior. The text discusses such activities in the section on police corruption, noting its historical pervasiveness. Chapter 6 also discusses how police departments have attempted to respond to police corruption.

The chapter also discusses terrorism's impact on policing. The attacks of September 11, 2001, has impacted many sectors of society and has significantly changed policing in the United States. Although the core mission of policing has not changed, law enforcement has had to focus time, energy, and resources to prepare for and prevent terrorist attacks. One of the interesting developments in this area is the concept of **intelligence-led policing**.

Other police issues discussed in Chapter 6 include drug testing of recruits and random testing of other employees. In addition, the dangers of police work (including exposure to blood evidence that might contain disease), deadly force, and police stress are discussed. Police civil liability issues and the very important topic of racial profiling are outlined as well.

The author discusses key issues related to resolving many of the issues facing police departments in the section on **professionalism** and **ethics**. Accrediting police departments, raising educational standards, and improving the recruitment and selection of officers are changes being made to address problem areas of policing. This chapter also discusses issues of ethnic and gender diversity in policing. Statistics show that the representation of underrepresented groups has dramatically increased, but women are still significantly underrepresented.

Chapter 6 concludes with a discussion of the growing private law enforcement industry. Indeed, the number of individuals employed in private security is higher than that in the other levels combined. Although the primary concern of the textbook is how local, state, and federal police respond to crime, discussion of private policing is important because of the growing influence of private security in criminal justice and the overlap of public and private security agencies.

Key Concepts

1983 Lawsuit   A civil suit brought under Title 42, Section 1983, of the U.S. Code, against anyone who denies others their constitutional rights to life, liberty, or property without due process of law.

Biological Weapon   A biological agent used to threaten human life (for example, anthrax, smallpox, or any infectious disease). *Source*: Technical Working Group on Crime Scene Investigation, *Crime Scene Investigation: A Guide for Law Enforcement* (Washington, DC: National Institute of Justice, 2000), p. 12.

***Bivens* Action**   A civil suit based upon the case of *Bivens* v. *Six Unknown Federal Agents*, brought against federal government officials for denial of the constitutional rights of others.

Civil Liability   Potential responsibility for payment of damages or other court-ordered enforcement as a result of a ruling in a lawsuit. Civil liability is not the same as criminal liability, which means "open to punishment for a crime." *Source*: Adapted from Gerald and Kathleen Hill, *The Real Life Dictionary of the Law*. Web posted at http://www.law.com. Accessed June 11, 2003.

Criminal Intelligence   Information compiled, analyzed, and/or disseminated in an effort to anticipate, prevent, or monitor criminal activity.

Deadly Force   Force likely to cause death or great bodily harm. Also, "the intentional use of a firearm or other instrument resulting in a high probability of death." *Source*: Sam W. Lathrop, "Reviewing Use of Force: A Systematic Approach," *FBI Law Enforcement Bulletin*, October 2000, p. 18.

Excessive Force   The application of an amount and/or frequency of force greater than that required to compel compliance from a willing or unwilling subject. *Source*: International Association of Chiefs of Police, *Police Use of Force in America 2001* (Alexandria, VA: IACP, 2001), p. 1.

Intelligence-led Policing   The collection and analysis of information to produce an intelligence end product designed to inform police decision making at both the tactical and strategic levels..

Internal Affairs   The branch of a police organization tasked with investigating charges of wrongdoing against other members of the department.

Knapp Commission   A committee that investigated police corruption in New York City in the early 1970s.

Less-Lethal Weapon   A weapon that is designed to disable, capture, or immobilize—but not kill—a suspect. Occasional deaths do result from the use of such weapons, however.

NLETS   The International Justice and Public Safety Information Sharing Network.

Peace Officer Standards and Training (POST) Program   The official program of a state or legislative jurisdiction that sets standards for the training of law enforcement officers. All states set such standards, although not all use the term *POST*.

Police Corruption   The abuse of police authority for personal or organizational gain. *Source*: Carl B. Klockers et al., "The Measurement of Police Integrity," *National Institute of Justice Research in Brief* (Washington, DC: NIJ, 2000), p. 1.

Police Ethics   The special responsibility to adhere to moral duty and obligation that is inherent in police work.

Police Professionalism   The increasing formalization of police work and the accompanying rise in public acceptance of the police.

Police Subculture   The set of informal values that characterize the police force as a distinct community with a common identity.

Police Use of Force   The use of physical restraint by a police officer when dealing with a member of the public. *Source*: National Institute of Justice, *Use of Force by Police: Overview of National and Local Data* (Washington, DC: NIJ, 1999).

Police Working Personality   All aspects of the traditional values and patterns of behavior evidenced by police officers who have been effectively socialized into the police subculture. Characteristics of the police personality often extend to the personal lives of law enforcement personnel.

Private Protective Services   Independent or proprietary commercial organizations that provide protective services to employers on a contractual basis.

Problem Police Officer A law enforcement officer who exhibits problem behavior, as indicated by high rates of citizen complaints and use-of-force incidents and by other evidence. *Source*: Samuel Walker, Geoffrey P. Alpert, and Dennis J. Kenney, *Responding to the Problem Police Officer: A National Study of Early Warning Systems* (Washington, DC: NIJ, 2000).

Racial Profiling Any police-initiated action that relies on the race, ethnicity, or national origin rather than [1] the behavior of an individual or [2] on information that leads the police to a particular individual who has been identified as being, or having been, engaged in criminal activity." *Source*: Deborah Ramierz, Jack McDevitt, and Amy Farrell, *A Resource Guide on Racial Profiling Data Collection Systems: Promising Practices and Lessons Learned* (Washington, DC: USDOJ, November 2000), p. 3.

KEY CASES

Biscoe v. *Arlington County*. Alvin Biscoe was awarded $5 million after he lost both legs in an accident with a police officer involved in a high-speed chase. This case demonstrates that officers who drive in a way that places others in danger may find themselves the subject of civil suits (*Biscoe* v. *Arlington County*, 238 U.S. App. D.C. 206, 738 F.2d 1352, 1362 [1984]).

Bivens v. *Six Unknown Federal Agents*. This case established a path for legal action against agents enforcing federal laws (*Bivens* v. *Six Unknown Federal Agents*, 403 U.S. 388 [1971]).

City of Canton, Ohio v. *Harris*. This case focuses on a department's training regimen. The Supreme Court held that a failure to train, when based on a deliberate indifference to the rights of persons, can lead to civil liability (*City of Canton, Ohio* v. *Harris*, 489 U.S. 378 [1989]).

Graham v. *Connor*. The Court established the standard of "objective reasonableness" by which an officer's use of deadly force could be assessed in terms of "reasonableness at the moment" (*Graham* v. *Connor*, 490 U.S. 386, 396–397 [1989]).

Hunter v. *Bryant*. This case applies to the issue of "qualified immunity" for officers in the line of duty. When making an arrest without a warrant, an officer is given immunity from civil liability when he or she makes a mistake; however, the determination of probable cause to make that arrest must have been reasonable (*Hunter* v. *Bryant*, 112 S.Ct. 534 [1991]).

Idaho v. *Horiuchi*. The holding in this case from the 9th U.S. Circuit Court of Appeals ruled that federal law enforcement officers are not immune from state prosecution when their actions violate state law with malice or excessive zeal (*Idaho* v. *Horiuchi*, No. 98-30149 [9th Cir. 06/05/2001]).

Malley v. *Briggs*. In this case, the Court decided that a police officer can be held liable for monetary damages if he or she makes an arrest or a search for property based on a bad warrant. An officer is liable if it can be shown that reasonably well-trained officers would have known that the warrant failed to establish probable cause (*Malley* v. *Briggs*, 475 U.S. 335, 106 sect. 1092 [1986]).

Maurice Turner v. *Fraternal Order of Police*. The court supported drug testing based on a reasonable suspicion of drug abuse (*Maurice Turner* v. *Fraternal Order of Police*, 500 A.2d 1005 [D.C. 1985]).

Tennessee v. *Garner*. This case specified the conditions under which deadly force could be used in the apprehension of suspected felons (*Tennessee* v. *Garner*, 471 U.S. 1 [1985]).

Learning Tips

Tests

Managing review time is essential for test preparation. Instant reviews, which should occur either directly after the class meeting or during your assigned readings, start the learning and memorization processes. Weekly reviews should be more focused than instant reviews. Last, final reviews are the most in-depth reviews, and they should be conducted in the week prior to the exam. Final reviews help demonstrate the big picture and further understanding of the information provided during the entire class. Used together, instant, weekly, and final reviews provide the foundation for successful test preparation.

Before the Test

Be sure to arrive early for exams. This will allow time for relaxation and general preparation. Avoid talking to other students about their test preparation. This will only cause more anxiety. Listen to all instructions while the exam is being distributed. As redundant as it may seem, read the directions twice. You may lose significant points for not following the simplest instructions. Before beginning, if you feel it is necessary, take a minute to release all test anxieties and to relax your mind.

CJ Brief on the World Wide Web

Web links to organizations and agencies related to the material in Chapter 6 include:

WEBSITE TITLE	URL
Abner Louima Torture Case	http://www.thesmokinggun.com /torture/torture.htm
California Law Enforcement Basic	http://www.clew.org/Tm/TmCtrs /BasicAcad.html
FBI's Counterterrorism Page	http://www.fbi.gov/aboutus /transformation/ct.htm
Ira Wilsker's Law Enforcement Sites	http://www.ih2000.net/ira
National Center for Disaster Preparedness	http://www.ncdp.mailman. columbia.edu/
Office of Community Oriented Policing Services	http://www.cops.usdoj.gov
Police Hall of Fame and Museum	http://www.aphf.org
Terrorism Research Center	http://www.terrorism.org/

Learner Activities

Activity 1

Read **Library Extra 6–1** on promoting police integrity. What does the author suggest are the key principles for promoting police integrity?

_____

_____

_____

_____

_____

_____

Activity 2

For this activity, first read the short research report on police use of force, as well as force against the police, posted at **Library Extras 6–13** and **6–14**. After reading the reports, summarize the findings in the space provided below. In your synopsis, be sure to answer the following questions: How often do the police use force? How often do suspects use force against the police? What type of force is used in arrest situations? What factors predict police use of force?

Library
EXTRA

_____

_____

_____

_____

_____

_____

Activity 3

Compile a list of the police civil liability cases discussed in this chapter. What are the major findings of each case?

_____

_____

_____

_____

_____

_____

Activity 4

Use the Cybrary (http://www.cybrary.info) to find four articles about racial profiling. Describe these studies and their findings.

_____

_____

_____

_____

_____

_____

Internet Activity

Use the Cybrary (http://www.cybrary.info) to find articles about police stress. What kinds of studies did you find? What do they deal with? What were the findings or results of each of these studies?

_____

_____

_____

_____

_____

_____

Distance Learning Activity

Visit a number of police memorial websites. What type of information is included at these websites? Assemble a notebook (or disk) containing the information you have gathered. Your instructor may request that you submit the material.

_____

_____

_____

_____

_____

_____

Student Study Guide Questions

True or False

_____   6-1. Most large law enforcement agencies have their own internal affairs division.

_____   6-2. Barker and Carter describe acts of occupational deviance as those that further the goals of law enforcement.

_____   6-3. Meat-eating police corruption is the most common form of police deviance, involving mostly small bribes or relatively small services.

_____   6-4. Police officers who have adopted a "working personality" are primarily concerned with fairness.

_____   6-5. The Knapp Commission investigated police use of deadly force in the late 1990s.

_____   6-6. In *Malley* v. *Briggs*, the Supreme Court banned random drug testing of police officers.

_____   6-7. More people are employed in private security than all local, state, and federal police agencies combined.

_____   6-8. Currently, the Fleeing Felon Rule guides police decision making in deadly force situations.

_____   6-9. Less-lethal weapons are designed to disable but not kill a suspect.

_____   6-10. A federal lawsuit against the police is often called a 2003 lawsuit.

Multiple Choice

6-11. Which type of police corruption occurs in order to further the organizational goals of law enforcement?
   a. meat eating
   b. grass eating
   c. occupational deviance
   d. abuse of authority

6-12. Which type of police corruption is motivated by the desire for personal benefit?
   a. meat eating
   b. grass eating
   c. occupational deviance
   d. abuse of authority

6-13. Which Supreme Court case is *not* directly relevant to police civil liability issues?
   a. *Malley* v. *Briggs*
   b. *City of Canton, Ohio* v. *Harris*
   c. *Tennessee* v. *Garner*
   d. *Board of County Commission of Bryan County, Oklahoma* v. *Brown*

6-14. Which division in a police department investigates charges that officers are guilty of wrongdoing?
   a. strategic investigations
   b. intelligence
   c. internal affairs
   d. officer supervision

6-15. Historically, officers were allowed to use deadly force to prevent the escape of a suspected felon. This was known as the
   a. deadly force statute.
   b. "shoot to kill" policy.
   c. escaping suspect doctrine.
   d. Fleeing Felon Rule.

6-16. A police officer can be sued for
   a. false arrest.
   b. failure to prevent a foreseeable crime.
   c. negligence in the care of persons in police custody.
   d. all of the above.

6-17. Officers who have adopted the police working personality are often
    a. cynical.
    b. authoritarian.
    c. prejudiced.
    d. all of the above.

6-18. What standard for deadly force was established in *Graham* v. *Connor*?
    a. objective reasonableness
    b. probable cause
    c. clear and present danger
    d. best guess

6-19. Which commission provided the grass-eating and meat-eating distinctions to describe types of police corruption?
    a. Johnson Commission
    b. Nixon Commission
    c. Knapp Commission
    d. Burger Commission

6-20. What area of police civil liability received a significant amount of media attention in the late 1990s?
    a. deadly force
    b. drug testing
    c. racial profiling
    d. false arrest

Fill-In

6-21. A(n) _____ is likely to have high rates of citizen complaints.

6-22. The _____ encompasses all aspects of the traditional values and patterns of behavior evidenced by police officers who have been effectively socialized into the police subculture.

6-23. _____ is the use of physical restraint by a police officer.

6-24. _____ developed the term *police working personality*.

6-25. A(n) _____ is an agent (such as anthrax) used to threaten human life.

6-26. _____ is the branch of the police department that investigates wrongdoing among members of the department.

6-27. _____ is the abuse of police authority for personal or organizational gain.

6-28. Civil suits brought under Title 42, Section 1983, of the U.S. Code are called _____.

6-29. _____ is the name given to civil suits brought against federal government officials for denial of the constitutional rights of others.

6-30. _____ is the increasing formalization of police work and the rise in public acceptance of the police that accompanies it.

Crossword Puzzle

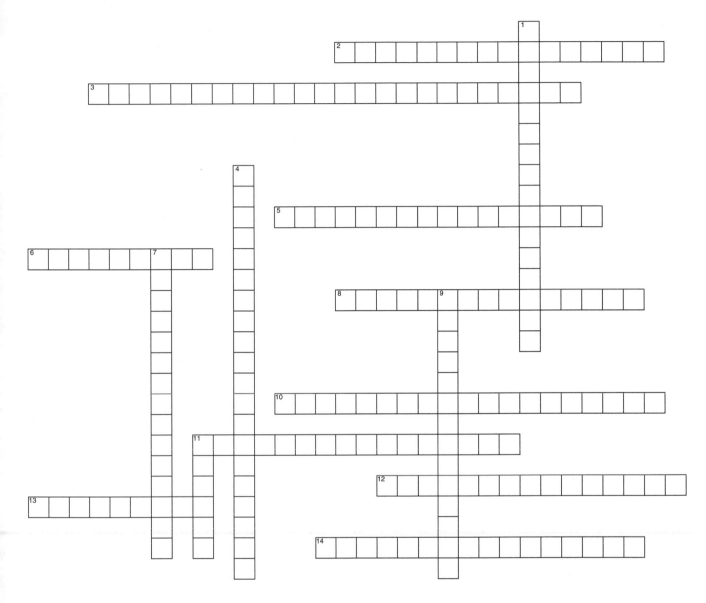

Across

2. Use of physical restraint by a police officer.
3. All aspects of the traditional values and patterns of behavior evidenced by police officers who have been effectively socialized into the police subculture.
5. Case that specified the conditions under which deadly force could be used in the apprehension of suspected felons.
6. Type of immunity generally given to police officers.
8. Famous police corruption commission.
10. When drug testing of police officers can occur.
11. Anthrax or smallpox.
12. Any police-initiated action that relies on a person's race, ethnicity, or national origin.

13. Type of force greater than is required for compliance.
14. Weapon designed to disable but not kill.

Down

1. Abuse of police authority for personal or organizational gain.
4. Police officer with a high rate of citizen complaints.
7. Department that polices the police.
9. Payment for a ruling in a lawsuit.
11. _____ v. *Six Unknown Federal Agents*.

Word Search Puzzle

```
V O T Q C F I N T E R N A L A F F A I R S V X L Q K P U N I
E W X U X O C B K F M U N C K W U R V T D G K J F T L Q L U
Z Y N T Q J L M X H D U J L N G R A S S E A T E R S C T F O
F Z M Q P G K Y S H R Y R C A H L M B S Y A D C H K W H K N
J C R E R Y G B T D D A W E I M E J T A N X U U L K O S O F
K I I M O A D M R N Z G C H C Z X U Z Q H J B Q Y E T I H Q
V V M Y B R N B E C S V I I P U R B S K C M H N Z W T F A P
T I H E L L R P S I B N J S A Z E M I P F E V V T P L L P C
H L Z Q E F E P S N B K J G L W H X V D S Z Y U T H F R F
J L P Z M F J S Y D Q I K L Y G P Y S G E Z H R P Y A D O X
A I E B P S X B S S E R O W S J P R P Q T N R F P J F E F K
O A X Q O G B G N L U A M L A Y N O O V N O S S C A P K I W
Y B S D L E C W E I E S D T O O V P H F C V I A O Y Y S L S
Z I T P I J K A G X N T S L I G O R R V I A C W C U F T I B
T L Y U C M L H F S C Q H S Y N I R C J B L B M A T Z I N V
A I A S E H W B J Y Y E S A K F C C U H U J I O L T I S G A
F T A F O W I R O K Y I S A L T O B A Y V I T N B T G O T A
K Y I X F X P G E D M K J S V W N R A L O E E Q G K C M N N
F K J M F X E W X M X D J E I O E P C N W A C S S Z X W Y J
K G Q P I F T V O W E B K O A V R A I E R E J M F H J K J D
E B F R C S I C N V S W Z Q N K E K P S U D A W J F S F K H
V R M R E E P I C E U Y P R R W G F C O I S A P O I S M N W
W S U N R P F E S H O B S Y C O D Z O E N Z B D O S E A L Z
R Z W D A M N I F H S U D R R S C W I R H S Y Q Q N M L X C
S B J N X M E A T E A T E R S R N S Q F C N F H L W C C W C
V B K R E A C V E X G H G S C V H L F A V E K N A R S W K F
A J B Y C O J Y V O R Z U X P O L I C E U S E O F F O R C E
O Z V F K P O L I C E W O R K I N G P E R S O N A L I T Y L
D Z R A F X F K U K Z Z H T U E H Q H X R S I T O I P J H Z
I Y Q D T P A M V T E Q L A G W O D V F O B W Y J A H V F W
```

Biological Weapon
Bivens Action
Civil Liability
Corruption
Deadly Force
Excessive Force
Grass Eaters
Internal Affairs
Knapp Commission

Less-Lethal Weapons
Meat Eaters
Police Use of Force
Police Working Personality
Problem Police Officer
Profiling
Racial Profiling
Stress

7 The Courts

Chapter Outline

- Introduction
- History and Structure of the American Court System
- The State Court System
- The Federal Court System
- Pretrial Activities

Learning Objectives

After reading this chapter, you should be able to

- Describe the development of the American court system.
- Explain the concept of the dual-court system in America.
- Identify some of the differences between the state and federal court systems.
- List and explain the steps typically taken during pretrial activities.
- Explain pretrial release, and describe the kinds of defendants that might be best qualified for release.
- Describe plea bargaining, and explain what purpose it serves in the American system of justice.

Chapter Summary

Chapter 7 provides an introduction to the American court system. It discusses the history of the dual-court structure in America, highlighting the decisions made at the various state and federal court levels. The text also describes the beginning stages of the court process, illustrating the process from arrest to arraignment. The chapter concludes with a discussion of **plea bargaining**.

The American court system is unique in many ways. One of its distinctive characteristics is that it is a dual-court system of state and federal courts. The founding fathers thought an essential feature of the new republic would be the power of individual states to retain authority and autonomy separate from federal control. However, the nation's founders also created a federal court system to mediate violations of federal law and to resolve violations of due process guarantees.

Most states have a three-level court structure. Trial courts are at the lowest level. Trial courts of limited or special jurisdiction hear only cases involving very minor crimes, such as misdemeanors and traffic violations; a judge, rather than a jury, usually resolves these cases. Trial courts of general jurisdiction, however, hear any criminal case and also provide the first level of appeal for cases decided in a court of limited jurisdiction. These decisions can then be appealed to the state intermediate appellate court. Appellate courts are concerned with reviewing the case on the record and will not conduct a new trial. Finally, all states have supreme courts, generally referred to as **courts of last resort**. The text provides a discussion of the Florida system to illustrate the various levels of a state court system.

The text also describes the **federal court system**. There are 94 district courts in the federal system; these courts are considered the trial courts of the federal system. The U.S. courts of appeal provide the first level of appeal in the federal system. These courts, often referred to as circuit courts, are responsible for reviewing decisions from the federal district courts. The federal Supreme Court is the most powerful court in the United States, and this Court reviews circuit court and state supreme court decisions.

Chapter 7 describes the early steps of the long and arduous court process. Usually within 48 hours after arrest, a suspect appears before a judge for his or her **first appearance**. During this stage, the legality of the arrest is assessed, the defendant is informed of the charges, and the decision on whether to release or detain pending trial is made. Judges have several bail options as well as a number of alternatives. Some alternative bail programs include **release on recognizance (ROR)**, property bond, deposit bail, conditional release, third-party custody, unsecured bond, and signature bond. Suspects then experience either a preliminary hearing or a grand jury hearing. There are significant differences between these two types of hearings, but the purpose of both is to filter cases out of the system if there is insufficient evidence to pursue the charges. Finally, the defendant is again informed of the charges and asked to make a plea at the arraignment stage. Defendants will plead guilty, not guilty, or ***nolo contendere*** (no contest).

This chapter concludes with a discussion of **plea bargaining**. Think of plea bargaining as a negotiation process that involves the defendant, the defense counsel, and the prosecutor. Defendants frequently waive their right to a trial and plead guilty, hoping to get something in return, such as a reduced sentence. Prosecutors and defense attorneys also benefit from the plea-bargaining process because it helps keep cases moving through the court system.

Key Concepts

Appeal   Generally, the request that a court with appellate jurisdiction review the judgment, decision, or order of a lower court and set it aside (reverse it) or modify it.

Appellate Jurisdiction   The lawful authority of a court to review a decision made by a lower court.

Bail Bond   A document guaranteeing the appearance of the defendant in court as required and recording the pledge of money or property to be paid to the court if he or she does not appear, which is signed by the person to be released and anyone else acting in his or her behalf.

Community Court   A low-level court that focuses on quality-of-life crimes that erode a neighborhood's morale, that emphasizes problem solving rather than punishment, and that builds upon restorative principles like community service and restitution.

Competent to Stand Trial   A finding by a court, when the defendant's sanity at the time of trial is at issue, that the defendant has sufficient present ability to consult with his or her attorney with a reasonable degree of rational understanding and that the defendant has a rational as well as factual understanding of the proceedings against him or her.

Court of Last Resort   The court authorized by law to hear the final appeal on a matter.

Danger Law   A law intended to prevent the pretrial release of criminal defendants judged to represent a danger to others in the community.

Dispute-Resolution Center   An informal hearing place designed to mediate interpersonal disputes without resorting to the more formal arrangements of a criminal trial court.

Federal Court System   The three-tiered structure of federal courts, comprising U.S. district courts, U.S. courts of appeal, and the U.S. Supreme Court.

First Appearance   An appearance before a magistrate during which the legality of a defendant's arrest is initially assessed and the defendant is informed of the charges on which he or she is being held. At this stage in the criminal justice process, bail may be set or pretrial release arranged. Also called initial appearance.

Judicial Review   The power of a court to review actions and decisions made by other agencies of government.

Jurisdiction   The territory, subject matter, or people over which a court or other justice agency may exercise lawful authority, as determined by statute or constitution.

Nolo Contendere   A plea of "no contest." A no-contest plea is used when the defendant does not wish to contest conviction. Because the plea does not admit guilt, however, it cannot provide the basis for later civil suits that might follow a criminal conviction.

Original Jurisdiction   The lawful authority of a court to hear or act upon a case from its beginning and to pass judgment on the law and the facts. The authority may be over a specific geographic area or over particular types of cases.

Plea   In criminal proceedings, a defendant's formal answer in court to the charge contained in a complaint, information, or indictment that he or she is guilty or is not guilty of the offense charged or does not contest the charge.

Plea Bargaining   The process of negotiating an agreement among the defendant, the prosecutor, and the court as to an appropriate plea and associated sentence in a given case. Plea bargaining circumvents the trial process and dramatically reduces the time required for the resolution of a criminal case.

Pretrial Release   The release of an accused person from custody, for all or part of the time before or during prosecution, upon his or her promise to appear in court when required.

Property Bond   The setting of bail in the form of land, houses, stocks, or other tangible property. In the event that the defendant absconds prior to trial, the bond becomes the property of the court.

Release on Recognizance (ROR)   The pretrial release of a criminal defendant on his or her written promise to appear in court as required. No cash or property bond is required.

State Court Administrator   A coordinator who assists with case-flow management, operating funds budgeting, and court docket administration.

State Court System   A state judicial structure. Most states have at least three court levels: generally, trial courts, appellate courts, and a state supreme court.

Trial *de Novo*   Literally, a "new trial." The term is applied to cases that are retried on appeal, as opposed to those that are simply reviewed on the record.

Key Cases

County of Riverside v. *McLaughlin*.   "A jurisdiction that provides judicial determinations of probable cause within 48 hours of arrest will, as a general matter, comply with the promptness requirement." Weekends and holidays are not excluded from this 48-hour provision, and in some cases, an even quicker arraignment may be appropriate (*County of Riverside* v. *McLaughlin*, 111 S.Ct. 1661 [1991]).

Herrera v. *Collins*.   New evidence of innocence is no reason for a federal court to order a new state trial if constitutional grounds are lacking (*Herrera* v. *Collins*, 113 S.Ct. 853, 122 L.Ed.2d 203 [1993]).

Keeney v. *Tamayo-Reyes*.   A defendant is entitled to a federal evidentiary hearing only "if he can show cause for his failure to develop the facts in the state-court proceedings and actual prejudice resulting from that failure, or if he can show that a fundamental miscarriage of justice would result from failure to hold such a hearing" (*Keeney* v. *Tamayo-Reyes*, 113 S.Ct. 853, 122 L.Ed.2d 203 [1992]).

Marbury v. *Madison*.   In this case, the court established its authority as the final interpreter of the U.S. Constitution (*Marbury* v. *Madison*, 1 Cranch 137 [1803]).

McNabb v. *U.S*.   This case established that any unreasonable delay in an initial court appearance would make confessions inadmissible if interrogating officers obtained them during the delay (*McNabb* v. *U.S*., 318 U.S. 332 [1943]).

Santobello v. *New York*.   This case established that plea bargaining is an important and necessary component of the American system of justice (*Santobello* v. *New York*, 404 U.S. 257 [1971]).

U.S. v. *Montalvo-Murillo*.   In this case, the Court found that a defendant has no right to freedom simply because of a "minor" violation of the provisions of the federal Bail Reform Act of 1984 (*U.S.* v. *Montalvo-Murillo*, 495 U.S. 711 [1990]).

Learning Tips

Learning to Write

One of the most important skills you can acquire is the ability to write well. The ability to communicate effectively in writing is essential for professional success. Although learning to write can be a painful learning process, the investment you make in developing your skills now will have long-term benefits. The best way to improve your writing skills is to have others review your work and provide constructive criticism. Thus, be a frequent visitor to your university writing center, ask friends and fellow students to critique your work, and learn from the feedback you receive from your professors.

Essay Questions on Exams

Essay questions cause anxiety for many students. To reduce anxiety, read the entire question first. Then reread the question, underlining key words and noting specific parts and instructions within the question. Write a quick outline. This will keep your answer focused as well as minimize your chances of forgetting important parts. Finally, because the grading of essay exams is partly subjective, it is good practice to write legibly, skip lines, keep your answers concise, and use only one side of the paper.

CJ Brief on the World Wide Web

Web links to organizations and agencies related to the material in Chapter 7 include:

WEBSITE TITLE	URL
Courts.Net	http://www.courts.net
Federal Courts	http://www.law.emory.edu /FEDCTS
Florida CyberCourt Home Page	http://www.flcourts.org
International Court of Justice	http://www.icj-cij.org
National Center for State Courts	http://www.ncsconline.org
Professional Bail Agents of the United States	http://www.pbus.com
Supreme Court of the United States	http://www.supremecourtus.gov
U.S. Federal Judiciary	http://www.uscourts.gov

Learner Activities

Activity 1

Choose two states, and search the World Wide Web to see if you can determine the court structure and jurisdiction of courts in those states. In the space provided, compare and contrast what you learn about the court systems in these states.

_____

_____

_____

_____

_____

_____

Activity 2

Determine whether there is a dispute-resolution center near you. If so, visit that center to learn more about it. Interview professionals and volunteers who work for the center to determine the types of cases handled, the caseloads, and the ways the center supports or replaces traditional court processes. If you are unable to locate a dispute-resolution center, then visit three websites that deal with dispute-resolution and mediation issues. The Web links listed provide several outstanding sites. Discuss what you learned about dispute-resolution centers in the space provided below.

_____

_____

_____

_____

_____

Activity 3

The Supreme Court is one of the most powerful institutions in America. The decisions of this Court have had significant impact on both social and criminal justice issues. Some of the greatest legal minds of American history served as justices of the Supreme Court. Through this activity, you will learn more about a justice who served on the Supreme Court. You can choose a current member of the Court or any other historical Justice. Use the Web and media databases to identify and gather information about the justice you selected. Use your university library to find additional information. In the space provided below, write a description of the justice you selected, and include a discussion of some of the important cases that he or she helped decide.

_____

_____

_____

_____

_____

Activity 4

Bail or No Bail?

1. Salvadore Lopez is a 52-year-old farmworker who cannot read. He has a wife and two children. Lopez was charged with smuggling guns, marijuana, and other narcotics across the Mexican border. The prosecutor, when discussing the case with the news media, says that he suspects Lopez was involved with guns and drugs for years but has avoided being arrested by authorities until now. Lopez claims that he is completely innocent and wouldn't know what marijuana looked like if he saw it. Should he be detained or released? How much bail would you set in order to release? What other information would you need to know?

2. Roger A. Kooney is a 27-year-old electrical engineer. Kooney is charged with vehicular homicide stemming from the death of Chris Pariano. Pariano was stepping out of his pickup truck when Kooney sped down the wrong side of the street. Kooney was drunk at the time, according to police. The police also learned that Kooney had eight previous convictions for drunk driving and 19 other serious vehicular offenses. Should he be detained or released? How much bail would you set in order to release? What other information would you need to know?

3. Edward Savitz is a 50-year-old single man who has a good-paying full-time job and lives in an expensive high-rise apartment. He is charged with the statutory rape of a 16-year-old, sexual abuse of two others, and corrupting the morals of a minor. It is alleged that Savitz paid to have sex with hundreds of boys, but on all occasions the young men agreed to participate. The maximum sentence that Savitz can receive for his crimes is five to ten years. Savitz has been diagnosed with the AIDS virus. Should he be detained or released? How much bail would you set in order to release? What other information would you need to know?

4. At the age of 19, Frank Anderson was convicted of rape and sentenced to prison for three years. Approximately one year after his release, he became a suspect in a number of robberies of women. He threatened a number of the victims with bodily harm if they filed complaints. One 21-year-old victim nevertheless agreed to cooperate with the authorities, and Anderson was arrested and charged with robbery. Shortly after his initial appearance, he was released on bail. Anderson then broke into the 21-year-old woman's house, beat her, kicked her numerous times, and stole $3,000 and a gun. The victim suffered a concussion and needed seven stitches. Anderson was identified, and again he was apprehended and charged with an additional count of robbery. Should he be detained or released? How much bail would you set in order to release? What other factors would you need to know?

5. An 18-year-old girl, Kim Walak, was arrested for shoplifting. She claimed to be indigent (poor), with no steady source of income; she lived with an unemployed boyfriend, and she had dropped out of school in the eleventh grade. Walak had one prior arrest for shoplifting, but those charges were dismissed for unknown reasons. Should she be detained or released? How much bail would you set in order to release? What other factors would you need to know?

_____

_____

_____

_____

_____

_____

Internet Activity

Use the Cybrary (http://www.cybrary.info) to locate a detailed description of a state court system (perhaps the court system in your home state). Describe the various courts that make up the system, the staff roles, and the administrative agencies (for example, the administrative office of state courts). Outline the functions of each.

_____

_____

_____

_____

_____

_____

Distance Learning Activity

This distance learning assignment is designed to help you learn more about the U.S. Supreme Court. Visit the Supreme Court's website at http://www.supreme courtus.gov. Explore the various links from this page. List ten facts that you learned about the Supreme Court from this exercise. Submit these facts if your instructor asks you to do so.

_____

_____

_____

_____

_____

Student Study Guide Questions

True or False

_____ 7-1. Grand juries meet in secret, and a person under investigation has no legal right to be present or even notified of a grand jury investigation.

_____ 7-2. The federal court system consists of three tiers, including the U.S. district courts, the U.S. courts of appeal, and the U.S. Supreme Court.

_____ 7-3. Federal judges are usually elected officials who then serve life terms on the bench.

_____ 7-4. The case of *Marbury* v. *Madison*, decided in 1803, was the first instance in which the U.S. Supreme Court declared its authority to review the actions of Congress to determine whether they comply or conflict with the Constitution.

_____ 7-5. In the 1993 case of *Herrera* v. *Collins*, the U.S. Supreme Court ruled that new evidence of innocence is not a sufficient reason for a federal court to order a new state trial if there are no constitutional grounds for appeal.

_____ 7-6. The U.S. Supreme Court has ruled that plea bargaining is an important and necessary component of the American system of justice.

_____ 7-7. The jurisdiction of a court can refer to the territory, subject matter, or person over which a court may lawfully exercise its authority.

_____ 7-8. According to the decision in *McNabb* v. *United States*, a person in custody must have an appearance in court within 48 hours of his or her arrest.

_____ 7-9. The courts have generally upheld the practice of detaining suspects indefinitely until they can appear before a magistrate.

_____ 7-10. Dispute-resolution centers are generally not allowed to mediate disputes when criminal charges are pending against either of the disputants.

Multiple Choice

7-11. States that don't use grand juries rely on what type of hearing to give the defendant an opportunity to challenge the legal basis of his or her detention?
   a. competency hearing
   b. arraignment
   c. preliminary hearing
   d. first appearance

7-12. State courts are generally divided into three levels, with _____ at the top of the hierarchy.
   a. courts of limited jurisdiction
   b. intermediate appellate courts
   c. courts of last resort
   d. trial courts

7-13. When the U.S. Supreme Court orders the lower court to "forward up the record" of a case that has been tried so that the high court can review it, it issues a
   a. writ of trial *de novo.*
   b. *nolo contendere.*
   c. writ of *mandamus.*
   d. writ of *certiorari.*

7-14. One purpose of bail is to
   a. examine the sufficiency of the evidence against the accused.
   b. ensure the appearance of the accused individual at trial.
   c. deter future offenses.
   d. protect the community from criminals.

7-15. The jurisdiction of a court is
   a. the geographic area it covers.
   b. the subject matter it deals with.
   c. its place in the hierarchy of the court system.
   d. all of the above.

7-16. State court administrators are responsible for all of the following *except*
   a. training support personnel.
   b. ruling on issues of law.
   c. managing court case flow.
   d. coordinating between state court levels and jurisdictions.

7-17. Which type of program releases defendants on their own after a promise to appear at court, with no requirement for posting a cash or property bond?
   a. voluntary community release
   b. signature bond
   c. preventive detention
   d. release on recognizance

7-18. A grand jury has all of the following characteristics and duties *except*
   a. determining if an accused individual should be held over for an actual trial
   b. meeting in secret, with no opportunity for the accused to cross-examine witnesses
   c. initiating prosecution independent of the prosecutor
   d. delivering a verdict of guilty or not guilty in criminal trials

7-19. The advantage of a plea of *nolo contendere* over a guilty plea is that it
   a. usually results in a lighter sentence for the offender.
   b. protects the accused in the event of a subsequent civil suit.
   c. limits the judge's sentencing alternatives.
   d. allows the defendant to use a legal loophole to avoid responsibility.

7-20. The 1803 case of _____ established the U.S. Supreme Court's authority as the final interpreter of the U.S. Constitution.
   a. *Marbury* v. *Madison*
   b. *Herrera* v. *Collins*
   c. *McNabb* v. *U.S.*
   d. *Brady* v. *U.S.*

Fill-In

7-21. An appearance before a magistrate when the legality of the defendant's arrest is reviewed and the defendant is informed of the charges is called the _____.

7-22. _____ of general jurisdiction are the first level of appeal from trial courts of limited jurisdiction.

7-23. _____ is the pretrial release of a defendant based on a written promise to appear at future hearings.

7-24. The _____ assists with the management of cases, budgeting, and docket administration.

7-25. _____ literally means a "new trial."

7-26. The highest-level appellate court in a state system is often referred to as the _____ because no legal recourse remains available to the defendant within the state system.

7-27. The lawful authority of a court to review a decision made by a lower court is called _____.

7-28. A(n) _____ is issued when an appellate court agrees to hear a case; it orders the lower court to forward up the records of the case.

7-29. A(n) _____ is a low-level court that focuses on quality-of-life crimes that erode a neighborhood's morale.

7-30. _____ is a plea of "no contest."

Crossword Puzzle

Across

4. Power of a court to review actions and decisions made by other agencies of government.
8. To review the judgment, decision, or order of a lower court.
9. No contest.
10. New trial.
11. Type of court that focuses on quality-of-life crimes.
12. Process of negotiating an agreement among the defendant, the prosecutor, and the court as to an appropriate plea and associated sentence in a given case.

Down

1. Authority of a court to hear a case from its beginning and to pass judgment.
2. Court stage at which bail is typically set.
3. U.S. district courts, U.S. courts of appeal, and U.S. Supreme Court.
5. Authority of a court to review a decision made by a lower court.
6. Court authorized by law to hear the final appeal on a matter.
7. Release by promise.

Word Search Puzzle

```
U A B L A P P E L L A T E J U R I S D I C T I O N K Z S X B
R P M Q B O X H J U S I Y F W L I S L G M L X O P N A C P E
R C H J U N W E F R P T Y B H S O L A X K F P Y Y K Y O T F
N Y A R D R I C M I J J A S B X M Y E Q X N I E I Y T M P X
M S A J D L Z L B Y R A A T X U Z L P N Y L K U T U T P I J
D H Q U Y Q M B Q T G S Q S E J N X M L I U I N Q H C E Y U
Q J W D D B O P X E V T T W R C K H U L M L A H H Z S T G R
J P E I W A W G B R S Q G A R T O Y K N Y O K G I I J E U I
R Z I C A M N Y M A Q P B I P E V U O D F J W K R Y U N X S
S L U I N U O G D B B B R K A P R E R J O L X G C G Z T K D
T C P A G B M T E Y G X A E B P E M T T O W S L M M Q T O I
C C B L V Y E U P R M S K A T E E A X U S F A L U J D O R C
Z D T R P F B D V C L I N S S R B H R T I Y P W R W H S I T
Q K C E I G N G H T B A Q L D F I A I A C Q S V W A Y T G I
N H O V U G X G V L M U W P C P C A I P N G Z T Y I N A I O
T O U I U U J T K V B F N I A L H U L L Y C G J E M D N N N
R P R E H Q P F A L L Y V N Q E U F A R B V E D C M G D A O
I J T W V G P R T Z W H R G Y A B Y C X E O B Z W N U T L E
A H O Z K M S X M V M G J G C B B J A W Q L N L P S W R J K
L K F U F B Y W O X R K T Y H A V G S W P Y E D P E C I U Z
D X L Q L O G A S W Y L P R K R I W J W X P F A P Z G A R G
E S A F S J J P W T J A B G V G G V G T T L T I S R M L I L
N L S B K A U P C K D Y Y X P A B B Q E P E L D K E T N S U
O M T B F Z T E P K J Y C E G I Y O D G Y A Z R W L C O D B
V R R A C I K A U K F M X I F N B S G A L D E S C Z L C I D
O W E W U V U L P U D Q Z W M I Z T K L I Q V G W J J Z C Y
B N S U X Q P C I T V Q A R D N E L Q S U X R R C Q H Y T G
U H O K B X E R O F U S Y Y P G V I C O E Q D Q Q N S W I F
N M R S P R O P E R T Y B O N D K X T U R H N W K V N K O B
D S T P O C O M M U N I T Y C O U R T F L L O E L V R Y N G
```

Appeal

Appellate Jurisdiction

Bail Bond

Community Court

Competent to Stand Trial

Court of Last Resort

Danger Law

First Appearance

Judicial Review

Jurisdiction

Original Jurisdiction

Plea

Plea Bargaining

Pretrial Release

Property Bond

State Court System

Trial *de Novo*

8 The Courtroom Work Group and the Criminal Trial

Chapter Outline

- Introduction
- The Courtroom Work Group: Professional Courtroom Actors
- Outsiders: Nonprofessional Courtroom Participants

- The Criminal Trial
- Stages in a Criminal Trial
- Improving the Adjudication Process

Learning Objectives

After reading this chapter, you should be able to

- Identify and explain the roles of the various professional members of the courtroom work group.
- Discuss indigent defense, and know what forms it takes in the United States.
- Identify and explain the roles of the various nonprofessional courtroom participants.
- Explain how professional and nonprofessional courtroom participants work together to bring most criminal trials to a successful close.
- Explain the roles of expert and lay witnesses in a criminal trial, and describe how their testimony might differ.

- Describe the various stages in a criminal trial.
- Explain the hearsay rule, and identify recognized exceptions to it.
- Explain the possible benefits of a professional jury system.
- Describe methods that have been suggested for improving the adjudication process.

Chapter Summary

A fundamental concept of criminal justice in the United States is that the criminal justice system is an **adversarial system**. Justice is achieved when a talented adversary is able to convince a judge or jury that his or her perspective is the correct one. Chapter 8 focuses on two issues central to understanding this adversarial system. First, the text describes the roles and responsibilities of "professional" members of the courtroom work group and "outsiders" to this group. Second, the text describes the trial process. The first professional courtroom work group member discussed in Chapter 8 is the **judge**. The primary responsibility of the judge is to ensure that justice prevails. The judge is probably the most powerful individual in the courtroom, able to influence the outcome of a case by ruling on matters of law, procedure, and sentence. The text describes the qualifications necessary to be a judge and the selection of judges. Some judges are elected officials, others are appointed, and others are selected by the Missouri Bar Plan. Although judges are generally well respected and highly ethical, the text describes several examples of judicial misconduct.

The **prosecutor** is responsible for representing the public and thus presents the state's case against the defendant. Prosecutors, typically with the help of several assistants, are responsible for deciding the appropriate charges for a defendant, preparing a case for each step of the court process, introducing evidence and witnesses to support the charges at trial, and perhaps advising the police. If the defendant is convicted, prosecutors make sentencing recommendations. The text also describes the significant amount of discretion possessed by prosecutors. Their discretion is limited, however, by a series of court decisions discussed in the text. For example, prosecutors are required to disclose any evidence that the defense requests (*U.S.* v. *Bagley*).

The prosecutor's main adversary is the **defense counsel**. While the prosecutor is responsible for case and trial preparation on behalf of the state, the defense attorney does the same for the defendant. The text describes the types of attorneys who provide criminal defense in the criminal justice system. In addition, it explains many of the important right-to-counsel cases. According to the Supreme Court's interpretation of the Sixth Amendment, defendants who face imprisonment if convicted and who are too poor to pay for an attorney are appointed counsel. These court decisions have forced states to provide counsel to indigent defendants using an assigned counsel, public defense, or contract arrangement system.

There are various other court professionals involved in the criminal trial process. The court reporter is responsible for the official trial record through use of a stenotype machine. The clerk of court (county clerk) maintains court records, swears in witnesses, and marks for identification all physical evidence introduced at trial; the **bailiff** keeps order in the courtroom and maintains physical custody of the jury. Similar to the activities of state court administrators discussed in Chapter 7, the duties of the local court administrator include being responsible for managing the local court. The court recorder creates the record of all that occurs at trial. Finally, **expert witnesses** have special knowledge and skills recognized by the court as relevant to the determination of guilt or innocence.

Chapter 8 then discusses the various "outsiders" or nonprofessionals of courtroom decision making. Although not considered members of the courtroom work group, these outsiders can have a significant impact on the trial process. **Lay witnesses** provide testimony relevant to a specific case; **jurors** hear the evidence presented and then make a determination of guilt or innocence. Crime victims have historically been considered the forgotten members of the criminal justice process, but their standing is changing. The defendants are also considered outsiders, but they have to be present at trial and can try to defend themselves. Finally, the press is often present in the courtroom, especially in celebrated cases, and may influence trial processes by publicizing facts about the case prior to trial or being present to record and publish trial testimony.

Chapter 8 concludes with a discussion of the trial process. Once the trial is initiated, the first step in the process is **jury selection**. Both the prosecutor and the defense attorneys question potential jurors through a process known as *voir dire*. Potential jurors can be dismissed by using challenges for cause and **peremptory challenges**. After the jury is selected, the prosecution and defense will make **opening statements**. After these statements are completed, the prosecution and the defense present various types of evidence, such as **real**, **circumstantial**, and **direct**. **Closing arguments** provide a review and a summation of the evidence. The judge then charges the jury and provides instructions on deliberation. Finally, the jury deliberates on the evidence presented during the trial and returns to the court with a verdict.

Key Concepts

Adversarial System The two-sided structure under which American criminal trial courts operate that pits the prosecution against the defense. In theory, justice is done when the most effective adversary is able to convince the judge or jury that his or her perspective on the case is the correct one.

Bailiff The court officer whose duties are to keep order in the courtroom and to maintain physical custody of the jury.

Change of Venue The movement of a trial or lawsuit from one jurisdiction to another or from one location to another within the same jurisdiction. A change of venue may be made in a criminal case to ensure that the defendant receives a fair trial.

Circumstantial Evidence Evidence that requires interpretation or that requires a judge or jury to reach a conclusion based upon what the evidence indicates. From the close proximity of a smoking gun to the defendant, for example, the jury might conclude that he or she pulled the trigger.

Closing Argument An oral summation of a case presented to a judge, or to a judge and jury, by the prosecution or by the defense in a criminal trial.

Courtroom Work Group The professional courtroom actors, including judges, prosecuting attorneys, defense attorneys, public defenders, and others who earn a living serving the court.

Defense Counsel (also **Defense Attorney**) A licensed trial lawyer, hired or appointed to conduct the legal defense of an individual accused of a crime and to represent him or her before a court of law.

Direct Evidence Evidence that, if believed, directly proves a fact. Eyewitness testimony and videotaped documentation account for the majority of all direct evidence heard in the criminal courtroom.

Evidence Anything useful to a judge or jury in deciding the facts of a case. Evidence may take the form of witness testimony, written documents, videotapes, magnetic media, photographs, physical objects, and so on.

Exculpatory Evidence Information having a tendency to clear a person of guilt of blame.

Expert Witness A person who has special knowledge and skills recognized by the court as relevant to the determination of guilt or innocence. Unlike lay witnesses, expert witnesses may express opinions or draw conclusions in their testimony.

Hearsay Something that is not based upon the personal knowledge of a witness. Witnesses who testify about something they have heard, for example, are offering hearsay by repeating information about a matter of which they have no direct knowledge.

Hearsay Rule The long-standing precedent that hearsay cannot be used in American courtrooms. Rather than accepting testimony based upon hearsay, the court will ask that the person who was the original source of the hearsay information be brought into court to be questioned and cross-examined. Exceptions to the hearsay rule may occur when the person with direct knowledge is dead or is otherwise unable to testify.

Judge An elected or appointed public official who presides over a court of law and who is authorized to hear and sometimes to decide cases and to conduct trials.

Juror A member of a trial or grand jury, selected for jury duty and required to serve as an arbiter of the facts in a court of law. Jurors are expected to render verdicts of "guilty" or "not guilty" as to the charges brought against the accused, although they may sometimes fail to do so (as in the case of a hung jury).

Jury Selection The process whereby, according to law and precedent, members of a particular trial jury are chosen.

Lay Witness An eyewitness, character witness, or any other person called upon to testify who is not considered an expert. Lay witnesses must testify to facts alone and may not draw conclusions or express opinions.

Opening Statement The initial statement of the prosecution and defense, made in a court of law to a judge, or to a judge and jury, describing the facts that he or she intends to present during trial to prove the case.

Peremptory Challenge The right to challenge a potential juror without disclosing the reason for the challenge. Prosecutors and defense attorneys routinely use peremptory challenges to eliminate from juries individuals who, although they express no obvious bias, are thought to be capable of swaying the jury in an undesirable direction.

Perjury The intentional making of a false statement as part of the testimony by a sworn witness in a judicial proceeding on a matter relevant to the case at hand.

Probative Value The degree to which a particular item of evidence is useful in, and relevant to, proving something important in a trial.

Prosecutor An attorney whose official duty is to conduct criminal proceedings on behalf of the state or the people against those accused of having committed criminal offenses.

Prosecutorial Discretion The decision-making power of prosecutors, based upon the wide range of choices available to them, in the handling of criminal defendants, the scheduling of cases for trial, the acceptance of bargained pleas, and so on. The most important form of prosecutorial discretion lies in the power to charge, or not to charge, a person with an offense.

Public Defender An attorney employed by a government agency or subagency, or by a private organization under contract to a government body, for the purpose of providing defense services to indigents, or an attorney who has volunteered such service.

Real Evidence Evidence that consists of physical material or traces of physical activity.

Rules of Evidence Court rules that govern the admissibility of evidence at criminal hearings and trials.

Scientific Jury Selection The use of correlational techniques from the social sciences to gauge the likelihood that potential jurors will vote for conviction or for acquittal.

Sequestered Jury A jury that is isolated from the public during the course of a trial and throughout the deliberation process.

Speedy Trial Act   A 1974 federal law requiring that proceedings against a defendant in a criminal case begin within a specified period of time, such as 70 working days after indictment. Some states also have speedy trial requirements.

Subpoena   A written order issued by a judicial officer or grand jury requiring an individual to appear in court and to give testimony or to bring material to be used as evidence. Some subpoenas mandate that books, papers, and other items be surrendered to the court.

Testimony   Oral evidence offered by a sworn witness on the witness stand during a criminal trial.

Verdict   The decision of the jury in a jury trial or of a judicial officer in a nonjury trial.

Victim Assistance Program   An organized program that offers services to victims of crime in the areas of crisis intervention and follow-up counseling and that helps victims secure their rights under the law.

Key Cases

Argersinger v. *Hamlin*.   The Supreme Court required legal representation for anyone facing a potential sentence of imprisonment (*Argersinger* v. *Hamlin*, 407 U.S. 25 [1972]).

Burns v. *Reed*.   "A state prosecuting attorney is absolutely immune from liability for damages for participating in a probable cause hearing, but not for giving legal advice to the police" (*Burns* v. *Reed*, 500 U.S. 478 [1991]).

Coy v. *Iowa*.   The Supreme Court ruled that a courtroom screen used to shield child witnesses from visual confrontation violated the Sixth Amendment confrontation clause (*Coy* v. *Iowa*, 487 U.S. 1012, 108 S.Ct. 2798 [1988]).

Crosby v. *U.S.*   A defendant may not be tried *in absentia* even if he or she was present at the beginning of a trial and his or her absence is due to escape or failure to appear (*Crosby* v. *U.S.*, 113 S.Ct. 748, 122 L.Ed.2d 25 [1993]).

Demarest v. *Manspeaker*.   Federal prisoners who are subpoenaed to testify are entitled to witness fees just as nonincarcerated witnesses would be (*Demarest* v. *Manspeaker*, 498 U.S. 184, 111 S.Ct. 599, 112 L.Ed.2d 608 [1991]).

Doggett v. *U.S.*   A delay of eight and a half years violated the speedy trial provisions because it resulted from government negligence (*Doggett* v. *U.S.*, 112 S.Ct. 2686 [1992]).

Edmonson v. *Leesville Concrete Co., Inc.*   Peremptory challenges based on race are not acceptable in civil lawsuits (*Edmonson* v. *Leesville Concrete Co., Inc.*, 500 U.S. 614, 111 S.Ct. 2077, 114 L.Ed.2d 660 [1991]).

Fex v. *Michigan*.   It ruled that the 180-day speedy trial provision does not commence until the prisoner's disposition request has actually been delivered to the court and to the prosecutor of the jurisdiction that lodged the detainer against him or her (*Fex* v. *Michigan*, 113 S.Ct. 1085, 122 L.Ed.2d 406 [1993]).

Georgia v. *McCollum*.   Defendants (and their attorneys) cannot use peremptory challenges to exclude potential jurors on the basis of race (*Georgia* v. *McCollum*, 505 U.S. 42 [1992]).

Gideon v. *Wainwright*.   This case extended the right to appointed counsel in state courts to all indigent defendants charged with a felony (*Gideon* v. *Wainwright*, 372 U.S. 335 [1963]).

Idaho v. *Wright*.   The Court stated that statements by children are fraught with unreliability, which the confrontation clause is designed to highlight and obviate (*Idaho* v. *Wright*, 497 U.S. 805 [1990]).

Imbler v. *Pachtman*.   It held that state prosecutors are absolutely immune from liability for their conduct in initiating a prosecution and in presenting the state's case (*Imbler* v. *Pachtman*, 424 U.S. 409 [1976]).

Maryland v. *Craig*.   Closed-circuit television can be used to shield children who testify in criminal courts (*Maryland* v. *Craig*, 497 U.S. 836, 845-847 [1990]).

Mu'Min v. *Virginia*.   Being aware of a case through pretrial publicity alone is not enough to disqualify a juror. If a prospective juror can be shown to be unbiased by the publicity, he or she can serve (*Mu'Min* v. *Virginia*, 500 U.S. 415 [1991]).

Powers v. *Ohio*.   The prosecution cannot systematically exclude jurors on the basis of race through the use of peremptory challenges (*Powers* v. *Ohio*, 499 U.S. 400 [1991]).

White v. *Illinois*.   In-court testimony given by a medical provider and the child's babysitter, who repeated what the child had said to them concerning the defendant's sexually abusive behavior, was not subject to hearsay restrictions and was permissible (*White* v. *Illinois*, 112 S.Ct. 736 [1992]).

Zafiro v. *U.S.*   Defendants charged in federal courts with similar or related offenses may be tried together—even when their defenses differ substantially (*Zafiro* v. *U.S.*, 113 S.Ct. 933, 122 L.Ed.2d 317 [1993]).

Learning Tips

Study Groups I

Group study can be very beneficial; however, make sure to select individuals who are attentive in class, who ask questions, and who participate and take notes. While it is good to join people who have similar academic standards, it is also useful to form groups of individuals from diverse backgrounds. The difference in backgrounds may offer a variety of perspectives and better insight into the course material. Last, keep the size to fewer than six people because large groups are often counterproductive to effective studying.

Study Groups II

A variety of purposes can be accomplished with study groups. Reviewing class lectures could help answer questions or clarify uncertainties in your notes, and group members can practice quizzing one another. Closer to test time, study groups are a great source for compiling potential test questions. Also, general discussions within the group are a great way to learn the material and reinforce your memory.

CJ Brief on the World Wide Web

Web links to organizations and agencies related to the material in Chapter 8 include:

WEBSITE TITLE	URL
American Bar Foundation	http://www.abf-sociolegal.org
Citizens for Effective Justice	http://www.reducecrime.org
Federal Magistrate Judges' Association	http://www.fedjudge.org

WEBSITE TITLE	URL
Illinois Office of the State Appellate Defender	http://www.state.il.us/defender
National Center for State Courts	http://www.ncsconline.org
New York State Defenders Association	http://www.nysda.org
Office of the U.S. Attorney General	http://www.usdoj.gov/ag
Trial Lawyers for Public Justice	http://www.tlpj.org

Learner Activities

Activity 1

Here are some ethical issues for the courtroom work groups. Put yourself in the place of each courtroom work group participant listed below, and explain how you would handle each dilemma.

The Prosecutor

1. While preparing the case against an accused arson defendant, you discover a witness who provides an alibi for the defendant. Do you tell the defense attorney about your discovery? Would it make any difference if the defendant were involved in organized crime? What if the defendant were charged with murder and arson?

2. After you have successfully prosecuted a rapist, you uncover evidence that indicates that the victim in the case created the story to avenge a love affair that went sour. What do you do? What would you do if you knew that the suspect was charged with rape on two other occasions but was not convicted due to legal technicalities?

The Defense Attorney

1. You are asked to represent a defendant who cannot afford to pay your full fee at the present time. Should you work out an arrangement so that your client pays you a $1,000 retainer now and pays the rest of the fee if and when she is acquitted (recognizing that conviction would result in incarceration and no real opportunity to earn the money for your fee)?

2. Your client informs you that she did in fact murder her mom. Should you inform the court of this information? Possessing such knowledge, should you allow your client to take the stand and deny her guilt?

_____

_____

_____

The Judge

1. At arraignment, you ask a defendant if he has obtained counsel yet. He replies that he wants to defend himself. He has a fifth-grade education and works as a day laborer for a local construction firm. He is charged with armed robbery and faces ten years in prison. Should you let him defend himself?

2. You are assigned to preside over a jury trial in a gruesome homicide case that has been widely publicized in the area. Although the defense does not request it, should you order a change of venue?

_____

_____

_____

_____

_____

_____

Activity 2

Historically, courts have resisted allowing cameras in our nation's courtrooms out of fear that it would adversely impact a defendant's right to a fair trial. Courts were concerned that the media's search for the sensational would turn our courtrooms into sideshows. For example, when Bruno Hauptmann was accused of kidnapping the Lindbergh baby, he was convicted in an atmosphere of circus sensationalism that degraded the entire judicial process. Among other things, the prosecutor gave newspaper interviews constantly; although the judge prohibited cameras from taking pictures, a reporter brought a camera into the courtroom and took pictures. During the trial, the public applauded state witnesses. Hauptmann was convicted, and appellate courts ruled that the publicity did not bias the final decision. Recently the U.S. Supreme Court decided that it was not unconstitutional for cameras to be in our nation's courtrooms. As discussed in the text, the majority of states now permit such coverage.

Do you think cameras should be allowed in trial courts of general jurisdiction? Be sure to discuss the pros and cons of having cameras in the courtroom. Do you think cameras influence jury verdicts? Why or why not?

_____

_____

_____

_____

_____

_____

Activity 3

Go to the Court TV website at http://www.courttv.com. This website provides a discussion of many current and famous cases that have received publicity across the country. Choose one of the cases presented on the website, and read the facts of the case. In the space provided below, write an opening statement for the prosecutor and an opening statement for the defense attorney. Be sure to use the facts of the case in your statement.

_____

_____

_____

_____

_____

Activity 4

Attend a trial at a local courthouse. In the space provided below, describe the case and the steps of the trial you saw. Were you able to see the complete trial? What was the verdict? Was a jury present? What trial stages did you see? What types of witnesses were called to present evidence? What types of evidence were presented? Was the victim present? What was the defendant's demeanor during testimony? Did the jury appear to be attentive?

_____

_____

_____

_____

_____

Internet Activity

Visit Cornell University Law School's Legal Information Institute at http://www.law.cornell.edu. Describe each of the site's features, paying special attention to the resources available in the sections titled "Court Opinions," "Law by Source or Jurisdiction," and "Constitutions and Codes." After exploring each feature, describe in detail those that you find most useful. Why do you especially like those features?

_____

_____

_____

_____

_____

_____

Distance Learning Activity

This distance learning exercise will be challenging and time-consuming, but it is an effective way to highlight the stages of the criminal trial. Search the World Wide Web for information about a specific criminal trial. In the space below, highlight the key facts of the case. What facts do you think the prosecutor will emphasize? What facts will the defense attorney emphasize?

_____

_____

_____

_____

_____

_____

Student Study Guide Questions

True or False

_____ 8-1. The process by which a potential juror is interviewed by the prosecutor and defense counsel is called _voir dire_.

_____ 8-2. If a defendant chooses not to testify at his or her trial, the prosecutor is allowed to point out to the jury that an innocent person would want to take the stand in an effort to clear his or her name.

_____ 8-3. When using a challenge for cause, a juror can be excused by either the defense or the prosecution, and no reason for doing so needs to be stated.

_____ 8-4. The prosecution must disclose any evidence related to a case that the defense requests.

_____ 8-5. The phrase "courtroom work group" refers to all persons who are licensed to practice law and who earn their living primarily in the courtroom.

_____ 8-6. A witness's statement that she didn't see the defendant commit the crime but she did see him arguing with and threatening the victim shortly before the crime occurred is an example of circumstantial evidence.

_____ 8-7. A sequestered jury is isolated from the public during the course of a trial and throughout the deliberation process.

_____ 8-8. A challenge to the array indicates that the defense attorney does not believe that the pool from which the jury is being selected is representative of the community at large.

_____ 8-9. A defense attorney who is aware that her client is about to commit perjury on the stand is obligated to inform the court of this fact, even if it violates the attorney–client privilege.

_____ 8-10. Hearsay evidence is automatically excluded from the courtroom, regardless of the circumstances.

Multiple Choice

8-11. Indigency refers to criteria used by
   a. the courts to establish the amount of bail.
   b. judges to determine eligibility of defendants for court-appointed counsel.
   c. the state police to establish crime-enforcement levels.
   d. the prosecutor's office to determine a witness's reliability.

8-12. The Missouri Bar Plan is a mechanism suggested by the American Bar Association for
   a. limiting judicial discretion during sentencing.
   b. using the merit plan for selection of judges.
   c. reducing endless appeals by defendants.
   d. speeding up the flow of cases through the courts.

8-13. As discussed in the text, criminal law is a field that
   a. attracts many prestigious lawyers.
   b. is a high-status segment of the legal profession.
   c. few law students actively choose to pursue.
   d. has high financial rewards for most practitioners.

8-14. Under the _____ system, legal services for defendants are provided by attorneys in private practice paid for by the court and selected from a roster of all practicing criminal attorneys within the jurisdiction of the court.
   a. retained counsel
   b. contract
   c. public defender
   d. court-appointed counsel

8-15. In _Gideon_ v. _Wainwright_ (1963), what ruling did the U.S. Supreme Court make?
   a. In federal cases, the right to counsel becomes applicable as soon as a defendant is arrested.
   b. The right to counsel applies not only to state trials of defendants charged with felonies but to all trials of defendants that might result in a jail sentence.
   c. A defendant has a right to counsel when submitting a guilty plea to the court for any offense.
   d. The right to appointed counsel applies to all indigent defendants in state court who are charged with a felony.

8-16. As discussed in your text, discovery is a request by the defense attorney to
   a. obtain detailed information about police activities.
   b. move the trial to a different part of the jurisdiction.
   c. suppress certain evidence that was illegally seized.
   d. examine all of the evidence that will be presented at trial.

8-17. In jury selection, challenges for cause are
   a. made only by the defense.
   b. not required to be justified by the attorney requesting the challenge.
   c. sound legal reasons for removing potential jurors.
   d. ruled on by the prosecuting attorney.

8-18. Changing the venue of a trial
   a. removes the defendant due to a conflict of interest.
   b. moves the trial to another location due to pretrial publicity.
   c. removes the prosecutor due to a conflict of interest.
   d. removes the judge due to a conflict of interest.

8-19. *Voir dire* is used to determine
   a. judicial bias.
   b. if prospective jurors are biased or hold preconceived notions of guilt or innocence
   c. the validity to a claim of prosecutorial misconduct
   d. whether the racial makeup of an impaneled jury violates Supreme Court guidelines

8-20. The murder weapon would primarily be considered _____ evidence.
   a. direct
   b. real
   c. testimonial
   d. damning

Fill-In

8-21. _____ is that which requires interpretation or that which requires the judge or jury to reach a conclusion based on what the evidence indicates.

8-22. _____ consists of physical material or traces of physical activity such as tire tracks.

8-23. Removing an unwanted potential juror without the need to disclose a reason for the removal is accomplished by means of a(n) _____.

8-24. _____ involves moving a trial from one jurisdiction to another.

8-25. The court officer who keeps order in the courtroom and maintains custody of the jury is the _____.

8-26. A(n) _____ is a person who has special knowledge recognized by the court as relevant to the determination of the guilt or innocence of the accused.

8-27. _____ is a false statement made by a sworn witness during a judicial proceeding.

8-28. A(n) _____ is a written order requiring someone to appear in court to testify.

8-29. An elected or appointed public official who presides over a court of law is a(n) _____.

8-30. _____ is a statement that is not based on the personal knowledge of a witness.

Crossword Puzzle

Across

4. Evidence that requires interpretation.
7. Elected or appointed public official who presides over a court of law and who is authorized to hear and sometimes to decide cases and to conduct trials.
9. What someone commits when he or she lies on the witness stand.
10. Person who tries to maintain order in the court.
11. A limited number of these types of challenges.
12. What established the time periods required for a case to be processed by the court system.
14. Oral evidence offered by a sworn witness.
15. Initial statement of an attorney.

Down

1. All who earn a living serving the court.
2. Type of evidence based on eyewitness testimony.
3. Jury isolated from the public.
5. Two-sided structure under which American criminal trial courts operate that pits the prosecution against the defense.
6. Motion used in a high-profile case.
8. Oral summation of a case.
13. Decision of the jury.

Word Search Puzzle

```
K Y V H R K W B F N Q W M N A Q E Z I X S A E N P P H K U D
K W E N N D J W D W D D C S K M R D R W K B S M V G I R T Y
Y O C Z C F E L T I Z B X B P U B L I C D E F E N D E R G Z
O A H H Y N G C M C R U H Y F N H S R S Q E V Q Y U H P M I
J O A H P A U W P H V E J T S B T D X M G P Q I L O H Y C K
V P N L T J D V L Z I W C Y X K Q R U O P X T K D H E H X G
L C G Z N S K J A A K N W T H C S L H H A R Q Y C E J E K K
X N E L E D R U A E Y J G U E W P U O Y W Z O V Y L N C F C
D K O Z F Y F R M H X W J F V U N E F O I Y S E Z P C R Q
A U F H K G M O Z T A Q I K P S I C Y D Q H B S E F X E E U
M N V R X W F R X G C S D T H E N D G E Z P N T A C K B X R
S G E I I B E H A J Q U V G N E N H E F F U X E W T U D C P
V D N B Q U U N J C Z D A T D E Q I Z N O K Y X M R I T M E
G Y U I A H O W I D G V V I S E S Y N C C P K E G S J H O M
W Y E B Y I T U A J F M V I Q T A S E G K E T M M P Y M E R
C P N I L K L U P B D E G B R R Z S P F S S A M P G R W C M
C R Q P X B A I G O L I S W Z Q N V O G Y T M G L V K F T R
G O N D R W E T F A S F Y C B E J P Z S I R A W B P U S Y L
D B J T S H L P E F H G V W F V I U L O O K I T W G I O Q H
V A M R R W E R J J I K S E R I R A D M S U X R E G X A F O
V T C M Q O K A X Y P P D M S O I I B G R C Y B U M A P Z B
L I L U D Z P N R C I X T J S R D D A C E U C S I G E K T A
Y V L P P R Y V G S V U P S A R R N C H J U U N A F E N T B
U E G W H C Z B B Y A Z P S U W M K U S V R O A R V G T T B
D V V E R D I C T Y S Y R F N I S R L T E L V S S P D X C I
B A L R I L M H J D V E E K W B Y H E B T E S T I M O N Y W
V L F W E W L R K W V U O C L O S I N G A R G U M E N T J U
Y U S C U G V S U D X W O A P J B P C P O E A V X U V O D M
N E U Q P T I C A Z Z A I Y R E X P E R T W I T N E S S M Y
J G Q P E N S M F H Q J F M C A J X R V R D K U X L I S N T
```

Adversarial System

Bailiff

Change of Venue

Closing Argument

Defense Counsel

Direct Evidence

Evidence

Expert Witness

Hearsay

Judge

Juror

Lay Witness

Opening Statement

Probative Value

Prosecutor

Public Defender

Real Evidence

Testimony

Verdict

9 Sentencing

Chapter Outline

- Introduction
- The Philosophy and Goals of Criminal Sentencing
- Indeterminate Sentencing
- Structured Sentencing
- Innovations in Sentencing
- The Presentence Investigation
- The Victim—Forgotten No Longer
- Modern Sentencing Options
- Death: The Ultimate Sanction

Learning Objectives

After reading this chapter, you should be able to

- Describe the five goals of contemporary criminal sentencing.
- Illustrate the difference between indeterminate and structured sentencing.
- Describe the different types of structured sentencing models in use today.
- Explain the importance of federal sentencing guidelines.
- Describe truth in sentencing.
- Define mandatory sentencing, and explain how it came about.
- Describe the nature and importance of the presentence investigation report.
- Describe the history of victims' rights and services, and discuss the growing role of the victim in criminal justice proceedings today.
- List the four traditional sentencing options.
- Outline the arguments for and against the death penalty.

Chapter Summary

Duane Harris, having recently pleaded guilty to one count of armed robbery, stood before Judge Joe Marist waiting to hear his sentence. The judge, known by his peers as "Hanging Joe," sentenced Harris to the maximum sentence possible under the law: 10 to 25 years in a maximum-security prison. Why did the judge decide to sentence Harris to the longest prison term possible? What factors did the judge consider to arrive at his sentence? What other options did he have? Could he have sentenced Harris to a longer term? Could he have sentenced Harris to death for the crime?

The text discusses several important aspects of sentencing in Chapter 9; it also describes five goals of contemporary sentencing: retribution, incapacitation, deterrence, rehabilitation, and restoration. **Retribution** corresponds to the just deserts model of sentencing and is best understood from the biblical reference to "eye for an eye, tooth for a tooth." **Incapacitation** seeks to isolate offenders from society. **Deterrence**, both **specific** and **general**, focuses on preventing crimes. **Rehabilitation** seeks to change the offender, and **restoration** seeks to make the victim "whole again."

Chapter 9 also describes types of sentencing practices. Harris was convicted in a state that uses an **indeterminate sentencing** model, and judges have the most discretion in states adhering to this model. A judge is expected to assess the differences among cases, situations, and offenders in an attempt to make the sentence both appropriate and proportionate. It is also believed that offenders will be more likely to participate in rehabilitation programs if they can reduce the amount of time served.

The text highlights several problems with the indeterminate sentencing model. The most significant criticism is the inequality of sentences. Harris received the maximum sentence possible under the law; however, it is possible that another offender, sentenced by another judge in an adjacent courtroom, could receive significantly fewer years in prison or probation. The personalities of different judges, race of the offender, race of the victim, and social class have all been shown to be factors contributing to disparities in sentences.

In response to the various problems of indeterminate sentencing systems, states and the federal government have revised sentencing practices in order to structure sentencing more precisely. For example, some states have adopted a **determinate sentencing model** that requires offenders to be sentenced to a fixed term; other states have developed **voluntary/advisory sentencing guidelines**, and some have adopted **presumptive sentencing guidelines**. Guideline jurisdictions specify a presumptive sentence for an offense but also allow the judge to consider **aggravating** and **mitigating** factors. Another type of structured sentencing discussed in the text is **mandatory sentencing**.

In general, judges try to make informed and fair sentencing decisions. The **presentence investigation report** assists judges with their decisions. Provided as a detailed report, an abbreviated report, or an oral report to the court, the presentence investigation report provides information about the defendant and the offense. It may also include a recommendation from the probation officer. Another factor that judges may consider when deciding the sentence is the impact of the crime on the victim. **Victim impact statements** provide an opportunity for crime victims, or surviving family members of a victim, to describe the suffering caused by the crime.

Finally, the text discusses the typical sentencing options available to the judge. Imprisonment and probation are mentioned but are discussed in more detail in later chapters of the text. The frequent use of fines as a criminal sanction is also discussed. Chapter 9 concludes with a discussion of **capital punishment**.

There are currently more than 3,800 offenders on death row. The number of offenders executed in a year is relatively small, but those numbers will probably increase because of Supreme Court rulings on *habeas corpus* review. The death penalty is one issue that generates considerable debate. Many people oppose the death penalty because they believe it is not an effective deterrent to crime, is not applied fairly, is costly, and always carries a risk of killing an innocent person. However, most of the public supports capital punishment; revenge, just deserts, and protection are the key supporting arguments of retentionists.

Key Concepts

Aggravating Circumstances   Circumstances relating to the commission of a crime that make it more grave than the average instance of that type of crime.

Alternative Sentencing   The use of court-ordered community service, home detention, day reporting, drug treatment, psychological counseling, victim-offender programming, or intensive supervision in lieu of other, more traditional sanctions, such as imprisonment and fines.

Capital Offense   A criminal offense punishable by death.

Capital Punishment   The death penalty. Capital punishment is the most extreme of all sentencing options.

Determinate Sentencing   A model of criminal punishment in which an offender is given a fixed term that may be reduced by good time or gain time. Under the model, for example, all offenders convicted of the same degree of burglary would be sentenced to the same length of time behind bars.

Deterrence   A goal of criminal sentencing that seeks to inhibit criminal behavior through the fear of punishment.

Diversion   The official suspension of criminal proceedings against an alleged offender at any point before the entering of a judgment, and the referral of that person to a treatment or care program administered by a nonjustice or private agency.

Equity   A sentencing principle, based upon concerns with social equality, that holds that similar crimes should be punished with the same degree of severity, regardless of the social or personal characteristics of the offenders.

Gain Time   The amount of time deducted from time to be served in prison on a given sentence for participation in special projects or programs.

General Deterrence   A goal of criminal sentencing that seeks to prevent others from committing crimes similar to the one for which a particular offender is being sentenced by making an example of the person sentenced.

Good Time   The amount of time deducted from time to be served in prison on a given sentence as a consequence of good behavior.

Incapacitation   The use of imprisonment or other means to reduce the likelihood that an offender will be capable of committing future offenses.

Indeterminate Sentencing   A model of criminal punishment that encourages rehabilitation via the use of general and relatively unspecified sentences (such as a term of imprisonment from one to ten years).

Just Deserts   A model of criminal sentencing that holds that criminal offenders deserve the punishment they receive at the hands of the law and that punishments should be appropriate to the type and severity of the crime committed.

Mandatory Sentencing   A structured sentencing scheme that allows no leeway in the nature of the sentence required and under which clearly enumerated punishments are mandated for specific offenses or for habitual offenders convicted of a series of crimes.

Mitigating Circumstances   Circumstances relating to the commission of a crime which may be considered to reduce the blameworthiness of the defendant.

Presentence Investigation   The examination of a convicted offender's background prior to sentencing. Presentence examinations are generally conducted by probation or parole officers and are submitted to sentencing authorities.

Presumptive Sentencing   A model of criminal punishment that meets the following conditions: (1) The appropriate sentence for an offender convicted of a specific charge is presumed to fall within a range of sentences authorized by sentencing guidelines that are adopted by a legislatively created sentencing body, usually a sentencing commission; (2) sentencing judges are expected to sentence within the range or to provide written justification for departure; (3) the guidelines provide for some review, usually appellate, of any departure from the guidelines.

Proportionality   A sentencing principle that holds that the severity of sanctions should bear a direct relationship to the seriousness of the crime committed.

Rehabilitation   The attempt to reform a criminal offender. Also, the state in which a reformed offender is said to be.

Restoration   A goal of criminal sentencing that attempts to make the victim "whole again."

Restorative Justice   A sentencing model that builds upon restitution and community participation in an attempt to make the victim "whole again."

Retribution   The act of taking revenge upon a criminal perpetrator.

Sentencing   The imposition of a criminal sanction by a judicial authority.

Social Debt   A sentencing principle that holds that an offender's criminal history should objectively be taken into account in sentencing decisions.

Specific Deterrence   A goal of criminal sentencing that seeks to prevent a particular offender from engaging in repeat criminality.

Structured Sentencing   A model of criminal punishment that includes determinate and commission-created presumptive sentencing schemes, as well as voluntary/advisory sentencing guidelines.

Truth in Sentencing   A close correspondence between the sentence imposed upon an offender and the time actually served prior to release from prison. *Source*: Lawrence A. Greenfeld, "Prison Sentences and Time Served for Violence," *Bureau of Justice Statistics Selected Findings*, No. 4, April 1995.

Victim-Impact Statement   The in-court use of victim- or survivor-supplied information by sentencing authorities wishing to make an informed sentencing decision.

Voluntary/Advisory Sentencing Guidelines   Recommended sentencing policies that are not required by law.

Writ of *Habeas Corpus*   A writ that directs the person detaining a prisoner to bring him or her before a judicial officer to determine the lawfulness of the imprisonment.

Key Cases

Apprendi v. *New Jersey*.   In this U.S. Supreme Court case, the Court ruled that other than prior conviction, any fact that enhances the sentence must be submitted to a jury and proved beyond a reasonable doubt (*Apprendi* v. *New Jersey*, 120 S.Ct 2348 [2000]).

Atkins v. *Virginia*.   The U.S. Supreme Court ruled that executing mentally retarded people violates the Constitution's ban on cruel and unusual punishment (*Atkins* v. *Virginia*, No. 00-8452 [U.S. Supreme Court 2002]).

Coker v. *Georgia.* The U.S. Supreme Court concluded that the death penalty is not an acceptable punishment for the crime of rape and that execution would be "grossly disproportionate" to the crime (*Coker* v. *Georgia*, 433 U.S. 584 [1977]).

Coleman v. *Thompson.* State prisoners condemned to die cannot cite "procedural default" (such as a defense attorney's failure to meet a filing deadline for appeals in state court) as the sole reason for an appeal to federal court (*Coleman* v. *Thompson*, 501 U.S. 722 [1991]).

Deal v. *U.S.* It is possible to try and to convict a defendant for six separate offenses in a single proceeding and use the federal sentencing guidelines to convict and sentence the defendant as a career offender as a consequence (*Deal* v. *U.S.*, 113 S.Ct. 1993, 124 L.Ed.2d 44 [1993]).

Furman v. *Georgia.* "Evolving standards of decency" might necessitate a reconsideration of the constitutionality of capital punishment. Allowing the jury to decide guilt and the punishment of death at the same time allowed for an arbitrary and capricious application of the death penalty (*Furman* v. *Georgia*, 408 U.S. 238 [1972]).

Gregg v. *Georgia.* The two-step process of a judge or jury deciding guilt and then undertaking a separate sentencing phase was specifically upheld by the Supreme Court (*Gregg* v. *Georgia*, 428 U.S. 153 [1976]).

In re Kemmler. Punishments are cruel when they involve torture or a lingering death, but the punishment of death is not cruel, within the meaning of that word as used in the Constitution (*In re Kemmler*, 136 U.S. 436 [1890]).

McClesky v. *Zandt.* This case limits the number of appeals available to a condemned person. After the first appeal, the defendant must show (1) why the subsequent appeal wasn't included in the first appeal and (2) how the defendant was harmed by the absence of the claim (*McClesky* v. *Zandt*, 499 U.S. 467, 493–494 [1991]).

Mistretta v. *U.S.* Congress acted appropriately in the creation of the federal sentencing guidelines, and the guidelines could be applied in federal cases nationwide (*Mistretta* v. *U.S.*, 488 U.S. 361, 371 [1989]).

Ring v. *Arizona.* The U.S. Supreme Court found that "Arizona's enumerated aggravating factors operate as the functional equivalent of an element of a greater offense" (*Ring* v. *Arizona*, No. 01-488 [U.S. Supreme Court, 2002]).

Schriro v. *Summerlin.* The court found that the rules established in *Apprendi* v. *New Jersey* and *Ring* v. *Arizona* could not be applied to sentences that had already been imposed because it was merely a new procedural rule and not a substantive change (*Schriro* v. *Summerlin*, 542 U.S. 348 [2004]).

Schlup v. *Delo.* The court ruled that before appeals based on claims of new evidence can be heard, a petitioner must show that "it is more likely than not that no reasonable juror would have found him guilty beyond a reasonable doubt" (*Schlup* v. *Delo*, 115 S.Ct. 851, 130 L.Ed.2d 1123 [1995]).

U.S. v. *Booker.* The court examined the constitutionality of the federal sentencing guidelines. One of the results of this case was that it made the federal sentencing guidelines advisory and increased the discretion of federal judges (*U.S.* v. *Booker*, 543 U.S. 220 [2005]).

Wilkerson v. *Utah.* This case upheld the use of the firing squad as a method of execution (*Wilkerson* v. *Utah*, 99 U.S. 130 [1878]).

Woodson v. *North Carolina.* Laws requiring the mandatory application of the death penalty for specific crimes are prohibited (*Woodson* v. *North Carolina*, 428 U.S. 280 [1976]).

Learning Tips

Reading and Outlining

When reading material, use the textbook's chapter outline and the *Student Study Guide's* chapter outline, or create an outline yourself to guide you through the information as you progress through the reading. Make the outlines more comprehensive by adding headings, notes, and thoughts. Whether using the provided outlines or your own method, outlining makes difficult material more understandable and allows you to see the larger picture rather than getting caught up in insignificant details or trivia.

Study Sessions

Avoid scheduling long study sessions. Four 2-hour study sessions are far more productive than one 8-hour session. The amount of time actually spent productively in excessively long study sessions is very small; however, if long study sessions are inevitable, be sure to give your mind and body a break for a few minutes each hour. Also, be sure to study a variety of subjects. Studying similar subjects back to back is usually unproductive.

CJ Brief on the World Wide Web

Web links to organizations and agencies related to the material in Chapter 9 include:

WEBSITE TITLE	URL
ACLU's Death Penalty Page	http://www.aclu.org/capital /facts/index.html
The Coalition for Federal Sentencing Reform	http://www.sentencing.org
Death Penalty Focus	http://www.deathpenalty.org
Death Penalty Information Center (DPIC)	http://www.deathpenaltyinfo.org
National Association of Sentencing Advocates (NASA)	http://www.sentencingproject .org/nasa
State Sentencing Commissions	http://www.ussc.gov/states /nascaddr.htm
United States Sentencing Commission	http://www.ussc.gov

Learner Activities

Activity 1

In the space provided, answer the questions at the end of each scenario.

1. Darryl Jackson is a 20-year-old unemployed male. He is addicted to cocaine, has no family, and is homeless. He has three prior felony convictions (all drug possession). He has recently been convicted of his fourth felony (a burglary), and you are the judge deciding his fate. The sentencing statute allows you to sentence Jackson with anything from a minor fine to life imprisonment (or any combination of punishments).

   Here are the specific facts of the case. On October 18, Darryl Jackson entered the apartment of Angela Starter. He entered by picking the lock on her back door. He stole her stereo ($1,500), jewelry ($3,500), and Matchbox car collection ($800). When Jackson was leaving her apartment, a security officer stopped and apprehended him for the burglary. Jackson claimed he needed to sell the goods so that he would have money for food.

What sentence would you give Darryl Jackson?

_____

_____

_____

_____

_____

_____

2. Ron Kuzak is a 20-year-old male. He is a college student with a 3.6 grade point average, he works part-time at McDonald's, and he goes to church on Sunday (he sings in the choir). He is also addicted to cocaine. Kuzak has three prior felony convictions (all drug possession); he has recently been convicted of his fourth felony (a burglary), and you are the judge deciding his fate. The sentencing statute allows you to sentence Kuzak with anything from a minor fine to life imprisonment (or any combination of punishments).

   Here are the specific facts of the case. On October 18, Ron Kuzak entered the apartment of Joni McDougal. He entered by picking the lock on her back door. He stole her watch ($1,500), diamond ring ($3,500), and Beanie Baby collection ($800). When Kuzak was leaving her apartment, a security officer stopped and apprehended him for the burglary. Kuzak claimed he needed to sell the goods so that he would have money for college tuition.

What sentence would you give Ron Kuzak?

_____

_____

_____

_____

_____

_____

Activity 2

What sentence would you give each of the following defendants? What factors would be most important to you? What other types of information would you want to know to make a more informed sentencing decision?

1. Ann Colby, a 32-year-old single mother, was convicted of reckless driving. On January 23, she was driving while intoxicated along State Street and hit a parked fire truck. The fire department was responding to an emergency medical call, attempting to transport an elderly man who had suffered a heart attack to the hospital. Because of the accident, the man could not be transported until another transport vehicle arrived. Colby was originally charged

with driving while intoxicated, but the prosecutor allowed her to plead guilty to reckless driving.

2. Daniel Driver, 35 years old, was convicted on felony child molestation charges. He was on parole for similar charges at the time of the current offense. Driver is divorced, works as a computer consultant for an electronics firm, and has been described as an "active churchgoer."

3. Maria Campo, age 40, pleaded guilty to two counts of passing bad checks. Campo had been purchasing new furniture for her apartment, paying with checks for which she had no funds; she has two previous convictions for forgery.

4. Thomas "Ziggy" Petruzzelli, age 16, was convicted on involuntary manslaughter charges. The fight that led to the stabbing happened on July 4 outside a convenience store. Petruzzelli was standing outside the store asking adults to buy him a pack of cigarettes, something he could not do as a minor. Bruce Pearl, age 33, agreed to buy the cigarettes, but when Pearl came back outside the store, the two began arguing. Ultimately, Petruzzelli's father got involved, intervening with a two-by-four; the father is currently awaiting trial on an assault with a deadly weapon charge.

_____

_____

_____

_____

_____

_____

Activity 3

Robert Jones, son of Debbie and Tom Jones, was murdered on his way home from work. Darrin Alexander was quickly apprehended near the scene of the crime, was identified by multiple eyewitnesses, and confessed to the crime. At trial, the jury took only 48 minutes to reach a guilty verdict in this death penalty case.

Robert Jones's parents had completed a written victim impact statement and had prepared oral statements; however, the judge did not allow them to speak. Alexander had 12 witnesses speak on his behalf. Despite Robert Jones's parents' objections, the sentencing phase of the trial occurred without their input. The jury, after considering the aggravating and mitigating factors in the case, decided to sentence Alexander to life imprisonment rather than to death.

Some victim advocates would argue that this would not have occurred if there existed a federal constitutional amendment that protected crime victims. Victim advocates believe that such an amendment would give victims complete protection of their rights.

Lawyers are split on their support for such an amendment. Some argue against it because it might put a halt to plea bargaining, it would overburden the system, courts are ill equipped to handle such a radical change, and it would give victims too much veto power. Others, however, support the amendment, arguing that it would protect victims from such harm as described above, would give victims a voice in all court proceedings, would lessen the traumatizing impact of crime, and would make the system more balanced. There are many additional arguments both for and against the amendment.

What do you think? This student activity requires you to take a position for or against this constitutional amendment. Make a strong argument for your position.

_____

_____

_____

_____

_____

_____

Activity 4

Visit **Library Extra 9–7** at cjbrief.com. Write a summary of the information provided in the report in the space below. Does this study influence your opinion about the
death penalty?

Library EXTRA

_____

_____

_____

_____

_____

_____

Internet Activity

Visit the Death Penalty Information Center at http://www.deathpenaltyinfo.org.
Review the various "Issues" listed on the site's home page. Look at each of the subareas (under Issues), including Arbitrariness, Clemency, Costs, Deterrence, Mental
Illness, and Race. Provide a brief description of the kinds of material each subarea
contains. Which of these subareas do you find the most interesting? Why?

_____

_____

_____

_____

_____

_____

Distance Learning Activity

In the space below, take a position on the death penalty. Visit three or four websites
to search for evidentiary support for your position. The following pages will be helpful: (1) ACLU Death Penalty page: http://www.aclu.org/capital/facts/index.html; (2)
Death Penalty Information Center page: http://www.deathpenaltyinfo.org. If your
instructor asks you to do so, participate in a class debate on the issue.

_____

_____

_____

_____

_____

_____

Student Study Guide Questions

True or False

_____ 9-1. Deterrence is based on the idea of "an eye for an eye."

_____ 9-2. Mitigating circumstances result in harsher sentences under the determinate model.

_____ 9-3. Sentencing philosophies are manifestly intertwined with issues of religion, morals, values, and emotions.

_____ 9-4. The overall goal of deterrence is crime prevention.

_____ 9-5. Presumptive sentencing guidelines eliminate judicial discretion.

_____ 9-6. Most judges ignore the presentence investigation report writer's recommendations.

_____ 9-7. Very few states currently use capital punishment as a sentencing option.

_____ 9-8. Justifications for the death penalty are collectively referred to as the retentionist position.

_____ 9-9. Truth in sentencing means that before sentencing, probation officers present their investigation reports based on the truths they uncovered.

_____ 9-10. General deterrence is a goal of criminal sentencing that seeks to prevent a particular offender from engaging in repeat criminality.

Multiple Choice

9-11. Modern sentencing practices are influenced by which of the following goals?
   a. retribution
   b. incapacitation
   c. deterrence
   d. rehabilitation
   e. all of the above

9-12. Which official is responsible for conducting presentence investigations in most jurisdictions?
   a. judge
   b. defense attorney
   c. prosecutor
   d. probation or parole officer

9-13. What philosophy of sentencing seeks to prevent others from committing crimes similar to the one for which an offender is being sentenced?
    a. rehabilitation
    b. retribution
    c. deterrence
    d. incapacitation

9-14. The retribution goal in sentencing corresponds to what model of sentencing?
    a. just deserts model
    b. medical model
    c. restoration model
    d. psychological healing model

9-15. What type of sentencing relies heavily on a judge's discretion to choose among types of sanctions and set upper and lower limits on the length of prison stays?
    a. intermediate
    b. indeterminate
    c. determinate
    d. deterrent

9-16. Much of the philosophical basis of today's victims' movement can be found in which model?
    a. restorative justice
    b. retribution
    c. restitution
    d. none of the above

9-17. What type of writ directs the person detaining a prisoner to bring him or her before a judicial officer to determine the lawfulness of the imprisonment?
    a. *certiori*
    b. *habeas corpus*
    c. particulars
    d. all of the above

9-18. A study of the efficacy of victim impact statements found that judicial sentencing decisions were _____ affected by them.
    a. greatly
    b. rarely
    c. modestly
    d. never

9-19. Which of the following is *not* one of the retentionist justifications for the death penalty?
    a. deterrence
    b. revenge
    c. just deserts
    d. protection

9-20. This U.S. Supreme Court case invalidated the death penalty because it allowed unguided discretion when imposing a capital sentence.
    a. *Furman* v. *Georgia*
    b. *Poyner* v. *Murray*
    c. *Stanford* v. *Kentucky*
    d. *Gregg* v. *Georgia*

Fill-In

9-21. A(n) _____ is an examination of a convicted offender's background prior to sentencing.

9-22. _____ is an attempt to have a close correspondence between the sentence imposed and the actual time served.

9-23. The attempt to reform a criminal offender is called _____.

9-24. _____ is a goal of criminal sentencing that attempts to prevent a particular offender from engaging in repeat criminal behavior.

9-25. A sentence of 2 to 12 years is an example of _____.

9-26. _____ is the act of taking revenge on a criminal perpetrator.

9-27. _____ is a model for criminal punishment that sets one particular punishment, or length of sentence, for each specific type of crime.

9-28. The amount of time deducted from time to be served in prison on a given sentence based on good behavior while in prison is called _____.

9-29. _____ are factors surrounding an offense that could result in a harsher sentence.

9-30. A(n) _____ is a criminal offense punishable by death.

Crossword Puzzle

Across

2. Sentencing principle that holds that the severity of sanctions should bear a direct relationship to the seriousness of the crime committed.

3. Another type of circumstances besides aggravating.

4. Amount of time deducted from time to be served in prison on a given sentence for good behavior.

7. Attempt to change the offender.

9. Goal of criminal sentencing that seeks to inhibit criminal behavior through the fear of punishment.

10. Also called fixed sentencing.

11. Sentencing scheme that allows no leeway in the nature of the sentence.

12. Offense that is punishable by death.

13. Use of imprisonment or other means to reduce the likelihood that an offender will be capable of committing future offenses.

14. Imposition of a criminal sanction by a judicial authority.

15. Model of sentencing to which retribution corresponds.

Down

1. Also called the death penalty.

5. Sentencing principle based on concerns for social equality.

6. What a probation officer usually conducts prior to sentencing.

7. Act to make the victim whole again.

8. "An eye for an eye."

Word Search Puzzle

```
Y D C S S Z V V J X S R W F B G M Y C E V W P S G Z L H C R
Y T A P P I M D B B Z B A U T V Z X V F I L R E R J Q M X O
Q Z P R E U B P P P T W U C H C S R Y V N A O N W L X I S D
A I I E C P W E W A Y E Y F P O U B E R C J P M T V E T E E
T N T S I Y R R R D O C D I I Z E W Q C A U O F Y N F I V T
E D A U F D D B I W I X R N F G F E U R P S R M O P N G I E
X E L M I E A J H T F R P Y O A M R I O A T T H S J S A C R
V T O P C T L C Z U O L L F S I V G T H C D I Y I R O T T M
Z E F T D E T V D D Z F L H T N B B Y D I E O Z U E R I I I
L R F I E R G Y V I V L H D B T F M D D T S N U R H E N M N
K M E V T R C E X X N O O A G I C H G X A E A F V A S G I A
K I N E E E D S N C M O I E B M X N P H T R L U M B T C M T
D N S S R N T P C E G A D Y M E I A A N I T I Q F I O I P E
C A E E R C G L O V R P N B V C A D M G O S T P E L R R A S
A T H N E E V T R F P A T D N M O S B F N Q Y U S I A C C E
P E F T N P M W R W R T L E A O R Z C C N L K X E T T U T N
I S V E C G R J D E W U T D I T W M S O I F I O N A I M S T
T E G N E O R N M L S N W O E N O M Y X R S X W T T V S T E
A N V C J C V H R C E T Z I H T E R S R K P K X E I E T A N
L T B I J P A M E S I Y O O H S E U Y S W O U D N O J A T C
P E Y N G V Z Q N H C H C R U Z C R B S O Z O S C N U N E I
U N V G T I D I I X H P G R A G X Z R G E C N U I Y S C M N
N C Y J Z Y H G X P L F B D G T T O T E I N I L N J T E E G
I I R S S T Z M J W E G Z A H E I P L G N R T A G G I S N E
S N P I U R L P H F V F Y T K O X O F A T C G E L M C L T E
H G S R R W U Q H Q O O J L I U W T N C T R E D N E G B I
M Z T Y A G G R A V A T I N G C I R C U M S T A N C E S L Z
E P R E S E N T E N C E I N V E S T I G A T I O N R I B X N
N O X R U N H S T R U C T U R E D S E N T E N C I N G N T B
T N Y L R H N O E G K B P G R E T R I B U T I O N O Q S G P
```

Aggravating Circumstances
Capital Offense
Capital Punishment
Determinate Sentencing
Deterrence
Equity
Gain Time
General Deterrence
Good Time
Incapacitation
Indeterminate Sentencing
Just Deserts
Mandatory Sentencing
Mitigating Circumstances

Presentence Investigation
Presumptive Sentencing
Proportionality
Rehabilitation
Restoration
Restorative Justice
Retribution
Sentencing
Social Debt
Specific Deterrence
Structured Sentencing
Truth in Sentencing
Victim Impact Statement
Writ of *Habeas Corpus*

10 Probation, Parole, and Community Corrections

Chapter Outline

- Introduction
- What Is Probation?
- What Is Parole?
- Probation and Parole: The Pluses and Minuses

- The Legal Environment
- The Job of Probation and Parole Officers
- Intermediate Sanctions
- The Future of Probation and Parole

Learning Objectives

After reading this chapter, you should be able to

- Explain the difference between probation and parole, and describe the advantages and disadvantages of each.
- Describe in detail the legal environment surrounding the use of probation and parole, including the names of significant court cases.
- Explain the nature of the job of probation and parole officers.

- List the advantages of intermediate sanctions over more traditional forms of sentencing.
- Describe the likely future of probation and parole.

Chapter Summary

Chapter 10 discusses many issues important to understanding **community corrections**. This chapter focuses primarily on probation and parole; however, there is also a discussion of intermediate sanctions. **Probation** is a sentence of imprisonment that is suspended. Offenders, if they abide by the specific and general conditions of probation, will serve their entire sentences in the community. This provides them with the opportunity to continue working or remain in school, maintain family and social ties, and use the treatment programs available in the community. Chapter 10 discusses the history of probation in the United States and describes it as the most common form of criminal sentencing today. As of 2004, there were 4 million offenders currently on probation, and 5% of people convicted of homicide were placed on probation.

Parole is often mistaken for probation, but the two sentences are different. When sentencing an offender to probation, a judge makes the decision that a prison sentence should be suspended and that the offender should serve his or her sentence in the community. An offender is on parole when he or she first serves time in prison and then is conditionally released by the paroling authority. However, similar to the constraints put on the probationer, the parolee must abide by general and specific conditions or face revocation of parole.

The text then describes the advantages and disadvantages of probation and parole. Advantages include lower cost than imprisonment, increased employment opportunities, opportunity to pay **restitution**, opportunity to receive community support, reduced risk of criminal socialization, and increased use of community services and opportunities for rehabilitation. Disadvantages include concerns about the lack of punishment, increased risk to the community, and increased social costs.

The legal environment of probation and parole is interesting because convicted offenders have fewer legal protections than someone accused of a crime. For example, the Supreme Court has decided that probation officers may conduct searches without a warrant or without probable cause (*Griffin* v. *Wisconsin*). Parole boards do not have to specify the evidence used in denying parole (*Greenholtz* v. *Nebraska*), and incriminating statements to a probation officer may be used as evidence if the probationer does not specify a right against self-incrimination (*Minnesota* v. *Murphy*). It is important to note, however, that probationers and parolees have some legal protections. The important *Gagnon* v. *Scarpelli* and *Morrissey* v. *Brewer* decisions declared that probationers and parolees deserve procedural safeguards when their probation or parole is being revoked.

The last section of Chapter 10 describes intermediate and innovative sentences. Judges have a wide variety of intermediate sanctions at their disposal. A **split sentence** requires the convicted person to serve a period of confinement in a facility followed by a period of probation. Similar to this type of sentence, **shock probation** (or **shock parole**) involves sentencing an offender to prison but then allowing him or her to be released early to probation. The first part of a split sentence is typically spent in a jail, and the first part of a shock probation sentence is spent in prison. **Shock incarceration** is a sentence to a military "boot camp"–style prison. **Intensive probation supervision** involves frequent face-to-face contacts between the probationary client and the probation officer. Other intermediate sanctions discussed in Chapter 10 include **mixed sentences**, **community service**, and **home confinement**.

Key Concepts

Caseload   The number of probation or parole clients assigned to one probation or parole officer for supervision.

Community Corrections The use of a variety of officially ordered program-based sanctions that permit convicted offenders to remain in the community under conditional supervision as an alternative to an active prison sentence.

Community Service A sentencing alternative that requires offenders to spend at least part of their time working for a community agency.

Conditional Release The release of an inmate from prison to community supervision with a set of conditions for remaining on parole. If a condition is violated, the individual can be returned to prison or face another sanction in the community. *Source*: Jeremy Travis and Sarah Lawrence, *Beyond the Prison Gates: The State of Parole in America* (Washington DC: The Urban Institute, 2002, p. 3).

Conditions of Parole (Probation) The general and special limits imposed upon an offender who is released on parole (or probation). General conditions tend to be fixed by state statute, while special conditions are mandated by the sentencing authority (court or board) and take into consideration the background of the offender and the circumstances of the offense.

Discretionary Release The release of an inmate from prison to supervision that is decided by a parole board or other authority.

Home Confinement House arrest. Individuals ordered confined to their homes are sometimes monitored electronically to ensure they do not leave during the hours of confinement. Absence from the home during working hours is often permitted.

Intensive Probation Supervision (IPS) A form of probation supervision involving frequent face-to-face contact between the probationer and the probation officer.

Intermediate Sanctions The use of split sentencing, shock probation or parole, home confinement, shock incarceration, or community service in lieu of other, more traditional, sanctions, such as imprisonment and fines.

Mandatory Release The release of an inmate from prison that is determined by statute or sentencing guidelines and is not decided by a parole board or other authority. *Source*: Jeremy Travis and Sarah Lawrence, *Beyond the Prison Gates: The State of Parole in America* (Washington DC: The Urban Institute, 2002, p. 3).

Mixed Sentence A sentence that requires that a convicted offender serve weekends (or other specified periods of time) in a confinement facility (usually a jail) while undergoing probation supervision in the community.

Parole The status of an offender who has been conditionally released from prison by a paroling authority prior to expiration of his or her sentence, is placed under the supervision of a parole agency, and is required to observe conditions of parole.

Parole Board A state paroling authority. Most states have parole boards that decide when an incarcerated offender is ready for conditional release and that may also function as revocation hearing panels.

Parole (Probation) Violation An act or a failure to act by a parolee (or probationer) that does not conform to the conditions of his or her parole (or probation).

Parole Revocation The administrative action of a paroling authority to remove a person from parole status in response to a violation of lawfully required conditions of parole, including the prohibition against commission of a new offense, and usually resulting in a return to prison.

Prisoner Reentry The managed return to the community of individuals released from prison. Also called reentry.

Probation A sentence of imprisonment that is suspended. Also, the conditional freedom granted by a judicial officer to an adjudicated adult or juvenile offender, as long as the person meets certain conditions of behavior.

Probation Revocation   A court order taking away a convicted offender's probationary status and usually withdrawing the conditional freedom associated with that status in response to a violation of the conditions of probation.

Recidivism   The repetition of criminal behavior. In statistical practice, a recidivism rate may be any of a number of possible counts or instances of arrest, conviction, correctional commitment, or correctional status change related to repetitions of these events within a given period of time.

Remote Location Monitoring   A supervision strategy that uses electronic technology to track offenders sentenced to house arrest or those who have been ordered to limit their movements while completing a sentence involving probation or parole.

Restitution   A court requirement that an alleged or convicted offender pay money or provide services to the victim of the crime or provide services to the community.

Revocation Hearing   A hearing held before a legally constituted hearing body (such as a parole board) to determine whether a probationer or parolee has violated the conditions and requirements of his or her probation or parole.

Shock Incarceration   A sentencing option that makes use of boot camp–type prisons to impress upon convicted offenders the realities of prison life.

Shock Probation   The practice of sentencing offenders to prison, allowing them to apply for probationary release, and enacting such release in surprise fashion. Offenders who receive shock probation may not be aware of the fact that they will be released on probation and may expect to spend a much longer time behind bars.

Split Sentence   A sentence explicitly requiring the convicted offender to serve a period of confinement in a local, state, or federal facility followed by a period of probation.

Key Cases

Bearden v. *Georgia.*   It held that probation cannot be revoked for failure either to pay a fine or to make restitution if it cannot be shown that the defendant was responsible for the failure. Alternative forms of punishment must be considered and be shown to be inadequate before the defendant can be incarcerated (*Bearden* v. *Georgia*, 461 U.S. 660, 103 S.Ct. 2064, 76 L.Ed.2d 221 [1983]).

Escoe v. *Zerbst.*   This case found that probation "comes as an act of grace to one convicted of a crime" and that the revocation of probation without hearing or notice to the probationer was acceptable (*Escoe* v. *Zerbst*, 295 U.S. 490 [1935]).

Gagnon v. *Scarpelli.*   It extended the due process rights granted to parolees in *Morrissey* (see below) to probationers, and it also required that two hearings be held before probation can be revoked—a preliminary hearing and a final hearing. The case also provided some indigence relief to probationers facing revocation hearings (*Gagnon* v. *Scarpelli*, 411 U.S. 778 [1973]).

Greenholtz v. *Nebraska.*   It found that parole boards do not have to specify the evidence used in deciding to deny parole (*Greenholtz* v. *Nebraska*, 442 U.S. 1 [1979]).

Griffin v. *Wisconsin.*   It established that probation officers may conduct searches of a probationer's residence without a search warrant or probable cause (*Griffin* v. *Wisconsin*, 483 U.S. 868, 107 S.Ct. 3164 [1987]).

Mempa v. *Rhay.*   It found that both notice and a hearing are required in order to revoke probation (*Mempa* v. *Rhay*, 389 U.S. 128 [1967]).

Minnesota v. *Murphy.*   This case established that a probationer's incriminating statements to a probation officer may be used as evidence if the probationer did not specifically claim a right against self-incrimination (*Minnesota* v. *Murphy*, 465 U.S. 420, 104 S.Ct. 1136, 79 L.Ed.2d 409 [1984]).

Morrissey v. *Brewer*.   This case found that procedural safeguards are required in revocation hearings involving parolees: (1) There must be written notice of alleged violations; (2) evidence of the violation must be disclosed; (3) a neutral and detached body must constitute the hearing authority; (4) the parolee should have the chance to appear and offer a defense, including testimony, documents, and witnesses; (5) the parolee has the right to cross-examine witnesses; and (6) a written statement should be provided to the parolee at the conclusion of the hearing that includes the body's decision, the testimony considered, and the reasons for revoking parole if such occurs (*Morrissey* v. *Brewer*, 408 U.S. 471 [1972]).

Pennsylvania Board of Probation and Parole v. *Scott*.   In this case, the U.S. Supreme Court declined to extend the exclusionary rule to searches by parole officers (*Pennsylvania Board of Probation and Parole* v. *Scott*, 524 U.S. 357 [1998]).

Samson v. *California*.   The U.S. Supreme Court found that the Fourth Amendment does not prohibit police officers from conducting a warrantless search of a person who is subject to a parole search condition, even when there is no suspicion of criminal wrongdoing (*Samson* v. *California*, 547 U.S. [2006]).

U.S. v. *Knights*.   This case expanded the search authority normally reserved for probation and parole officers to police officers in certain circumstances (*U.S.* v. *Knights*, 534 U.S. 112, 122 S.Ct. 587, 151. L.Ed.2d 497 [2001]).

Learning Tips

Taking Notes

Pay special attention to key words; names, vocabulary words, and quotations are examples of key words. Focusing on key words will eliminate excess material from cluttering your notes. More important, key words are wonderful review mechanisms because they help you recall images.

Reviewing Notes

Because short-term memory is indeed short, it is important to review your class notes as soon as possible, especially within 24 hours. Extensively review your notes, correct misspellings, write out abbreviations, insert any information you were unable to write in your notes during the class, and write as legibly as possible. Not only can these strategies save valuable time when studying for tests, but they also help transfer information from short-term to long-term memory.

CJ Brief on the World Wide Web

Web links to organizations and agencies related to the material in Chapter 10 include:

WEBSITE TITLE	URL
Alternative Dispute Resolution Resources, Mediation Essays, and Web Page Hosting for Mediators	http://www.adrr.com
American Probation & Parole Association (APPA)	http://www.appa-net.org

WEBSITE TITLE	URL
Center for Community Alternatives	http://www.dreamscape.com /ccacny/ccahome.htm
Electronic Monitoring	http://www.housearrest.com
Institute for Dispute Resolution	http://www.cpradr.org
International Community Corrections Association	http://www.iccaweb.org
Justice Concepts Incorporated	http://www.justiceconcepts.com
Mediation Works, Inc.	http://www.mwi.org
National Center on Institutions and Alternatives	http://www.igc.org/ncia
The Sentencing Project	http://www.sentencingproject.org
Victim-Offender Reconciliation Program Resources	http://www.vorp.com

Learner Activities

Activity 1

According to the Bureau of Justice Statistics study discussed at the beginning of Chapter 10, 5% of murderers and 21% of sexual offenders are sentenced to probation. Do you think that murderers and sexual offenders should be sentenced to probation? Why or why not? What factors contribute to courts relying on probation for these types of offenders? Are there any offenses for which you would exclude probation as a sentencing option? Explain your answer.

_____

_____

_____

_____

_____

_____

Activity 2

One of the significant pressures affecting the criminal justice system is overcrowding in the prison system. Most prisons operate above capacity, and some state systems are under court mandate to reduce overcrowding. At the same time, however, many states are considering abolishing parole, which has traditionally been one mechanism that can reduce overcrowding by allowing the early release of inmates. Do you think parole should be eliminated? Why or why not? Are there other mechanisms that states can use to reduce prison populations? Explain your answer.

_____

_____

_____

_____

_____

_____

Activity 3

Visit **Library Extra 10–2** and read the publication on trends in state parole. In the
space below, describe the major trends identified. What trends do you think will
influence parole in the next ten years? Explain your answer.

Library
EXTRA

_____

_____

_____

_____

_____

_____

Activity 4

Locate a probation or parole agency in your state. Visit or call that agency, and interview an officer in each agency. Find out about the types of intermediate sanctions
available in your state. In the space provided below, describe at least three of the
intermediate sanctions available.

_____

_____

_____

_____

_____

_____

Internet Activity

Visit the American Probation and Parole Association (APPA) at http://www.
appa-net.org. Use the site map on the home page to locate APPA position statements.
What topics do these statements cover? Select three or four position statements, and
read and summarize them. Your instructor may request that you submit your findings.

_____

_____

_____

_____

_____

_____

Distance Learning Activity

Visit the Dispute Resolution Resources web page at http://www.adrr.com. This website provides essays on mediation and dispute resolution. Read one of the essays posted, and provide a summary of its key ideas. If your instructor asks you to do so, organize a class discussion that provides an opportunity to compare and contrast the findings from the different essays.

_____

_____

_____

_____

_____

_____

Student Study Guide Questions

True or False

_____ 10-1. When using shock probation, the judge sentences an offender to a prison term and then suspends the sentence before the offender actually starts to serve the sentence in a jail or prison.

_____ 10-2. Community service is a sentencing alternative that requires offenders to spend at least part of their time working for a community agency.

_____ 10-3. A split sentence requires an offender to serve at least part of his or her sentence in a jail or prison followed by a longer period on probation.

_____ 10-4. Restitution is a court requirement that an offender pay money or provide services to the victim of the crime or provide services to the community.

_____ 10-5. Parole is the status of an offender conditionally released from a prison by a paroling authority prior to the expiration of his or her sentence.

_____ 10-6. Probation is the conditional freedom granted by a judicial officer to an adjudicated adult or juvenile offender after a period of incarceration.

_____ 10-7. Statutory decrees grant parole based on a board's discretion.

_____ 10-8. If a judge orders that a convicted offender's sentence be suspended and places the offender on probation, no further steps can be taken to reinstate the suspended prison time regardless of the offender's behavior while on probation.

_____ 10-9. The number of probation and parole clients assigned to a probation or a parole officer for supervision is referred to as the officer's caseload.

_____ 10-10. Any act or failure to act by a probationer (or parolee) that does not conform to the conditions of probation (or parole) is a violation.

Multiple Choice

10-11. Probation and parole
    a. are essentially the same and are terms that are used interchangeably.
    b. use different supervision techniques but are usually administered by the same office.
    c. are sentences handed down by the courts.
    d. are distinctly different forms of community corrections administered by different authorities.

10-12. The most common method of release from prison is
    a. escape.
    b. discretionary parole.
    c. appeal.
    d. mandatory parole.

10-13. In the 1973 case of *Gagnon* v. *Scarpelli*, the U.S. Supreme Court
    a. affirmed the privilege against self-incrimination revocation hearings.
    b. extended the holding in *Morrissey* v. *Brewer* to include probationers.
    c. stressed the rehabilitative nature of probation.
    d. ruled against the use of hearsay evidence in probation revocation hearings.

10-14. Parole boards grant _____ parole.
    a. mandatory
    b. conditional
    c. discretionary
    d. limited

10-15. In what case did the court (Court) rule that the search authority of probation and parole officers might be extended to police officers in certain situations?
    a. *U.S.* v. *Knights*
    b. *Mempa* v. *Rhay*
    c. *Griffin* v. *Wisconsin*
    d. *Pennsylvania Board of Probation and Parole* v. *Scott*

10-16. In the event of a technical violation of probation, the _____ would be responsible for initiating violation proceedings.
    a. police officer
    b. probation officer
    c. judge
    d. prosecutor

10-17. In the 1983 case of *Bearden* v. *Georgia*, the U.S. Supreme Court determined that
    a. a restitution order cannot be vacated through a filing of bankruptcy.
    b. probation cannot be revoked for failure either to pay a fine or to make restitution if it can be shown that the defendant was not responsible for the failure.
    c. a probationer's incriminating statements made to a probation officer may be used as evidence against him or her.
    d. Probation "comes as an act of grace to one convicted of a crime."

10-18. _____ allows for a three- to six-month regimen of military drill, drug treatment, exercise, and academic work in return for having several years removed from an inmate's sentence.
    a. "Good time" law
    b. Shock incarceration
    c. Intensive parole
    d. Intensive probation

10-19. All of the following are considered advantages of probation and parole *except*
    a. relative lack of punishment.
    b. reduced risk of criminal socialization.
    c. lower cost.
    d. increased employment opportunities.

10-20. In the 1967 case of _____, the U.S. Supreme Court determined that both notice of the charges and a hearing are required in order to revoke an offender's probation.
    a. *Gagnon* v. *Scarpelli*
    b. *Morrissey* v. *Brewer*
    c. *Mempa* v. *Rhay*
    d. *Griffin* v. *Wisconsin*

Fill-In

10-21. _____ are state-ordered limits imposed on all offenders who are released on either probation or parole.

10-22. _____ is the practice of sentencing offenders to prison, allowing them to apply for probationary release, and enacting such release in a surprise fashion.

10-23. A(n) _____ is used to decide if an offender has violated the terms of his or her probation or parole by committing a new offense or failing to live up to the conditions of probation or parole.

10-24. Split sentencing, shock probation and parole, home confinement, shock incarceration, and community service are all examples of _____.

10-25. _____ is also called house arrest.

10-26. A(n) _____ requires an offender to serve a period of confinement in a local, state, or federal facility followed by a period of probation.

10-27. _____ makes use of "boot camp"–type prisons to impress on convicted offenders the realities of prison life.

10-28. A(n) _____ requires that a convicted offender serve weekends in jail and be on supervised probation in the community during the week.

10-29. _____ is a sentencing alternative that requires offenders to spend at least part of their time working for a community agency.

10-30. _____ is a form of probation supervision involving frequent face-to-face contacts between the probationary client and the probation officer.

Crossword Puzzle

Across

2. System usually utilized by home confinement.
3. Also called alternative sanctions.
4. Act or failure to act by a probationer that does not conform to the conditions of his or her probation.
7. Sentence explicitly requiring the convicted offender to serve a period of confinement in a local, state, or federal facility followed by a period of probation.
8. _____ v. *Scarpelli*.
10. Shock _____.
11. Hearing to determine whether a probationer has violated probation.
12. Court requirement that an alleged or convicted offender pay money or provide services to the victim.
13. Sentence that requires offenders to spend time working for a community agency.
14. Suspended sentence.
15. Number of clients assigned to a probation officer.
16. IPS.

Down

1. Also called community-based corrections.
5. State paroling authority.
6. _____ v. *Wisconsin*.
7. Like "boot camp."
9. Also called house arrest.

Word Search Puzzle

```
W Q K V M Y Q P B J S C R Z K M I U D L X Z P L Y J R F I W
E L L B X T Z F S Z X L O M T E E R K V Q U X H E M R U L I
C W R E M O T E L O C A T I O N M O N I T O R I N G E D M N
O Y E M B W H B J O J M A T G Q K G T W N U D G D M V U R T
M L W X J L P F O R G N O T K U B N P T J D R C K Q O X L E
M F K P C A S E L O A D Q A O E E F M I P Z L M K F C F K N
U J F Z J T Q W P U V Z G R E M E K L W I Y O M B R A M D S
N W U R L F N W L S F K H L E O S R L R A W W P C U T W M I
I F N J Y V P R B F Q G F N Q G A V G S O X X Z F S I T M V
T I Z I Z G T A C U L J I I R Y H B T P U L X I U C O J I E
Y C H E Y O Y W R D G F I C C K Y U L E W Y T C U O N P U P
S O A S J Y T U Z O N C Z B K E A N F Y Y F N Z E N H Q S R
E M N Y M X V A X O L O B R R N T F J C C S N Q K D E Y H O
R M V P Y I S C C D M E M X E V Y H R P E X F U T I A R O B
V U G G V Z X E J B H T B I Q S P Q I N Q M Z N Y T R D C A
I N M E U G M E D Z T N X O S A T G S J P M B X B I I Q K T
C I Y P N O C M D V P K A I A R L I K U W O F V I O N H P I
E T U A H U H C F S W R Z Z S R E G T F A P B E F N G X R O
L Y R R U S O N S Z E O O K E A D Q X U M E M J W S R N O N
S C G O B P B H E T B N F B V Q G V E F T W E G I O M C B S
F O I L X X Z T M H H F T I A Q T M H O O I O R L F U A A U
H R T E Y R R S K W Z E B E Y T D I P L M T O X A P U C T P
A R L Q Q L E W F D M D T A N J I Q G Q R B S N G A H A I E
D E T E T A A D W X F J A C J C X O J Z O I I A M R N E O R
T C H X Q M B Q H I U G E J F I E E N R I T R L R O K K N V
J T A R T I A H Z S Y Z J X N X C B W J Y B E W I L K B T I
H I H P A P R O B A T I O N R E V O C A T I O N X E A N Z S
H O B O F V F O Q S Z Z R L L A U I O V G L W I T T M G I
Y N V U P E Z W A A K W U Z G W Q X H V T M C W S M K X K O
L S S U X C V S P L I T S E N T E N C E R R U L J P E T X N
```

Caseload

Community Corrections

Community Service

Conditions of Parole

Home Confinement

Intensive Probation Supervision

Mixed Sentence

Parole

Parole Board

Probation

Probation Revocation

Remote Location Monitoring

Restitution

Revocation Hearing

Shock Probation

Split Sentence

11 Prisons and Jails

Chapter Outline

- Introduction
- Prisons

- Jails
- Private Prisons

Learning Objectives

After reading this chapter, you should be able to

- Discuss the major characteristics and purposes of today's prisons.
- Describe the prison population in America today.
- Describe the just deserts model, and explain how it has led to an increased use of imprisonment and to prison overcrowding.
- Discuss how changes in the rate of criminal offending relate to changes in the rate of imprisonment.

- Explain the role that jails play in American corrections, and discuss the issues that jail administrators face.
- Describe the trend toward privatization in the corrections field.

Chapter Summary

Chapter 11 discusses three areas related to imprisonment in the United States today: **prisons**, **jails**, and **private prisons**.

Today, there are approximately 1,325 state prisons and 84 federal prisons. On January 1, 2006, the nation's state and federal prisons held 1,470,045 inmates, with most prison facilities operating above rated capacity. There are more men than women in prison, and there are significant disparities by race. For example, the incarceration rate for African-Americans is eight times greater than the figure for whites. Most people in state prisons were convicted of violent crimes, and most prisoners in federal prisons were convicted of drug crimes. Imprisonment varies tremendously by state. The size of prison facilities varies greatly and the costs are substantial. In 2001, it cost $60 billion to run the nation's prisons.

Chapter 11 also discusses the philosophy of imprisonment. It is important to note that the driving philosophy behind imprisonment changes over time. For example, prisons in this country were originally built to satisfy rehabilitation objectives. Today, the justice model is the operating principle underlying many corrections initiatives. Since this model supports strict and severe punishment, the number of offenders sent to prison has increased dramatically. In the 1990s, as national crime rates declined substantially, rates of imprisonment increased dramatically.

Prisons are categorized according to security level. The most well-known type of prison is the maximum-custody prison. These prisons are well known because of their frequent portrayal in popular culture. The typical prison, however, is either medium- or minimum-custody. This chapter also discusses the federal prison system. The federal system consists of 104 institutions classified in five security levels: administrative-maximum (**ADMAX**), high-security, medium-security, low-security, and minimum-security.

Jails are another type of confinement facility discussed in Chapter 11. Jails, the responsibility of local governments, generally house either pretrial detainees or offenders with a sentence of a year or less. There are approximately 747,530 inmates in the 3,360 jails in the United States. This section of the text also discusses women as the largest growth group in jails nationwide. Women in jails pose unique challenges to jail administrators because most jurisdictions do not have separate housing for female inmates. The text also discusses the fact that many jurisdictions are using citizen volunteer programs, jail "boot camps," and regional jail systems.

The last section of Chapter 11 discusses **private prisons**. An increasing number of jurisdictions are contracting with private firms to provide their confinement responsibilities. By 2005, privately operated facilities held over 98,000 state and federal prisoners across 34 states and the District of Columbia. Legal issues, and the relationship between the state-run and privately managed facilities, are interesting topics that have emerged since the privatization of prisons began.

Key Concepts

ADMAX Administrative maximum. The term is used by the federal government to denote ultra-high-security prisons.

Classification System A system used by prison administrators to assign inmates to custody levels based on offense history, assessed dangerousness, perceived risk of escape, and other factors.

Design Capacity (Bed Capacity) The number of inmates a prison was intended to hold when it was built or modified.

Direct-Supervision Jail   A temporary confinement facility that eliminates many of the traditional barriers between inmates and correctional staff. Physical barriers in direct-supervision jails are far less common than in traditional jails, allowing staff members the opportunity for greater interaction with, and control over, residents.

Ex Post Facto   Latin for "after the fact." The Constitution prohibits the enactment of *ex post facto* laws, which make acts committed before the laws in question were passed punishable as crimes.

Jail   A confinement facility administered by an agency of local government, typically a law enforcement agency, intended for adults but sometimes also containing juveniles, which holds persons detained pending adjudication and/or persons committed after adjudication, usually those committed on sentences of a year or less.

Justice Model   A contemporary model of imprisonment based upon the principle of just deserts.

Operational Capacity   The number of inmates a prison can effectively accommodate based on management considerations.

Prison   A state or federal confinement facility that has custodial authority over adults sentenced to confinement.

Prison Capacity   The size of the correctional population an institution can effectively hold. There are three types of prison capacity: rated, operational, and design. *Source*: Bureau of Justice Statistics, *Prisoners in 1998* (Washington, DC: BJS, 1999), p. 7.

Private Prison   A correctional institution operated by a private firm on behalf of a local or state government.

Privatization   The movement toward the wider use of private prisons.

Rated Capacity   The number of inmates a prison can handle according to the judgment of experts.

Regional Jail   A jail that is built and run using the combined resources of a variety of local jurisdictions.

Learning Tips

Attending Class

One of the most important things that you can do to ensure success is to attend class. You may think that attending class is not necessary because you have a friend, a roommate, or a neighbor who attends and who allows you to copy the notes. However, it is important to have your own notes that you created by attending the lectures because this will help you learn and retain the information more effectively and will make it easier for you to prepare for examinations.

Active Learning

Attending class is important, but it is also imperative that you try to be actively engaged in the lecture. Get to class early so that you can find a seat and are ready to focus on the material. Try to sit near the front of the class, and do not sit near students who are constantly talking or shuffling in their seats. Try not to daydream; stay focused on the professor's lecture, ask questions, and take clear and complete notes.

CJ Brief on the World Wide Web

Web links to organizations and agencies related to the material in Chapter 11 include:

WEBSITE TITLE	URL
American Correctional Association	http://www.corrections.com/aca
Correctional News Online	http://www.correctional news.com
Corrections (NCJRS)	http://www.virlib.ncjrs.org /Corrections.asp
Federal Bureau of Prisons	http://www.bop.gov/
National Juvenile Detention Association	http://www.njda.com
The Other Side of the Wall	http://www.prisonwall.org
Prison Industry Links	http://www.corrections.com /industries
Prison Legal News	http://www.prisonlegalnews.org

Learner Activities

Activity 1

Consider the following case. Michael Faye was an 18-year-old American living with his parents in Singapore when he was arrested for spray-painting cars during ten days of vandalism. He confessed to these crimes but later said that his confession was coerced from police officials who severely beat him. He was convicted and sentenced to four strokes with a rattan cane—a punishment in which the prisoner is flogged, tearing open the skin and producing permanent scars. Was his punishment a violation of Michael Faye's rights? Remember that his crime took place in Singapore, a legal system that balances individual and community rights in a way very different from ours. Indeed, more than 1,000 prisoners are caned per year in Singapore. Do you think we should use similar types of punishment in the United States? Would you recommend the use of any of the other early punishments described in Chapter 11? Why or why not?

_____

_____

_____

_____

_____

_____

Activity 2

Visit **Library Extras 11–3** and **11–4**. This link provides a discussion on the Federal Bureau of Prisons. Summarize what you read in the space provided below.

_____

_____

_____

_____

_____

_____

Activity 3

Collect data to answer the following questions about the prisons in the state where your campus is located. How many inmates are incarcerated in the state? How many prisons are there? How many maximum-security? Medium-security? Minimum-security? How has the number of prisoners changed over time? Present the data you collected in the space below, and then discuss how the data on your state system are similar to and different from the national data presented in Chapter 11.

_____

_____

_____

_____

_____

_____

Activity 4

Many private companies, such as Corrections Corporation of America and Corrections Concepts, have been able to convince legislators to turn over the operation of some prisons (or prison functions) to private companies. Do you think the use of private companies to run state prison systems is a good idea? What are some problems with using private companies? Do you think the prisons run by private companies will be more effective than state-run prisons? Explain your answer.

_____

_____

_____

_____

_____

_____

Internet Activity

Visit the Corrections Connection Web site at http://www.corrections.com. View (and click on) the topics in the "Focus" section. Write a brief summary of three different items. Your instructor may request that you submit these summaries.

_____

_____

_____

_____

_____

_____

Distance Learning Activity

Visit the Correctional News website or some other major industry legal publication (see Correctional News Online: http://www.correctionalnews.com; or Prison Legal News: http://www.prisonlegalnews.org). In the space below, summarize one of the articles or cases posted on the website. If your instructor asks you to do so, share your summary with other students in the class, and participate in a class discussion about the issues that students wrote about.

_____

_____

_____

_____

_____

Student Study Guide Questions

True or False

_____   11-1. A state or federal confinement facility that has custodial authority over adults sentenced to confinement for less than one year is called a prison.

_____   11-2. There are significantly more federal than state prisons in operation today.

_____   11-3. The number of offenders sent to prison has steadily declined since 1980.

_____   11-4. Federal prison camps are classified as minimum-security prisons in the federal system.

_____   11-5. The movement toward the wider use of private prisons is called corporationalization.

_____   11-6. Close to 50% of the offenders in prison are women.

_____   11-7. The just deserts model was a late-nineteenth-century correctional model based on both the use of the indeterminate sentence and the belief in the possibility of rehabilitation of offenders.

_____   11-8. There are more high-security prisons in the federal prison system than any other category of prison classification.

_____   11-9. Most people sentenced to state prisons were convicted of drug crimes.

_____ 11-10. Direct-supervision jails are temporary confinement facilities that eliminate many of the traditional barriers between inmates and correctional staff.

Multiple Choice

11-11. What is the term used by the federal government to denote ultra-high-security prisons?
   a. ULTRAMAX
   b. SUPERMAX
   c. ADMAX
   d. MAXIMAX

11-12. Most facilities in the federal prison system are
   a. federal prison camps.
   b. low-security facilities.
   c. medium-security facilities.
   d. high-security prisons.

11-13. Which of the following house the most serious offenders and are characterized by double and triple security patterns?
   a. maximum-security prisons
   b. reformatories
   c. medium-security prisons
   d. minimum-security prisons

11-14. What percent of jail facilities house more than half of all jail inmates in the nation?
   a. 6
   b. 20
   c. 50
   d. 75

11-15. What aspect of the corrections system has been called the "shame of the criminal justice system"?
   a. boot camps
   b. federal prisons
   c. state prisons
   d. jails

11-16. Jail occupancy, in 2005, was at about _____ percent of rated capacity?
   a. 95
   b. 104
   c. 85
   d. 70

11-17. The federal system's only ADMAX unit is located in
   a. Florence, Colorado.
   b. Auburn, New York.
   c. Battle Creek, Virginia.
   d. Huntsville, Texas.

11-18. The 1981 U.S. Supreme Court case of _Rhodes_ v. _Chapman_ dealt with the issue of prison overcrowding and held that
   a. placing two inmates in one cell is cruel and unusual punishment.
   b. placing two inmates in one cell is not cruel and unusual punishment.
   c. inmates must show that prison officials exhibited "deliberate indifference" by not dealing with overcrowding sooner.
   d. inmates have a reasonable expectation of privacy that is violated by having to share a cell with another inmate.

11-19. What type of facility houses inmates in dormitory-like settings where inmates are generally free to visit most of the prison?
  a. maximum-security prison
  b. reformatory
  c. medium-security prison
  d. minimum-security prison

11-20. The number of inmates a prison was intended to hold when it was built or modified is its
  a. prison capacity.
  b. rated capacity.
  c. operational capacity.
  d. design capacity.

Fill-In

11-21. _____ capacity is the size of the inmate population a facility can handle according to the judgment of experts.

11-22. A(n)_____ is used by prison administrators to assign inmates to custody levels.

11-23. _____ capacity is the number of inmates a prison can effectively accommodate based on management consideration.

11-24. _____ capacity is the number of inmates a prison was architecturally intended to hold when it was built or modified.

11-25. _____ capacity is a general term referring to the size of the correctional population an institution can effectively hold.

11-26. _____ is the Latin term meaning "after the fact."

11-27. _____ are jails designed to eliminate many of the traditional barriers between inmates and staff.

11-28. _____ are correctional institutions operated by private firms on behalf of local and state governments.

11-29. The _____ is a contemporary model of imprisonment based on the social philosophy of just deserts.

11-30. A(n) _____ jail is built and run using the combined resources of a variety of local jurisdictions.

Crossword Puzzle

Across

1. Repetition of criminal behavior.
3. Just deserts.
4. Number of inmates a prison can effectively accommodate based on management considerations.
7. Temporary confinement facility that allows greater interaction between inmates and staff.
8. Facility that holds committed individuals with sentences of a year or less.
9. Size of the correctional population an institution can effectively hold.
11. Jail run using the combined resources of a variety of local jurisdictions.

Down

2. Number of inmates a prison was intended to hold when it was built or modified.
5. Movement toward the wider use of private prisons.
6. Administrative maximum.
10. State or federal confinement facility.

Word Search Puzzle

```
R G P T R B G B T X X G B Z Y Z M O Q Z O Y O J L D L E H D
R K R F V D D A B U G V B C E R T V G S P W V J B J F V B R
Z R I K I A P O T R T E D Y A C B W Q R Q J C X I S Z K K U
J Y V I S H G U I C A Y B O A E V U O F Z P A M Y V A V U Z
A V A C J E M G J L Q S B F K E P M K E I Z C I N E B E Y F
L D T P J N F F S B B I T S G D P R U H Z H Q B L K A G L H
Q E I K R X S S D L B S W E U R E G I O N A L J A I L O E P
Q V Z I E I U W K Z O J G U A N W Q T V A F Q G Q U K E K Z
M V A W Z Y S M F P H Z Q X Y P F Z Z O A X H Y L G K E Z P
D L T Z H M Z O X V S H V G L H P L W P Y T T G L Z D N C X
I P I O X P O E N D W R D V Y M B Y U E W I E L P Q R Z S N
R X O E O F E K C O E H J N T L S L C R C R N P B K J D Z Y
E B N J W V R P J Y S F G S F K R W Q A T G F L R B E A U D
C Y I G P U C O E U Y S A B X D J L P T W J Z X A I W E T N
T B F H R N A E S R Y Q G E P E T A A I D U W H T N S H O W
S Z P K D L I X N B R C N M L Q C J A O I S N M E K E O B S
U P Z I Y R Y V Z T A S J B X N S V X N J T J Y D U O O N N
P T R U C A I Y D I Q O O V G A Q K D A G I I Q C R A W H H
E I K I R Y W O G H T I W I I F J R Z L R C N B A D O U V S
R S V A S B M Q Q H M F S G Q Z F E Z C L E V D P Q T E Z R
V T W R I O B Z F X B E I V Q K D R M A E M N F A C M T Z E
I M H A R N N F F K D L X I X Y O J U P H O Y R C S J U Z P
S G D P A Q A C Y D F C W A U X U Z L A M D S R I P G Q G P
I B T O Y B T D A E U T K J K F O D B C Z E S V T Y A A F D
O T Q H N G R I D P C H E Z J Q J T M I U L I S Y L D B Q Q
N Q R K G Z X T Z J A J Y O J X V B C T Y D J C Z T M R J X
J Y G B M N U P X K L C R W R W G Q Y Y I P Y F H K A C W Z
A G Z J W C D R J V K H I R C F K A Q C O T K B M L X T Y O
I T H G C I W H F Y A M X T W S T M E T B X G E V Z E H C M
L H L A E C S I C D Y K C Q Y C K R A H J T M V U G K G A Y
```

ADMAX

Design Capacity

Direct-Supervision Jail

Ex Post Facto

Jail

Justice Model

Operational Capacity

Prison

Prison Capacity

Private Prison

Privatization

Rated Capacity

Recidivism

Regional Jail

12 Prison Life

Chapter Outline

- Introduction
- The Male Inmate's World
- The Female Inmate's World
- The Staff World
- Prison Riots
- Prisoners' Rights
- Issues Facing Prisons Today

Learning Objectives

After reading this chapter, you should be able to

- Describe the realities of prison life and subculture from the inmate's point of view.
- Explain the concept of prisonization.
- Illustrate the significant differences between men's prisons and women's prisons.
- Describe the realities of prison life from the correctional officer's point of view.
- Describe the causes of riots, and list the stages through which prison riots progress.
- Explain the nature of the hands-off doctrine, and discuss the status of that doctrine today.
- Discuss the legal aspects of prisoners' rights, and explain the consequences of precedent-setting U.S. Supreme Court cases in the area of prisoners' rights.
- Explain the balancing test established by the U.S. Supreme Court as it relates to prisoners' rights.
- Explain state-created rights within the context of corrections.
- Describe the major problems and issues that prisons face today.

Chapter Summary

Chapter 12 describes life in prison. The text focuses on the various social realities that coexist among correctional officers and inmates in male and female institutions, including prison riots, prisoners' rights, and other issues facing prisons today.

The discussion of the realities of the male inmate's world revolves around the areas of **total institutions** and **prison subcultures**. Since inmates share all aspects of their lives on a daily basis, prison life is shaped by both the official structure and rules and the values and behavioral patterns of the inmates. New inmates undergo a process of **prisonization**, learning the values, language (**prison argot**), and rules of the institution. The text also describes nine inmate types who occupy various positions in the prison hierarchy.

Chapter 12 also describes the realities of life in prison for women. Although accounting for only 6.9% of the U.S. prison inmate population, the number of women in prison is growing rapidly. Two important factors contributing to this growth are female involvement in drug and drug-related offenses and the demise of the "chivalry factor." Although there is some disagreement among scholars attempting to describe the social structure of women's prisons, many researchers find that females are more likely to be involved in prison "families." Also, the amount and type of violence in female institutions are significantly different from those in male institutions. The text describes several types of female inmates, including the "square," the "cool," the "life," and "crack kids."

Correctional officers also undergo a process of socialization into the prison culture. Due to overcrowded prisons and limitations in the number of staff, the primary mission of correctional officers is custody and control. The text describes six types of correctional officers and how they relate to inmates. The field of corrections is growing and is undergoing significant changes. Among the efforts to adapt to these changes is the professionalization of correctional officers.

Chapter 12 also discusses prison riots, emphasizing the explosive decade of prison riots; several significant riots occurred between 1970 and 1980, beginning with the Attica riots and ending with the Santa Fe prison riots. Research indicates that the causes of prison riots include an insensitive prison administration and neglected inmates' demands, the lifestyles most inmates are familiar with on the streets, the dehumanizing prison conditions, the ways riots regulate inmate society and redistribute power, and the power vacuums created by a variety of factors. The text also discusses the five typical stages of a riot and the control of riots.

Chapter 12 provides an examination of the legal rights of inmates. Historically, courts have adhered to a policy of nonintervention with regard to prison management. However, this **hands-off doctrine** was abandoned in the late 1960s. Courts have since provided precedent in many areas important to life in prison, including communications, religious practices, visitation, legal access to courts, privacy, medical care, and disciplinary proceedings. The **balancing test** is the important test applied to these areas of prison life. This test, articulated in the *Pell* v. *Procunier* decision, attempts to weigh the rights of an individual against the authority of the state to make laws or otherwise restrict a person's freedom.

Chapter 12 concludes with a discussion of three issues facing prisons today. First, it discusses AIDS in prisons, describing the number of inmates infected and some of the strategies in place to reduce the transmission of this disease. Second, it discusses the growing geriatric offender population. With longer sentences and the "graying" of the population, administrators must implement policies to deal with the special needs of geriatric and long-term inmates. Third, the special needs of mentally ill inmates are discussed.

Key Concepts

Balancing Test   A principle, developed by the courts and applied to the corrections arena by *Pell* v. *Procunier* (1974), that attempts to weigh the rights of an individual, as guaranteed by the Constitution, against the authority of states to make laws or to otherwise restrict a person's freedom in order to protect the state's interests and its citizens.

Civil Death   The legal status of prisoners in some jurisdictions who are denied the opportunity to vote, hold public office, marry, or enter into contracts by virtue of their status as incarcerated felons. While civil death is primarily of historical interest, some jurisdictions limit the contractual opportunities available to inmates.

Deliberate Indifference   A wanton disregard by correctional personnel for the well-being of inmates. Deliberate indifference requires both actual knowledge that a harm is occurring and disregard of the risk of harm. A prison official may be held liable under the Eighth Amendment for acting with deliberate indifference to inmate health or safety only if he or she knows that inmates face a substantial risk of serious harm and disregards that risk by failing to take reasonable measures to abate it.

Grievance Procedure   A formalized arrangement, usually involving a neutral hearing board, whereby institutionalized individuals have the opportunity to register complaints about the conditions of their confinement.

Hands-Off Doctrine   A policy of nonintervention with regard to prison management that U.S. courts tended to follow until the late 1960s. For the past 30 years, the doctrine has languished as judicial intervention in prison administration has dramatically increased, although there is now some evidence that a new hands-off era is approaching.

Prison Argot   The slang characteristic of prison subcultures and prison life.

Prison Subculture   The values and behavioral patterns characteristic of prison inmates. Prison subculture has been found to be surprisingly consistent across the country.

Prisonization   The process whereby newly institutionalized offenders come to accept prison lifestyles and criminal values. Although many inmates begin their prison experience with only a few values that support criminal behavior, the socialization experience they undergo while incarcerated leads to a much wider acceptance of such values.

Security Threat Group (STG)   An inmate group, gang, or organization whose members act together to pose a threat to the safety of correctional staff or the public, or who prey on other inmates, or who threaten the secure and orderly operation of a correctional institution.

Total Institutions   An enclosed facility separated from society both socially and physically, where the inhabitants share all aspects of their daily lives.

Key Cases

Block v. *Rutherford*.   This case ruled that in the interests of security, jails can prohibit all visits from friends and relatives (*Block* v. *Rutherford*, 486 U.S. 576 [1984]).

Bounds v. *Smith*.   This case not only confirmed the right of prisoners to have access to the courts and to legal assistance but also required states to assist inmates in the preparation and filing of legal papers. This assistance can be given through trained personnel or through the creation and availability of a law library for inmates (*Bounds* v. *Smith*, 430 U.S. 817, 821 [1977]).

Cruz v. *Beto*. Based on this case, inmates must be given a "reasonable opportunity" to pursue their religious faith even if it differs from traditional forms of worship (*Cruz* v. *Beto*, 405 U.S. 319 [1972]).

Estelle v. *Gamble*. This case required prison officials to provide for inmates' medical care, and it established the concept of "deliberate indifference" in determining whether prison administrators are meeting the medical needs of prisoners (*Estelle* v. *Gamble*, 429 U.S. 97 [1976]).

Helling v. *McKinney*. In this case, an inmate sued due to involuntary exposure to secondhand cigarette smoke. The Court indicated that prison officials are responsible not only for "inmates' current serious health problems" but also for creation of environmental conditions under which health problems might be prevented (*Helling* v. *McKinney*, 113 S.Ct. 2475, 125 L.Ed.2d 22 [1993]).

Houchins v. *KQED*. The court stated that news personnel cannot be denied correspondence with inmates, but they have no constitutional right to interview inmates or to inspect correctional facilities beyond the areas available to the general public (*Houchins* v. *KQED*, 438 U.S. 11 [1978]).

Hudson v. *Palmer*. The Court ruled that the need for prison officials to conduct thorough and unannounced searches precludes inmates' right to privacy in personal possessions (*Hudson* v. *Palmer*, 468 U.S. 517 [1984]).

Johnson v. *Avery*. This case established that inmates have a right to consult "jailhouse lawyers" for advice if assistance from trained legal professionals is not available (*Johnson* v. *Avery*, 393 U.S. 483 [1968]).

Jones v. *North Carolina Prisoners' Labor Union*. The Court ruled that prisons must establish some formal opportunity for the airing of inmates' grievances (*Jones* v. *North Carolina Prisoners' Labor Union*, 433 U.S. 119, 53 L.Ed.2d 629, 641 [1977]).

Katz v. *U.S.* The Court, in this case, stated that when a person makes an effort to keep something private, even in a public place, it requires a judicial decision, in the form of a warrant issued for probable cause, to unveil it (*Katz* v. *U.S.*, 389 U.S. 347, 88 S.Ct. 507, 19 L.Ed.2d 576 [1967]).

Overton v. *Bazzetta*. The Court found that new visitation restrictions imposed by the Michigan Department of Corrections to counter security problems was acceptable (*Overton* v. *Bazzetta*, 539 U.S. 126, 286 F.3d 311 [2003]).

Pell v. *Procunier*. The Supreme Court established a balancing test to guide prison authorities in determining what rights an inmate should have. Inmates should have the same rights as nonincarcerated citizens, provided that the legitimate needs of the prison for security, custody, and safety are not compromised (*Pell* v. *Procunier*, 417 U.S. 817, 822 [1974]).

Pennsylvania Department of Corrections v. *Yeskey*. The Supreme Court held that the Americans with Disabilities Act of 1990 applies to prisons and prison inmates (*Pennsylvania Department of Corrections* v. *Yeskey*, 524 U.S. 206, 209 [1998]).

Ruiz v. *Estelle*. This case challenged the structure of the Texas prison system and specifically required major changes in the handling of inmates' medical care. The Court ordered an improvement in record keeping, physical facilities, and general medical care while it continued to monitor the progress of the department (*Ruiz* v. *Estelle*, 503 F.Supp. 1265 [S.D. Texas, 1980]).

Sandin v. *Conner*. This case signaled an apparent return to the hands-off doctrine when the Court rejected the argument that any state action taken for a punitive reason encroaches on a prisoner's constitutional right to be free from the deprivation of liberty (*Sandin* v. *Conner*, 63 U.S.L.W. 4601 [1995]).

Wolff v. *McDonnell.* This case established that sanctions cannot be levied against inmates without appropriate due process, which was the beginning of the concept of "state-created liberty interests" (*Wolff* v. *McDonnell*, 94 S.Ct. 2963 [1974]).

Learning Tips

Multiple-Choice Questions

Multiple-choice questions can be very confusing and challenging, but the following four-step process will assist you in tackling these types of questions. First, check to see how many answers you are supposed to choose for each question. Second, read and answer the questions without looking at the test answers. If your answer matches one of the test answers, choose it. This will avoid additional confusion brought on by the other test answers. Third, if you don't know the exact answer, read each choice because answers are often quite similar. Fourth, skip questions that you cannot answer immediately, and go back to them when you have time.

Multiple-Choice Answers

Whenever you are not penalized for wrong answers on multiple-choice questions and you are completely unable to answer the question, there are three ways to choose the best answer. One strategy is to eliminate any answer you know to be wrong and guess from the remaining choices. Another strategy is to assess if two answers are very similar, except for a couple of words, and to choose one of these two answers. A third strategy states that if it is a question involving numbers and the answers are listed in numerical order, choose an answer that lies in the middle.

CJ Brief on the World Wide Web

Web links to organizations and agencies related to the material in Chapter 12 include:

WEBSITE TITLE	URL
15 Years to Life	http://www.15yearstolife.com
Bureau of Justice Prison Statistics	http://www.ojp.usdoj.gov/bjs /prisons.htm
Federal Bureau of Prisons	http://www.bop.gov/
Pennsylvania Department of Corrections	http://www.cor.state.pa.us
Prison Activist Resource Center	http://www.prisonactivist.org/
Prison Legal News	http://www.prisonlegalnews.org
Prison Zone	http://www.prisonzone.com/
Stop Prisoner Rape	http://www.spr.org/
Weight Lifting and Recreation	http://www.strengthtech.com/

Learner Activities

Activity 1

Your text outlines in great detail the adaptation process that inmates go through when entering a prison setting and describes the prisonization process. How are these adaptations similar to and different from the adaptations that students have to make at a college campus? What subcultures exist on your campus? Is there an argot unique to college campuses?

_____

_____

_____

_____

_____

Activity 2

Mike and his sister Michelle committed several bank robberies together. After they were caught, tried, and convicted, the judge sentenced them both to 25 to 50 years in a maximum-security prison. Their sentencing hearing occurred about two years ago. Recently, they exchanged their first letters describing their lives in prison. What did each of them say? Be sure to discuss the physical characteristics of the prison, the needs that are fulfilled by the prison, and the different social realities of the prison.

_____

_____

_____

_____

_____

_____

Activity 3

Visit **Library Extra 12–2**. Read this document, and in the space below write a summary of the information provided about the positive and negative impacts of imprisonment.

_____

_____

_____

_____

_____

_____

_____

Activity 4

Contact a local correctional facility (either a prison or a jail). Interview an administrator of that facility about the issues discussed in Chapter 12. How is that facility responding to AIDS? How is it managing the aging inmate population? Mentally ill inmates? In the space below, discuss what you learn.

_____

_____

_____

_____

_____

_____

Internet Activity

Read **Library Extras 12–8** and **12–9**. Describe the medical issues facing corrections officials in the space below. Your instructor may request that you submit this material.

_____

_____

_____

_____

_____

_____

Distance Learning Activity

Write a short essay about life in prison from the perspective of a correctional officer or from the perspective of an inmate. Search the World Wide Web for materials to be included in your essay.

_____

_____

_____

_____

_____

_____

Student Study Guide Questions

True or False

_____ 12-1. Few states have a substantial capacity for the psychiatric treatment of mentally disturbed inmates.

_____ 12-2. In 1935, an Indiana University sociology professor completed a groundbreaking study of prison life when he voluntarily served three months in prison as a participant-observer to discover what being an inmate was really like.

_____ 12-3. Prison argot is a secret language that no one except the prisoners knows and that prisoners use to communicate.

_____ 12-4. In all state and federal prison facilities combined, the number of incarcerated male prisoners is greater than the number of females incarcerated by a ratio of slightly more than 2 to 1.

_____ 12-5. African-American women are eight times more likely than white women to be incarcerated in prison.

_____ 12-6. A prisoner's private mail from immediate family members may not be opened and censored by prison authorities.

_____ 12-7. Prison riots are generally unplanned and tend to occur spontaneously, the result of some relatively minor precipitating event.

_____ 12-8. Most male sexual aggressors in prisons are committed to their heterosexual sexual identity.

_____ 12-9. Inmates have a right to consult "jailhouse lawyers" for advice if the prison does not provide assistance from trained legal professionals.

_____ 12-10. The U.S. Supreme Court case of *Hudson* v. *Palmer* asserts that the need for prison officials to conduct thorough and unannounced searches is greater than inmates' right to privacy in personal possessions.

Multiple Choice

12-11. _____ develop independently of the plans of prison administrators.
   a. Prison subcultures
   b. Total institutions
   c. Women's prisons
   d. Parole boards

12-12. What was established by the U.S. Supreme Court in *Pell* v. *Procunier* that has served as a guideline generally applicable to all prison operations?
   a. either-or doctrine
   b. balancing test
   c. writ of *habeas corpus*
   d. prisonization process

12-13. What is the average inmate-to-staff ratio in state prisons?
   a. 1 inmate for each correctional officer
   b. 4 inmates for each correctional officer
   c. 12 inmates for each correctional officer
   d. 30 inmates for each correctional officer

12-14. What was the policy followed by the courts until the 1960s in refusing to hear inmate complaints about the conditions of incarceration and the constitutional deprivations of inmate life called?
    a. fingers-crossed model
    b. bloody codes
    c. hands-off doctrine
    d. inmate code

12-15. The hands-off doctrine ended when the federal court declared that the entire prison system of which state was in violation of the constitutional ban against cruel and unusual punishment?
    a. Arkansas
    b. New Mexico
    c. Indiana
    d. New York

12-16. What is the term for an inmate who is quick to fight and fights like a wild man?
    a. opportunist
    b. mean dude
    c. hedonist
    d. retreatist

12-17. In *The Society of Captives*, Gresham Sykes claims that prisoners are deprived of all of the following *except*
    a. liberty.
    b. goods and services.
    c. homosexual relationships.
    d. autonomy.

12-18. Which of the following is *not* listed as contributing to the "graying" of America's prison population?
    a. increasing crime among those over age 50
    b. gradual aging of the society from which prisoners come
    c. trend toward longer sentences
    d. reduction in the number of older habitual offenders in prison

12-19. Inmates adopt a series of lifestyles in an attempt to survive the prison experience. Which ones build their lifestyle around the limited pleasures that can be had within the confines of prison?
    a. mean dudes
    b. hedonists
    c. opportunists
    d. retreatists

12-20. What is a female inmate who is likely to be a career offender called?
    a. square
    b. cool
    c. life
    d. none of the above

Fill-In

12-21. _____ is the slang characteristic of prison subcultures and prison life.

12-22. _____ are enclosed facilities in which the inhabitants share all aspects of their daily lives.

12-23. _____ is the case that required that inmates be given a "reasonable opportunity" to pursue their religious faith even if it differs from traditional forms of worship.

12-24. _____ are formalized arrangements prisoners have to register complaints about the conditions of their confinement.

12-25. The _____ attempts to weigh the constitutional rights of an individual against the authority of the state to make laws to protect its interests and its citizens.

12-26. The values and behavioral patterns characteristic of prison inmates make up the _____.

12-27. The _____ was a policy of nonintervention with regard to prison management that American courts tended to follow until the late 1960s.

12-28. _____ is the process whereby institutionalized individuals come to accept prison lifestyles and criminal values.

12-29. _____ is the legal status of prisoners in some jurisdictions who are denied the opportunity to vote, hold public office, or enter into contracts by virtue of their status as incarcerated felons.

12-30. A wanton disregard by corrections personnel for the well-being of inmates is called _____.

Crossword Puzzle

Across

2. *Block* v. _____.
3. Enclosed facilities, separated from society both socially and physically, where the inhabitants share all aspects of their lives daily.
5. Case beginning the concept of state-created liberty interests.
7. *Hudson* v. *Palmer* focuses on this issue.
9. Policy of nonintervention of prison management.
12. Standard set by *Cruz* v. *Beto*. [reasonable opportunity]
15. State of prisoners who are denied the opportunity to vote and hold public office.
16. Author of *The Society of Captives*.
17. Standard set by *Estelle* v. *Gamble*.

Down

1. Process whereby newly institutionalized offenders come to accept prison lifestyles and criminal values.
4. Inmate lawyer.
6. Official way prisoners can complain about the conditions of their confinement.
8. Scholar who coined the term *total institution*.
10. *Pell* v. _____.
11. Test established by *Pell* v. *Procunier*.
13. Language of inmates.
14. Values and behavioral patterns of prison inmates.

Word Search Puzzle

```
V B G G N N V A L K M A C O W R Y R O M K U T B W D C J N F
J W G D R Q R V H K M V M E V R R A K N M B E M I W I D S U
L R O W P S H S K K C I O Z F U Z E F Q H J A K J N Z K C G
E C R R E A S O N A B L E O P P O R T U N I T Y G B J J B F
T E K Y D N W Q P U P S O K L C X K C H O R S O S A U M P H
V W D H A N D S O F F D O C T R I N E F V W E L J L T T D A
J R P F O S E C U R I T Y T H R E A T G R O U P S A T W K B
C A R M X X Q G R I E V A N C E P R O C E D U R E N O L G B
N C I Q C L Q T C R M P Q A G A J E X V K P L A I C T F Q J
L V S L H Z M E N T A L L Y I L L I N M A T E S W I A N K R
F K O N H A S Q I L D A S L R I I N Y B B Y R T I N L U K C
B J N Z T O R V A V V E G V Z V H U U K U C J O A G I F H Z
E Y I C B J U G T Q I E Z W E K F D P U C T S R J T N G W H
I W Z I I U P S O B C S X B V Z N O M V D K N M E E S N J E
Z I A V T G M G E T P Q I B M L B P T X U W X M C S T W K F
O S T I S P L C C L X Q Q T J J Y A R K E T I L V T I F E K
E T I L J A K O L V A M N Y A J J O D I D N X X K Z T B P Y
L R O D G Z H X U W M W W B A T A P L R S P A N J T U E S L
N F N E D W B Z I E N N Y F W M I K M P D O L X H V T H U N
D H A A D E X Y T R Z J G E Y G O O U H J O N E N E I E B C
P L F T Z Q P I C T B Q C D R L G L N W S V W R L D O C C R
F P Q H G P I Y U B E Z D U G A K S G O K C X Z I M N Q U B
Y G W V L M L B P Z S D I E R C K F V U G H I B T O V G L R
E D E L I B E R A T E I N D I F F E R E N C E U X G T N T J
R R Z I W E K W W G C S B B T P D L G P Y H M O C M J O U P
E G S O D Y M Z U T U L E U H Z T J V O S G N J P G X H R V
M Z Z J B W Z M Q U R Z U T U J R Y F U K J U N U S U N E C
C Q W L U T G I B N I Y D C Z Y E N W N W B P J V Y S T W Z
C Q U C B R Q Z N R T U Z R F G D U K I X A X P B E Z N N R
K U J V Y Q T Q R Q Y H S C V M Z W W C W X Z B O G T P B E
```

Argot

Balancing Test

Civil Death

Deliberate Indifference

Grievance Procedure

Hands-Off Doctrine

Jailhouse Lawyer

Mentally Ill Inmates

Prisonization

Prison Riot

Reasonable Opportunity

Security

Security Threat Groups

Subculture

Total Institution

Visitation

13 Juvenile Justice

Chapter Outline

- Introduction
- Juvenile Justice throughout History
- The Legal Environment

- The Juvenile Justice Process Today
- The Post–Juvenile Court Era

Learning Objectives

After reading this chapter, you should be able to

- Describe the history and evolution of the juvenile justice system in the Western world.
- List and define the categories of children in today's juvenile justice system.
- Name the important U.S. Supreme Court decisions of relevance to juvenile justice, and describe their impact on the handling of juveniles by the system.

- Explain the similarities and differences between the juvenile and adult systems of justice.
- Identify possible future directions in juvenile justice.

Chapter Summary

Juvenile crime is a perplexing problem for the criminal justice system. It is perplexing because research indicates that the amount of violent crime committed by juveniles is decreasing, but public demand for severe punishments for juveniles has increased. Moreover, the public's desire for a crackdown on juvenile crime, and the demand that juvenile punishments be equivalent to adult punishments, is inconsistent with the underlying philosophy of the juvenile court.

This chapter examines four areas of juvenile justice: First, it examines the historical development of the juvenile justice system; second, it compares the juvenile justice system to the adult system; third, it discusses the juvenile justice system process; and finally, it discusses several criticisms of the juvenile system.

The text discusses the historical beginnings of the juvenile justice system throughout the world and in America and traces this history through several important Supreme Court cases decided in the 1970s and 1980s. The text's examination of the historical evolution of the juvenile justice system begins with a discussion of treatment of juveniles in the earliest times, when they were treated differently from adults. For example, the laws of King Aethelbert made no special provisions for offenders because of age. The common law principle of *parens patriae* is important to an understanding of juvenile justice because it means that the state can assume the role of the parent and take custody of a child.

In America, the criminal justice response to juveniles began in the early nineteenth century with the development of houses of refuge. The child-savers movement began in the mid-1800s, influencing the development of reform schools. The early model, embodied in the Chicago Reform School, focused on emulating family environments to provide security and build moral character, emphasizing traditional values such as hard work. Finally, the text discusses the beginnings of the juvenile court era from early legislation in Massachusetts and New York to the Illinois juvenile law that was modeled by most states and the federal government's Juvenile Court Act. Most legislation included six categories of children subject to the jurisdiction of the juvenile court: **delinquent children, undisciplined children, dependent children, neglected children, abused children**, and **status offenders**.

Chapter 13 also provides an excellent overview of several important court decisions affecting juveniles. The most significant is *In re Gault*. This decision guaranteed several procedural rights to juveniles, including the right to have notice of the charges, the right to counsel, the right to confront and cross-examine witnesses, and the right to appeal. Other cases discussed include *In re Winship*, *McKeiver* v. *Pennsylvania*, *Breed* v. *Jones*, *Kent* v. *U.S.*, and *Schall* v. *Martin*. Juveniles, however, are not provided all the protections guaranteed to adult defendants. For example, juveniles do not have a constitutional right to a jury trial.

The juvenile justice system, as a process, involves four stages: intake, adjudication, disposition, and postadjudication review. **Intake** involves the filing of a juvenile petition by some party, such as the police, alleging illegal behavior by the juvenile. Adjudication is the trial process for juveniles. Adjudicatory hearings are similar to the adult trial, but with some exceptions. A **dispositional hearing**, similar to an adult sentencing hearing, occurs to determine the action the court should take against a juvenile. Judges have several options at disposition, including outright release, probation, or confinement to a secure institution.

Chapter 13 concludes by considering the future of the juvenile justice system, acknowledging that it will increase penalties, reduce privacy, and eliminate diversionary opportunities for juveniles.

Key Concepts

Abused Child   A child who has been physically, sexually, or mentally abused. Most states also consider a child who is forced into delinquent activity by a parent or guardian to be abused.

Adjudicatory Hearing   The fact-finding process wherein the juvenile court determines whether there is sufficient evidence to sustain the allegations in a petition.

Blended Sentence   A juvenile court disposition that imposes both a juvenile sanction and an adult criminal sentence on an adjudicated delinquent. The adult sentence is suspended on the condition that the juvenile offender successfully complete the term of the juvenile disposition and refrain from committing any new offense *Source*: Howard N. Synder and Melissa Sickmund, Juvenile Offenders and Victims: 2006 National Report (Washington, D.C.: OJJDP, 2006).

Delinquency   In the broadest usage, juvenile actions or conduct in violation of criminal law, juvenile status offenses, and other juvenile misbehavior.

Delinquent Child   A child who has engaged in activity that would be considered a crime if the child were an adult. The term *delinquent* is used to avoid the stigma associated with the term *criminal*.

Dependent Child   A child who has no parents or whose parents are unable to care for him or her.

Dispositional Hearing   The final stage in the processing of adjudicated juveniles, in which a decision is made on the form of treatment or penalty that should be imposed on the child.

Intake   The first step in decision making regarding a juvenile whose behavior or alleged behavior is in violation of the law or could otherwise cause a juvenile court to assume jurisdiction.

Juvenile   A youth at or below the upper age of juvenile court jurisdiction in a particular state.

Juvenile Court   Any court that has jurisdiction over matters involving juveniles.

Juvenile Disposition   The decision of a juvenile court, concluding a disposition hearing, that an adjudicated juvenile be committed to a juvenile correctional facility; be placed in a juvenile residence, shelter, or care or treatment program; be required to meet certain standards of conduct; or be released.

Juvenile Justice System   Government agencies that function to investigate, supervise, adjudicate, care for, or confine youthful offenders and other children subject to the jurisdiction of the juvenile court.

Juvenile Petition   A document filed in juvenile court alleging that a juvenile is a delinquent, a status offender, or a dependent, and asking that the court assume jurisdiction over the juvenile, or that an alleged delinquent be transferred to a criminal court for prosecution as an adult.

Neglected Child   A child who is not receiving the proper level of physical or psychological care from his or her parent(s) or guardian(s) or who has been placed for adoption in violation of the law.

Parens Patriae   A common law principle that allows the state to assume a parental role and to take custody of a child when he or she becomes a delinquent, is abandoned, or is in need of care that the natural parents are unable or unwilling to provide.

Status Offender   A child who commits an act that is contrary to the law by virtue of the juvenile's status as a child. Purchasing cigarettes, buying alcohol, and being truant are examples of such behavior.

Status Offense   An act or conduct that is declared by statute to be an offense, but only when committed by or engaged in by a juvenile, and that can be adjudicated only by a juvenile court.

Teen Court   An alternative approach to juvenile justice in which juvenile offenders are judged and sentenced by a jury of their peers.

Undisciplined Child   A child who is beyond parental control, as evidenced by his or her refusal to obey legitimate authorities, such as school officials and teachers.

Key Cases

Breed v. *Jones.*   This case severely restricts the conditions under which transfers from juvenile to adult court may occur. Such transfers must occur prior to an adjudicatory hearing in juvenile court (*Breed* v. *Jones*, 421 U.S. 519 [1975]).

In re Gault.   The Court decided that juveniles have a right to notice of charges, right to counsel, right to confront and to cross-examine witnesses, and must be provided protection against self-incrimination (*In re Gault*, 387 U.S. 1 [1967]).

In re Winship.   Allegations of delinquency must be established beyond a reasonable doubt. Status offenses, however, can be established with the preponderance of the evidence standard (*In re Winship*, 397 U.S. 358 [1970]).

Kent v. *U.S.*   This case ended the hands-off era in juvenile justice and recognized that at least minimal due process must be provided in juvenile court hearings (*Kent* v. *U.S.*, 383 U.S. 541 [1966]).

McKeiver v. *Pennsylvania.*   This case held that juveniles do not have the constitutional right to a jury trial (*McKeiver* v. *Pennsylvania*, 403 U.S. 528 [1971]).

Roper v. *Simmons.*   The court set a new standard in this case when it ruled that an offender is not eligible for the death penalty if committing the crime when younger than 18 (*Roper* v. *Simmons*, 543 U.S. 551 [2005]).

Schall v. *Martin.*   This case upheld the practice of preventive detention but stated that it cannot be imposed without prior notice, an equitable detention hearing, and a statement by the judge setting the reasons for the detention (*Schall* v. *Martin*, 467 U.S. 253 [1984]).

Learning Tips

Open-Book or Open-Note Exams

While an open-book or open-note test may seem extremely easy, these exams are often the most difficult. Significant preparation is even more imperative with these exams. To eliminate excess time spent flipping through pages of notes or chapters of a book, prepare thoroughly by marking pages, marking tabs, highlighting key words, including an outline in your notes, and knowing the progression of the notes or chapters backward and forward.

Short Answers

Short-answer questions usually ask for a definition or description and the significance of the question relative to the coursework. Problems arise when students go off on tangents and write everything they know on the topic. It is important to stay focused on the question, be brief, and answer the question directly. In addition, be sure to use facts and key words.

CJ Brief on the World Wide Web

Web links to organizations and agencies related to the material in Chapter 13 include:

WEBSITE TITLE	URL
American Bar Association's Juvenile Justice Center	http://www.abanet.org/crimjust /juvjus/home.html
Center on Juvenile and Criminal Justice (CJCJ)	http://www.cjcj.org
Juvenile Court Section Juvenile Justice (NCJRS)	http://www.virlib.ncjrs.org /JuvenileJustice.asp
The Juvenile Justice Clearinghouse	http://www.fsu.edu/~crimdo /jjclearinghouse
Juvenile Justice Magazine Online	http://www.juvenilejustice.com
National Council on Crime and Delinquency	http://www.nccd-crc.org
National Youth Gang Center (NYGC)	http://www.iir.com/nygc
Office of Juvenile Justice and Delinquency Prevention (OJJDP)	http://www.ojjdp.ncjrs.org
An Urban Ethnography of Latino Street Gangs	http://www.csun.edu/~hcchs006 /gang.html

Learner Activities

Activity 1

Youth violence has long been a concern for the criminal justice system. In the early 1900s, for example, legislators across the country decided that juvenile delinquents who commit a crime should be treated differently from adult criminals. Thus, the juvenile justice system was created with the important purpose of providing opportunities for juveniles to reform rather than strictly punishing them for their acts.

However, an increasing number of juveniles, some as young as 13, have been waived out of the juvenile justice system into adult court—13- and 14-year-old children are being sent to maximum-security prisons. Currently, it appears that the system is more concerned with punishing delinquents than reforming them. After reading about the juvenile justice system in Chapter 13, combined with what you learned about criminal justice in this class, do you think the juvenile justice system should be abolished? Why or why not?

_____

_____

_____

_____

_____

_____

Activity 2

There are many theories that might be helpful in attempting to explain juvenile delinquency. For example, some critics argue that the reliance on various sources of media by children is a major contributing cause of delinquency. Video games, cartoons, music—especially rap and heavy metal—and violence on television have all been criticized for poisoning the minds of youth. Do you think media images of violence cause children to become delinquents? Why or why not? What types of media images do you think are most harmful to children? Explain your answer. (Note that there is a very large body of research attempting to examine the links between viewing violence and committing violence. It may be helpful to visit the World Wide Web or your library to do some background reading on this topic).

_____

_____

_____

_____

_____

_____

Activity 3

Judge Gayle Garner has the following three juvenile cases on her docket:

1. Jarred Owens is a 17-year-old high school dropout. He has recently been convicted of two burglaries. His criminal record includes three other crimes: two shoplifting incidents and a theft. His parents are frustrated with his behavior and admit to having trouble controlling him. Jarred's two brothers are well behaved and have no criminal records.

2. Anne Yeerns is 15 years old and was convicted of attempting to steal a car. This was her first offense. However, she is also a runaway. On two prior occasions, she has run away from her father. The first time she went back home after three days, the second time the police brought her back after one week, and this time she claims she was stealing the car to get as far away as possible. Anne's father did not attend the dispositional hearing.

3. Patrick Darvy is 12 years old and was recently initiated into a juvenile gang. He was caught selling drugs; it was his first offense. Patrick lives with his mother, who is divorced. Ms. Darvy is very concerned about recent changes in his behavior and would like the court's help in changing his behavior.

Make a recommendation to Judge Garner for the dispositions of these three cases. Discuss the sentences you would recommend, and provide the rationale for your recommendations.

_____

_____

_____

_____

_____

Activity 4

Near the end of Chapter 13, the text discusses three ongoing efforts directed at reforming the juvenile justice system. These efforts include lessening the degree of privacy, increasing penalties for certain kinds of delinquent acts, and reducing diversionary opportunities for habitual, violent, and serious offenders. The President's Commission on Juvenile Justice would like you to recommend one of these reform efforts. In the space provided below, discuss which one of these reforms you think would have the most positive impact on the juvenile justice system and provide your rationale for excluding the other two reforms.

_____

_____

_____

_____

_____

_____

Internet Activity

Visit the Cybrary at http://www.cybrary.info. Click on the topic "Juvenile Justice," and review the sites that appear. Which of those sites is identified as one of the "Top 100" sites? Are there other juvenile justice sites that you think should be among the "Top 100" identified by the Cybrary? If so, use the feedback link at the bottom of the Cybrary's home page to tell the Cybrary staff what you think. Submit your findings to your instructor if requested to do so.

_____

_____

_____

_____

_____

_____

Distance Learning Activity

Visit the American Bar Association's website on juvenile justice issues at http://www.abanet.org/crimjust/juvjus/jjnews.html. Read one of the essays posted and provide a summary of its key ideas. If your instructor asks you to do so, participate in a class discussion that compares and contrasts the findings from the different essays.

_____

_____

_____

_____

_____

_____

Student Study Guide Questions

True or False

_____   13-1. Juveniles have a constitutional right to a jury trial.

_____   13-2. Roman Law created our current juvenile justice system by allowing special allowances for the age of the offender.

_____   13-3. The first house of refuge opened in Philadelphia in 1824.

_____   13-4. The provisions established in *Miranda* v. *Arizona* do not apply to juveniles.

_____   13-5. Very few juvenile correctional institutions are overcrowded.

_____   13-6. A delinquent child is one who has no parents or whose parents are unable to care for him or her.

_____   13-7. Juveniles charged with a status offense have the same procedural rights afforded to adults charged with a criminal offense.

_____   13-8. If a juvenile is charged as a status offender, his or her guilt must be proved using a preponderance of evidence standard.

_____   13-9. Juvenile trials are open to the public and to the news media.

_____   13-10. If a juvenile is charged with a criminal offense, his or her guilt must be proved beyond a reasonable doubt.

Multiple Choice

13-11. Which of the following was *not* emphasized by the reform school movement?
   a. the worth of hard work
   b. wholesome family environments
   c. affection necessary to build moral character
   d. All of the above were emphasized by the reform school movement.

13-12. According to *Roper* v. *Simmons*, at what age is an offender eligible for the death penalty?
   a. 18
   b. 16
   c. 14
   d. 21

13-13. Which of the following is *not* a status offense?
   a. truancy
   b. running away from home
   c. robbery
   d. incorrigibility

13-14. What is the evidentiary standard that must be met at a delinquency hearing?
   a. preponderance of the evidence
   b. beyond a reasonable doubt
   c. in most instances
   d. the "feel good" standard

13-15. Which of the following U.S. Supreme Court cases ruled that juveniles are entitled to representation by attorneys who must have access to their records when the juveniles are being transferred to adult court?
    a. *Breed* v. *Jones*
    b. *Schall* v. *Martin*
    c. *Kent* v. *U.S.*
    d. *Ex parte Crouse*

13-16. _____ children are defined as those who do not receive proper care from their parents or guardians.
    a. Dependent
    b. Neglected
    c. Abused
    d. Undisciplined

13-17. Teen court is
    a. a place where status offenders are given due process.
    b. another name of the juvenile justice system.
    c. a place where children ages 13–17 are tried.
    d. a place where alleged offenders are judged and sentenced by a jury of their peers.

13-18. Which step of the juvenile court process is similar to an adult trial?
    a. intake
    b. adjudication
    c. disposition
    d. postadjudicatory review

13-19. A common law principle that allows the state to assume a parental role and to take custody of a child who becomes delinquent, is abandoned, or is in need of care that the natural parents are unable or unwilling to provide is
    a. arrest.
    b. community outreach.
    c. *parens patriae.*
    d. intake.

13-20. Most states' juvenile court systems were modeled after the court system in which state?
    a. Indiana
    b. Illinois
    c. New York
    d. Ohio

Fill-In

13-21. The term applied to a child in order to avoid the stigma that comes from application of the term *criminal* is _____

13-22. A child who is beyond parental control, as evidenced by refusal to obey legitimate authorities such as school officials and teachers, is termed a(n) _____.

13-23. A(n) _____ is a youth at or below the upper age of juvenile court jurisdiction in a particular state.

13-24. A child who has been forced into delinquent activity by a parent or guardian is termed a(n) _____.

13-25. _____ is the principle that allows the state to assume a parental role.

13-26. _____ is the fact-finding process where the court determines whether or not there is sufficient evidence to sustain the allegations in a petition.

13-27. A document filed in juvenile court alleging that a juvenile is delinquent, a status offender, or a dependent and asking that the court assume jurisdiction over the child is a(n) _____.

13-28. A child who commits an act that is contrary to the law by virtue of the juvenile's status as a child is a(n) _____.

13-29. A child not receiving the proper level of physical or psychological care from parents is a(n) _____.

13-30. A child who has no parent(s) or whose parent(s) is (are) unable to care for him or her is a(n) _____.

Crossword Puzzle

Across

1. Child who is not receiving the proper level of physical or psychological care from his or her parents.
4. Juvenile court document.
6. When a juvenile breaks the law.
10. Child who has been physically, sexually, or mentally abused.
11. Child who has no parents or whose parents are unable to care for him or her.
12. Alternative approach to juvenile justice in which juvenile offenders are judged and sentenced by a jury of their peers.
15. Minors purchasing cigarettes, buying alcohol, and being truant are examples.
16. Term meaning the state assumes responsibility for the welfare of problem children.

17. Case that ended the Supreme Court's hands-off era in juvenile justice.

Down

2. First step of the juvenile justice process.
3. Child beyond parental control.
5. _____ v. *Martin*.
7. Final stage of the juvenile justice process.
8. System that responds to crimes committed by youthful offenders.
9. Juvenile justice hearing to determine whether there is sufficient evidence to sustain allegations.
13. _____ v. *Pennsylvania*.
14. Case that established that allegations of delinquency must be established beyond a reasonable doubt.

Word Search Puzzle

```
G J N X Z U P A R E N S P A T R I A E J W X T E W B K U C A
M X M M C E S D B Y A B U S E D C H I L D O N R S X R C B O
G S Z W A T U I H O L U Y H C K O N Q F Y G U Z K E N Y K W
N M Y K P J U V E N I L E J U S T I C E S Y S T E M M G D A
D D P N T T D W P S U N D I S C I P L I N E D C H I L D T D
Z G B S B P H O F X E C V P U B N B Z D P I O U J K T W F J
V B Y F S Y J U V E N I L E P E T I T I O N L W D U B J H U
Z F K I P Y K F J H U M K L C Q Z O V S G R Y M I A Y B Z D
Q H O M D G O T B B N K K K D Z X W R P M P R Z K J S V I
Q Y W J K S J D R L E Y S L E W J P S O T N B I R X I Y Z C
Y T E J G L U X S E R P R Y L F J G B S B E K V U W G O I A
H L V Y W D V Z I N E Q Y D I D V K E I J W E L L X W C B T
H X N J X V E N E D G F W I N L E E Q T U K W N X X T E T O
B K N E I A N D T E E I G G Q M H P K I B C S V C I X Z W R
K V W Z G D I X B D R Q B X U A X M E O V R I H D O R J V Y
B F F N I L L N W S M O G M E T R T U N Z X X P H K U P W H
T U B U Q S E J E E A G O V N F S Z R A D F Y N I I W R I E
J G E W L B D C O N M W C W T A T V Y L I E L O Y A V U T A
H L R Z C O I Y T T V X Y I C Y A D Q H A B N V L X X P M R
N Z R L N S S Z T E B B D F H A T S I E Z J U T J F Q L I I
W S N H F T P D L N D N D Q I B U J U A K M U T C J R S O N
D R E B F Q O G L C L C C V L K S P Z R W N T O I H O K M G
R M C A V Z S G J E X H H E D D O P A I Y O R Y P Q I V X I
D J L D N D I F Z T H F K I C P F F G N P V P V J E U L F Z
S Q G N O V T U F P S A B Y L K F H S G K V C L P X C R D T
S W S T H W I C Q T T Z L S I D E L I N Q U E N C Y U L P L
N I I W J X O N Q N C V C N C Q N T P N P V R Z S P C P X Z
H F W K V Y N A I W E G Z I V N D F M I I P X L F A H N E W
H T O E B W F S H Z K Y O S H K E Z U V I H U V X K W L Z C
Y W N Q C N F U G S H G W L Q Y R V B M G S V E J G J S U E
```

Abused Child	Juvenile Disposition
Adjudicatory Hearing	Juvenile Justice System
Blended Sentence	Juvenile Petition
Delinquency	Neglected Child
Delinquent Child	*Parens Patriae*
Dependent Child	Status Offender
Dispositional Hearing	Teen Court
Intake	Undisciplined Child

A Answers to Odd-Numbered Questions

Chapter 1

1-1. False
1-3. True
1-5. False
1-7. False
1-9. False
1-11. d
1-13. d
1-15. c
1-17. d
1-19. a
1-21. public-order advocate
1-23. Herbert Packer
1-25. criminal justice nonsystem
1-27. Social justice
1-29. bail

Chapter 2

2-1. False
2-3. True
2-5. True
2-7. False
2-9. True
2-11. d
2-13. a
2-15. e
2-17. b
2-19. d
2-21. Forcible rape
2-23. Date rape
2-25. Hate crimes
2-27. Cyberstalking
2-29. motor vehicle theft

Chapter 3

3-1. True
3-3. False
3-5. False
3-7. True
3-9. False
3-11. a
3-13. c
3-15. c
3-17. d
3-19. d
3-21. Civil law
3-23. M'Naghten rule
3-25. Durham rule
3-27. Jurisprudence
3-29. *Mens rea*

Chapter 4

4-1. False
4-3. False
4-5. True
4-7. False
4-9. True
4-11. d
4-13. d
4-15. c
4-17. a
4-19. a
4-21. watchman
4-23. Strategic policing
4-25. Directed patrol
4-27. Federal Bureau of Investigation
4-29. service

Chapter 5

5-1. True
5-3. False
5-5. False
5-7. True
5-9. False
5-11. d
5-13. b
5-15. b
5-17. c
5-19. a
5-21. *U.S.* v. *Leon*
5-23. *Aguilar* v. *Texas*
5-25. *Warden* v. *Hayden*
5-27. *Terry* v. *Ohio*
5-29. *Mapp* v. *Ohio*

Chapter 6

6-1. True
6-3. False
6-5. False
6-7. True
6-9. True
6-11. d
6-13. c
6-15. d
6-17. d
6-19. c
6-21. problem police officer
6-23. Use of force
6-25. biological weapon
6-27. Police corruption
6-29. *Bivens* action

Chapter 7

7-1. True
7-3. False
7-5. True
7-7. True
7-9. False
7-11. c
7-13. d
7-15. d
7-17. d
7-19. b
7-21. first appearance
7-23. Release on recognizance
7-25. Trial *de novo*
7-27. appellate jurisdiction
7-29. community court

Chapter 8

8-1. True
8-3. False
8-5. True
8-7. True
8-9. True
8-11. b
8-13. c
8-15. d
8-17. c
8-19. b
8-21. Circumstantial evidence
8-23. peremptory challenge
8-25. bailiff
8-27. Perjury
8-29. judge

Chapter 9

9-1. False
9-3. True
9-5. False
9-7. False
9-9. False
9-11. e
9-13. c
9-15. b
9-17. b
9-19. a
9-21. presentence investigation
9-23. rehabilitation
9-25. indeterminate sentencing
9-27. Determinate sentencing
9-29. Aggravating circumstances

Chapter 10

10-1. False
10-3. True
10-5. True

10-7. False

10-9. True

10-11. d

10-13. b

10-15. d

10-17. b

10-19. a

10-21. General conditions

10-23. revocation hearing

10-25. Home confinement

10-27. Shock incarceration

10-29. Community service

Chapter 11

11-1. False

11-3. False

11-5. False

11-7. False

11-9. False

11-11. c

11-13. a

11-15. d

11-17. a

11-19. d

11-21. Rated

11-23. Operational

11-25. Prison

11-27. Direct-supervision jails

11-29. justice model

Chapter 12

12-1. True

12-3. False

12-5. True

12-7. True

12-9. True

12-11. a

12-13. b

12-15. a

12-17. c

12-19. b

12-21. Prison argot

12-23. *Cruz* v. *Beto*

12-25. balancing test

12-27. hands-off doctrine

12-29. Civil death

Chapter 13

13-1. False

13-3. False

13-5. False

13.7. False

13.9. False

13-11. d

13-13. c

13-15. a

13-17. d

13-19. c

13-21. delinquent child

13-23. juvenile

13-25. *Parens patriae*

13-27. juvenile petition

13-29. neglected child

B The Constitution of the United States

WE THE PEOPLE of the United States, in Order to form a more perfect Union, establish Justice, insure domestic Tranquility, provide for the common defence, promote the general Welfare, and secure the Blessings of Liberty to ourselves and our Posterity, do ordain and establish this CONSTITUTION for the United States of America.

Article I.

SECTION 1. All legislative Powers herein granted shall be vested in a Congress of the United States, which shall consist of a Senate and House of Representatives.

SECTION 2. The House of Representatives shall be composed of Members chosen every second Year by the People of the several States, and the Electors in each State shall have the Qualifications requisite for Electors of the most numerous Branch of the State Legislature.

No Person shall be a Representative who shall not have attained to the Age of twenty-five Years, and been seven Years a Citizen of the United States, and who shall not, when elected, be an Inhabitant of that State in which he shall be chosen.

Representatives and direct Taxes shall be apportioned among the several States which may be included within this Union, according to their respective Numbers, which shall be determined by adding to the whole Number of free Persons, including those bound to Service for a Term of Years, and excluding Indians not taxed, three fifths of all other Persons. The actual Enumeration shall be made within three Years after the first Meeting of the Congress of the United States, and within every subsequent Term of ten Years, in such Manner as they shall by Law direct. The Number of Representatives shall not exceed one for every thirty Thousand, but each State shall have at Least one Representative; and until such enumeration shall be made, the State of New Hampshire shall be entitled to chuse three, Massachusetts eight, Rhode-Island and Providence Plantations one, Connecticut five, New York six, New Jersey four, Pennsylvania eight, Delaware one, Maryland six, Virginia ten, North Carolina five, South Carolina five, and Georgia three.

When vacancies happen in the representation from any State, the Executive Authority thereof shall issue Writs of Election to fill such Vacancies.

The House of Representatives shall chuse their Speaker and other Officers; and shall have the sole Power of Impeachment.

SECTION 3. The Senate of the United States shall be composed of two Senators from each State, chosen by the Legislature thereof for six Years; and each Senator shall have one Vote.

Immediately after they shall be assembled in Consequence of the first Election, they shall be divided as equally as may be into three Classes. The Seats of the Senators of the first Class shall be vacated at the Expiration of the second Year, of the second Class at the Expiration of the fourth Year, and of the third Class at the

Expiration of the sixth Year, so that one third may be chosen every second Year; and if Vacancies happen by Resignation, or otherwise, during the recess of the Legislature of any State, the Executive thereof may make temporary Appointments until the next Meeting of the Legislature, which shall then fill such Vacancies.

No Person shall be Senator who shall not have attained to the Age of thirty Years, and been nine Years a Citizen of the United States, and who shall not, when elected, be an Inhabitant of that State for which he shall be chosen.

The Vice President of the United States shall be President of the Senate, but shall have no Vote, unless they be equally divided.

The Senate shall chuse their other Officers, and also a President pro tempore, in the absence of the Vice President, or when he shall exercise the Office of President of the United States.

The Senate shall have the sole Power to try all Impeachments. When sitting for that Purpose, they shall be on Oath or Affirmation. When the President of the United States is tried, the Chief Justice shall preside: And no Person shall be convicted without the Concurrence of two thirds of the Members present.

Judgment in Cases of Impeachment shall not extend further than to removal from Office, and disqualification to hold and enjoy any Office of honor, Trust, or Profit under the United States: but the Party convicted shall nevertheless be liable and subject to Indictment, Trial, Judgment and Punishment, according to Law.

SECTION 4. The Times, Places and Manner of holding Elections for Senators and Representatives, shall be prescribed in each State by the Legislature thereof; but the Congress may at any time by Law make or alter such Regulations, except as to the Place of chusing Senators.

The Congress shall assemble at least once in every Year, and such Meeting shall be on the first Monday in December, unless they shall by law appoint a different Day.

SECTION 5. Each House shall be the Judge of the Elections, Returns and Qualifications of its own Members, and a Majority of each shall constitute a Quorum to do Business; but a smaller Number may adjourn from day to day, and may be authorized to compel the Attendance of absent Members, in such Manner, and under such Penalties as each House may provide.

Each House may determine the Rules of its Proceedings, punish its Members for disorderly Behaviour, and, with the Concurrence of two thirds, expel a Member.

Each House shall keep a Journal of its Proceedings, and from time to time publish the same, excepting such Parts as may in their Judgment require Secrecy; and the Yeas and Nays of the Members of either House on any question shall, at the Desire of one fifth of those Present, be entered on the journal.

Neither House, during the Session of Congress, shall, without the Consent of the other, adjourn for more than three days, nor to any other Place than that in which the two Houses shall be sitting.

SECTION 6. The Senators and Representatives shall receive a Compensation for their Services, to be ascertained by Law, and paid out of the Treasury of the United States. They shall in all Cases, except Treason, Felony and Breach of the Peace, be privileged from Arrest during their Attendance at the Session of their respective Houses, and in going to and returning from the same; and for any Speech or Debate in either House, they shall not be questioned in any other Place.

No Senator or Representative shall, during the Time for which he was elected, be appointed to any civil Office under the Authority of the United States, which shall have been created, or the Emoluments whereof shall have been encreased during such time; and no Person holding any Office under the United States, shall be a Member of either House during his Continuance in Office.

SECTION 7. All Bills for raising Revenue shall originate in the House of Representatives; but the Senate may propose or concur with Amendments as on other Bills.

Every Bill which shall have passed the House of Representatives and the Senate, shall, before it become a Law, be presented to the President of the United

States; If he approve he shall sign it, but if not he shall return it, with his Objections to that House in which it shall have originated, who shall enter the Objections at large on their Journal, and proceed to reconsider it. If after such Reconsideration two thirds of that House shall agree to pass the Bill, it shall be sent, together with the Objections, to the other House, by which it shall likewise be reconsidered, and if approved by two thirds of that House, it shall become a Law. But in all such Cases the Votes of both Houses shall be determined by Yeas and Nays, and the Names of the Persons voting for and against the Bill shall be entered on the Journal of each House respectively. If any Bill shall not be returned by the President within ten Days (Sundays excepted) after it shall have been presented to him, the Same shall be a Law, in like Manner as if he had signed it, unless the Congress by their Adjournment prevent its Return, in which Case it shall not be a Law.

Every Order, Resolution, or Vote to which the Concurrence of the Senate and House of Representatives may be necessary (except on a question of Adjournment) shall be presented to the President of the United States; and before the Same shall take Effect, shall be approved by him, or being disapproved by him, shall be repassed by two thirds of the Senate and House of Representatives, according to the Rules and Limitations prescribed in the Case of a Bill.

SECTION 8. The Congress shall have Power to lay and collect Taxes, Duties, Imposts and Excises, to pay the Debts and provide for the common Defence and general Welfare of the United States; but all Duties, Imposts and Excises shall be uniform throughout the United States;

To borrow Money on the credit of the United States;

To regulate Commerce with foreign Nations, and among the several States, and with the Indian Tribes;

To establish an uniform Rule of Naturalization, and uniform Laws on the subject of Bankruptcies throughout the United States;

To coin Money, regulate the Value thereof, and of foreign Coin, and fix the Standard of Weights and Measures;

To provide for the Punishment of counterfeiting the Securities and current Coin of the United States;

To establish Post Offices and post Roads;

To promote the Progress of Science and useful Arts, by securing for limited times to Authors and Inventors the exclusive Right to their respective Writings and Discoveries;

To constitute Tribunals inferior to the supreme Court;

To define and punish Piracies and Felonies committed on the high Seas, and Offences against the Law of Nations;

To declare War, grant Letters of Marque and Reprisal, and make Rules concerning Captures on Land and Water;

To raise and support Armies, but no Appropriation of Money to that Use shall be for a longer Term than two Years;

To provide and maintain a Navy;

To make Rules for the Government and Regulation of the land and naval Forces;

To provide for calling forth the Militia to execute the Laws of the Union, suppress Insurrections and repel Invasions;

To provide for organizing, arming, and disciplining the Militia, and for governing such Part of them as may be employed in the Service of the United States, reserving to the States respectively, the Appointment of the Officers, and the Authority of training the Militia according to the discipline prescribed by Congress;

To exercise exclusive Legislation in all Cases whatsoever, over such District (not exceeding ten Miles square) as may, by Cession of particular States, and the Acceptance of Congress, become the Seat of the Government of the United States, and to exercise like Authority over all Places purchased by the Consent of the Legislature of the State in which the Same shall be, for the Erection of Forts, Magazines, and Arsenals, dock-Yards, and other needful Buildings;—And

To make all Laws which shall be necessary and proper for carrying into Execution the foregoing Powers, and all other Powers vested by this Constitution in the Government of the United States, or in any Department or Officer thereof.

SECTION 9. The Migration or Importation of such Persons as any of the States now existing shall think proper to admit, shall not be prohibited by the Congress prior to the Year one thousand eight hundred and eight, but a Tax or duty may be imposed on such Importation, not exceeding ten dollars for each Person.

The privilege of the Writ of Habeas Corpus shall not be suspended, unless when in Cases of Rebellion or Invasion the public Safety may require it.

No Bill of Attainder or ex post facto Law shall be passed.

No Capitation, or other direct, Tax shall be laid, unless in Proportion to the Census or Enumeration herein before directed to be taken.

No Tax or Duty shall be laid on Articles exported from any State.

No Preference shall be given by any Regulation of Commerce or Revenue to the Ports of one State over those of another: nor shall Vessels bound to, or from, one State, be obliged to enter, clear, or pay Duties in another.

No Money shall be drawn from the Treasury, but in Consequence of Appropriations made by Law; and a regular Statement and Account of the Receipts and Expenditures of all public Money shall be published from time to time.

No Title of Nobility shall be granted by the United States: And no Person holding any Office of Profit or Trust under them, shall, without the Consent of the Congress, accept of any present, Emolument, Office, or Title, of any kind whatever, from any King, Prince, or foreign State.

SECTION 10. No State shall enter into any Treaty, Alliance, or Confederation; grant Letters of Marque and Reprisal; coin Money; emit Bills of Credit; make any Thing but gold and silver Coin a Tender in Payment of Debts; pass any Bill of Attainder, ex post facto Law, or Law impairing the Obligation of Contracts, or grant any Title of Nobility.

No State shall, without the consent of the Congress, lay any Imposts or Duties on Imports or Exports, except what may be absolutely necessary for executing it's inspection Laws: and the net Produce of all Duties and Imposts, laid by any State on Imports or Exports, shall be for the Use of the Treasury of the United States; and all such Laws shall be subject to the Revision and Control of the Congress.

No State shall, without the Consent of Congress, lay any Duty of Tonnage, keep Troops, or Ships of War in time of Peace, enter into any Agreement or Compact with another State, or with a foreign Power, or engage in War, unless actually invaded, or in such imminent Danger as will not admit of delay.

Article II.

SECTION 1. The executive Power shall be vested in a President of the United States of America. He shall hold his Office during the Term of four Years, and, together with the Vice President, chosen for the same Term, be elected, as follows

Each State shall appoint, in such Manner as the Legislature thereof may direct, a Number of Electors, equal to the whole Number of Senators and Representatives to which the State may be entitled in the Congress: but no Senator or Representative, or Person holding an Office of Trust or Profit under the United States, shall be appointed an Elector.

The Electors shall meet in their respective States, and vote by Ballot for two persons, of whom one at least shall not be an Inhabitant of the same State with themselves. And they shall make a List of all the Persons voted for, and of the Number of Votes for each; which List they shall sign and certify, and transmit sealed to the Seat of the Government of the United States, directed to the President of the Senate. The President of the Senate shall, in the Presence of the Senate and House of Representatives, open all the Certificates, and the Votes shall then be counted. The Person having the greatest Number of Votes shall be the President, if such

Number be a Majority of the whole Number of Electors appointed; and if there be more than one who have such Majority, and have an equal Number of Votes, then the House of Representatives shall immediately chuse by Ballot one of them for President; and if no Person have a Majority, then from the five highest on the List the said House shall in like Manner chuse the President. But in choosing the President, the Votes shall be taken by States, the Representation from each State having one Vote; A quorum for this Purpose shall consist of a Member or Members from two thirds of the States, and a Majority of all the States shall be necessary to a Choice. In every Case, after the Choice of the President, the Person having the greatest Number of Votes of the Electors shall be the Vice President. But if there should remain two or more who have equal Votes, the Senate shall chuse from them by Ballot the Vice President.

The Congress may determine the Time of chusing the Electors, and the Day on which they shall give their Votes; which Day shall be the same throughout the United States.

No person except a natural born Citizen, or a Citizen of the United States, at the time of Adoption of this Constitution, shall be eligible to the Office of President; neither shall any Person be eligible to that Office who shall not have attained to the Age of thirty five Years, and been fourteen Years a Resident within the United States.

In Case of the Removal of the President from Office, or of his Death, Resignation, or Inability to discharge the Powers and Duties of the said Office, the same shall devolve on the Vice President, and the Congress may by Law provide for the Case of Removal, Death, Resignation or Inability, both of the President and Vice President, declaring what Officer shall then act as President, and such Officer shall act accordingly, until the Disability be removed, or a President shall be elected.

The President shall, at stated Times, receive for his Services, a Compensation, which shall neither be encreased nor diminished during the Period for which he shall have been elected, and he shall not receive within that Period any other Emolument from the United States, or any of them.

Before he enter on the Execution of his Office, he shall take the following Oath or Affirmation:—"I do solemnly swear (or affirm) that I will faithfully execute the Office of President of the United States, and will to the best of my Ability, preserve, protect and defend the Constitution of the United States."

SECTION 2. The President shall be Commander in Chief of the Army and Navy of the United States, and of the Militia of the several States, when called into the actual Service of the United States; he may require the Opinion in writing, of the principal Officer in each of the executive Departments, upon any subject relating to the Duties of their respective Offices, and he shall have Power to grant Reprieves and Pardons for Offenses against the United States, except in Cases of Impeachment.

He shall have Power, by and with the Advice and Consent of the Senate, to make Treaties, provided two thirds of the Senators present concur; and he shall nominate, and by and with the Advice and Consent of the Senate, shall appoint Ambassadors, other public Ministers and Consuls, Judges of the supreme Court, and all other Officers of the United States, whose Appointments are not herein otherwise provided for, and which shall be established by Law: but the Congress may by Law vest the Appointment of such inferior Officers, as they think proper, in the President alone, in the courts of Law, and in the Heads of Departments.

The President shall have Power to fill up all Vacancies that may happen during the Recess of the Senate, by granting Commissions which shall expire at the End of their next Session.

SECTION 3. He shall from time to time give to the Congress Information of the State of the Union, and recommend to their Consideration such Measures as he shall judge necessary and expedient; he may, on extraordinary Occasions, convene both Houses, or either of them, and in Case of Disagreement between them, with Respect to the Time of Adjournment, he may adjourn them to such Time as he shall think proper; he shall receive Ambassadors and other public Ministers; he shall take Care that the Laws be faithfully executed, and Shall Commission all the Officers of the United States.

SECTION 4. The President, Vice President and all civil Officers of the United States, shall be removed from Office on Impeachment for, and Conviction of, Treason, Bribery, or other high Crimes and Misdemeanors.

Article III.

SECTION 1. The judicial Power of the United States, shall be vested in one supreme Court, and in such inferior Courts as the Congress may from time to time ordain and establish. The Judges, both of the supreme and inferior Courts, shall hold their Offices during good Behavior, and shall, at stated Times, receive for their Services, a Compensation, which shall not be diminished during their Continuance in Office.

SECTION 2. The judicial Power shall extend to all Cases, in Law and Equity, arising under this Constitution, the Laws of the United States, and Treaties made, or which shall be made, under their Authority;—to all Cases affecting Ambassadors, other public Ministers and Consuls;—to all Cases of admiralty and maritime Jurisdiction;—to Controversies to which the United States shall be a Party;—to Controversies between two or more States;—between a State and Citizens of another State;—between citizens of different States;—between Citizens of the same State claiming Lands under Grants of different States, and between a State, or the Citizens thereof, and foreign States, Citizens or Subjects.

In all Cases affecting Ambassadors, other public Ministers and Consuls, and those in which a State shall be Party, the supreme Court shall have original Jurisdiction. In all the other Cases before mentioned, the supreme Court shall have appellate Jurisdiction, both as to Law and Fact, with such exceptions, and under such Regulations as the Congress shall make.

The Trial of all Crimes, except in Cases of Impeachment, shall be by Jury; and such Trial shall be held in the State where the said Crimes shall have been committed; but when not committed within any State, the Trial shall be at such Place or Places as the Congress may by Law have directed.

SECTION 3. Treason against the United States, shall consist only in levying War against them, or in adhering to their Enemies, giving them Aid and Comfort. No Person shall be convicted of Treason unless on the Testimony of two Witnesses to the same overt Act, or on Confession in open Court.

The Congress shall have Power to declare the Punishment of Treason, but no Attainder of Treason shall work Corruption of Blood, or Forfeiture except during the Life of the Person attainted.

Article IV.

SECTION 1. Full Faith and Credit shall be given in each State to the public Acts, Records, and judicial Proceedings of every other State. And the Congress may by general Laws prescribe the Manner in which such Acts, Records and Proceedings shall be proved, and the Effect thereof.

SECTION 2. The Citizens of each State shall be entitled to all Privileges and Immunities of Citizens in the several States.

A Person charged in any State with Treason, Felony, or other Crime, who shall flee from Justice, and be found in another State, shall on Demand of the executive Authority of the State from which he fled, be delivered up, to be removed to the State having Jurisdiction of the Crime.

No Person held to Service or Labour in one State, under the Laws thereof, escaping into another, shall, in Consequence of any Law or Regulation therein, be discharged from such Service or Labour, but shall be delivered up on Claim of the Party to whom such Service or Labour may be due.

SECTION 3. New States may be admitted by the Congress into this Union; but no new State shall be formed or erected within the Jurisdiction of any other State; nor any State be formed by the Junction of two or more States, or parts of States, without the Consent of the Legislatures of the States concerned as well as of the Congress.

The Congress shall have Power to dispose of and make all needful Rules and Regulations respecting the Territory or other Property belonging to the United States; and nothing in this Constitution shall be so construed as to Prejudice any Claims of the United States, or of any particular State.

SECTION 4. The United States shall guarantee to every State in this Union a Republican Form of Government, and shall protect each of them against Invasion; and on Application of the Legislature, or of the Executive (when the Legislature cannot be convened) against domestic Violence.

Article V.

The Congress, whenever two thirds of both Houses shall deem it necessary, shall propose Amendments to this Constitution, or, on the Application of the Legislatures of two thirds of the several States, shall call a Convention for proposing Amendments, which, in either Case, shall be valid to all Intents and Purposes, as Part of this Constitution, when ratified by the Legislatures of three fourths of the several States, or by Conventions in three fourths thereof, as the one or the other Mode of Ratification may be proposed by the Congress; Provided that no Amendment which may be made prior to the Year One thousand eight hundred and eight shall in any Manner affect the first and fourth Clauses in the Ninth Section of the first Article; and that no State, without its Consent, shall be deprived of its equal Suffrage in the Senate.

Article VI.

All Debts contracted and Engagements entered into, before the Adoption of this Constitution, shall be as valid against the United States under this Constitution, as under the Confederation.

This Constitution, and the Laws of the United States which shall be made in Pursuance thereof; and all Treaties made, or which shall be made, under the Authority of the United States, shall be the supreme Law of the Land; and the Judges in every State shall be bound thereby; any Thing in the Constitution or Laws of any State to the Contrary notwithstanding.

The Senators and Representatives before mentioned, and the Members of the several State Legislatures, and all executive and judicial Officers, both of the United States and of the several States, shall be bound by Oath or Affirmation, to support this Constitution; but no religious Test shall ever be required as a Qualification to any Office or public Trust under the United States.

Article VII.

The Ratification of the Conventions of nine States shall be sufficient for the Establishment of this Constitution between the States so ratifying the Same.

Articles in Addition to, and Amendment of, the Constitution of the United States of America, Proposed by Congress, and Ratified by the Legislatures of the Several States, Pursuant to the Fifth Article of the Original Constitution.

Amendment I. (1791)

Congress shall make no law respecting an establishment of religion, or prohibiting the free exercise thereof; or abridging the freedom of speech, or of the press; or the right of the people peaceably to assemble, and to petition the Government for a redress of grievances.

Amendment II. (1791)

A well regulated Militia, being necessary to the security of a free State, the right of the people to keep and bear Arms, shall not be infringed.

Amendment III. (1791)

No Soldier shall, in time of peace be quartered in any house, without the consent of the Owner, nor in time of war, but in a manner to be prescribed by law.

Amendment IV. (1791)

The right of the people to be secure in their persons, houses, papers, and effects, against unreasonable searches and seizures, shall not be violated, and no Warrants shall issue, but upon probable cause, supported by Oath or affirmation, and particularly describing the place to be searched, and the persons or things to be seized.

Amendment V. (1791)

No person shall be held to answer for a capital, or otherwise infamous crime, unless on a presentment or indictment of a Grand Jury, except in cases arising in the land or naval forces, or in the Militia, when in actual service in time of War or public danger; nor shall any person be subject for the same offence to be twice put in jeopardy of life or limb; nor shall be compelled in any criminal case to be a witness against himself, nor be deprived of life, liberty, or property, without due process of law; nor shall private property be taken for public use, without just compensation.

Amendment VI. (1791)

In all criminal prosecutions, the accused shall enjoy the right to a speedy and public trial, by an impartial jury of the State and district wherein the crime shall have been committed, which district shall have been previously ascertained by law, and to be informed of the nature and cause of the accusation; to be confronted with the witnesses against him; to have compulsory process for obtaining Witnesses in his favor, and to have the Assistance of Counsel for his defence.

Amendment VII. (1791)

In Suits at common law, where the value in controversy shall exceed twenty dollars, the right of trial by jury shall be preserved, and no fact tried by a jury, shall be otherwise reexamined in any Court of the United States, than according to the rules of the common law.

Amendment VIII. (1791)

Excessive bail shall not be required, nor excessive fines imposed, nor cruel and unusual punishments inflicted.

Amendment IX. (1791)

The enumeration of the Constitution, of certain rights, shall not be construed to deny or disparage others retained by the people.

Amendment X. (1791)

The powers not delegated to the United States by the Constitution, nor prohibited by it to the States, are reserved to the States respectively, or to the people.

Amendment XI. (1798)

The Judicial power of the United States shall not be construed to extend to any suit in law or equity, commenced or prosecuted against one of the United States by Citizens of another State, or by Citizens or Subjects of any Foreign State.

Amendment XII. (1804)

The Electors shall meet in their respective states and vote by ballot for President and Vice-President, one of whom, at least, shall not be an inhabitant of the same state with themselves; they shall name in their ballots the person voted for as President, and in distinct ballots the person voted for as Vice-President, and they shall make distinct lists of all persons voted for as President, and of all persons voted for as Vice-President, and of the number of votes for each, which lists they shall sign and certify, and transmit sealed to the seat of the government of the United States, directed to the President of the Senate;—The President of the Senate shall, in the presence of the Senate and House of Representatives, open all the certificates and the votes shall then be counted;—The person having the greatest number of votes for President, shall be the President, if such number be a majority of the whole number of Electors appointed; and if no person have such majority, then from the persons having the highest numbers not exceeding three on the list of those voted for as President, the House of Representatives shall choose immediately, by ballot, the President. But in choosing the President, the votes shall be taken by states, the representation from each state having one vote; a quorum for this purpose shall consist of a member or members from two-thirds of the states, and a majority of all the states shall be necessary to a choice. And if the House of Representatives shall not choose a President whenever the right of choice shall devolve upon them, before the fourth day of March next following, then the Vice-President shall act as President, as in the case of the death or other constitutional disability of the President. The person having the greatest number of votes as Vice-President, shall be the Vice-President, if such number be a majority of the whole number of Electors appointed, and if no person have a majority, then from the two highest numbers on the list, the Senate shall choose the Vice-President; a quorum for the purpose shall consist of two-thirds of the whole number of Senators, and a majority of the whole number shall be necessary to a choice. But no person constitutionally ineligible to the office of President shall be eligible to that of Vice-President of the United States.

Amendment XIII. (1865)

SECTION 1. Neither slavery nor involuntary servitude, except as a punishment for crime whereof the party shall have been duly convicted, shall exist within the United States, or any place subject to their jurisdiction.

SECTION 2. Congress shall have power to enforce this article by appropriate legislation.

Amendment XIV. (1868)

SECTION 1. All persons born or naturalized in the United States, and subject to the jurisdiction thereof, are citizens of the United States and of the State wherein they reside. No State shall make or enforce any law which shall abridge the privileges or immunities of citizens of the United States; nor shall any State deprive any person of life, liberty, or property, without due process of law; nor deny to any person within its jurisdiction the equal protection of the law.

SECTION 2. Representatives shall be apportioned among the several States according to their respective numbers, counting the whole number of persons in each State, excluding Indians not taxed. But when the right to vote at any election for the choice of electors for President and Vice-President of the United States, Representatives in Congress, the Executive and Judicial officers of a State, or the members of the Legislature thereof, is denied to any of the male inhabitants of such State, being twenty-one years of age, and citizens of the United States, or in any way abridged, except for participation in rebellion, or other crime, the basis of representation therein shall be reduced in the proportion which the number of such male citizens shall bear to the whole number of male citizens twenty-one years of age in such State.

SECTION 3. No person shall be a Senator or Representative in Congress, or elector of President and Vice-President, or hold any office, civil or military, under the United States, or under any State, who, having previously taken an oath, as a member of Congress, or as an officer of the United States, or as a member of any State legislature, or as an executive or judicial officer of any State, to support the Constitution of the United States, shall have engaged in insurrection or rebellion against the same, or given aid or comfort to the enemies thereof. But Congress may by a vote of two-thirds of each House, remove such disability.

SECTION 4. The validity of the public debt of the United States, authorized by law, including debts incurred for payment of pensions and bounties for services in suppressing insurrection or rebellion, shall not be questioned. But neither the United States nor any State shall assume or pay any debt or obligation incurred in aid of insurrection or rebellion against the United States, or any claim for the loss or emancipation of any slave; but all such debts, obligations and claims shall be held illegal and void.

SECTION 5. The Congress shall have power to enforce, by appropriate legislation, the provisions of this article.

Amendment XV. (1870)

SECTION 1. The right of citizens of the United States to vote shall not be denied or abridged by the United States or by any State on account of race, color, or previous condition of servitude.

SECTION 2. The Congress shall have power to enforce this article by appropriate legislation.

Amendment XVI. (1913)

The Congress shall have power to lay and collect taxes on incomes, from whatever source derived, without apportionment among the several States, and without regard to any census or enumeration.

Amendment XVII. (1913)

The Senate of the United States shall be composed of two Senators from each State, elected by the people thereof, for six years; and each Senator shall have one vote. The electors in each State shall have the qualifications requisite for electors of the most numerous branch of the State legislatures.

When vacancies happen in the representation of any State in the Senate, the executive authority of such State shall issue writs of election to fill such vacancies: *Provided*, That the legislature of any State may empower the executive thereof to make temporary appointments until the people fill the vacancies by election as the legislature may direct.

This amendment shall not be so construed as to affect the election or term of any Senator chosen before it becomes valid as part of the Constitution.

Amendment XVIII. (1919)

SECTION 1. After one year from the ratification of this article the manufacture, sale, or transportation of intoxicating liquors within, the importation thereof into, or the exportation thereof from the United States and all territory subject to the jurisdiction thereof for beverage purposes is hereby prohibited.

SECTION 2. The Congress and the several States shall have concurrent power to enforce this article by appropriate legislation.

SECTION 3. This article shall be inoperative unless it shall have been ratified as an amendment to the Constitution by the legislatures of the several States, as provided in the Constitution, within seven years from the date of the submission hereof to the States by the Congress.

Amendment XIX. (1920)

The right of citizens of the United States to vote shall not be denied or abridged by the United States or by any State on account of sex.

Congress shall have power to enforce this article by appropriate legislation.

Amendment XX. (1933)

SECTION 1. The terms of the President and Vice President shall end at noon on the 20th day of January, and the terms of Senators and representatives at noon on the 3d day of January, of the years in which such terms would have ended if this article had not been ratified; and the terms of their successors shall then begin.

SECTION 2. The Congress shall assemble at least once in every year, and such meeting shall begin at noon on the 3d day of January, unless they shall by law appoint a different day.

SECTION 3. If, at the time fixed for the beginning of the term of the President, the President elect shall have died, the Vice President elect shall become President. If a President shall not have been chosen before the time fixed for the beginning of his term, or if the President elect shall have failed to qualify, then the Vice President elect shall act as President until a President shall have qualified; and the Congress may by law provide for the case wherein neither a President elect nor a Vice President elect shall have qualified, declaring who shall then act as President, or the manner in which one who is to act shall be selected, and such person shall act accordingly until a President or Vice President shall have qualified.

SECTION 4. The Congress may by law provide for the case of the death of any of the persons from whom the House of Representatives may choose a President whenever the right of choice shall have devolved upon them, and for the case of the death of any of the persons from whom the Senate may choose a Vice President whenever the right of choice shall have devolved upon them.

SECTION 5. Sections 1 and 2 shall take effect on the 15th day of October following the ratification of this article.

SECTION 6. This article shall be inoperative unless it shall have been ratified as an amendment to the Constitution by the legislatures of three-fourths of the several States within seven years from the date of submission.

Amendment XXI. (1933)

SECTION 1. The eighteenth article of amendment to the Constitution of the United States is hereby repealed.

SECTION 2. The transportation or importation into any State, Territory, or possession of the United States for delivery or use therein of intoxicating liquors, in violation of the laws thereof, is hereby prohibited.

SECTION 3. This article shall be inoperative unless it shall have been ratified as an amendment to the Constitution by conventions in the several States, as provided in the Constitution, within seven years from the date of the submission hereof to the States by the Congress.

Amendment XXII. (1951)

SECTION 1. No person shall be elected to the office of the President more than twice, and no person who has held the office of President, or acted as President, for more than two years of a term to which some other person was elected president shall be elected to the office of the President more than once. But this Article shall not apply to any person holding office of President when this Article was proposed by the Congress, and shall not prevent any person who may be holding the office of President, or acting as President, during the term within which this Article becomes operative from holding the office of President or acting as President during the remainder of such term.

SECTION 2. The article shall be inoperative unless it shall have been ratified as an amendment to the Constitution by the legislatures of three-fourths of the several States within seven years from the date of its submission to the States by the Congress.

Amendment XXIII. (1961)

SECTION 1. The District constituting the seat of Government of the United States shall appoint in such manner as the Congress may direct:

A number of electors of President and Vice President equal to the whole number of Senators and Representatives in Congress to which the District would be entitled if it were a State, but in no event more than the least populous State; they shall be in addition to those appointed by the States, but they shall be considered, for the purposes of the election of President and Vice President, to be electors appointed by a State; and they shall meet in the District and perform such duties as provided by the twelfth article of amendment.

SECTION 2. The Congress shall have power to enforce this article by appropriate legislation.

Amendment XXIV. (1964)

SECTION 1. The right of citizens of the United States to vote in any primary or other election for President or Vice President, for electors for President or Vice President, or for Senator or Representative in Congress, shall not be denied or abridged by the United States or any State by reason of failing to pay any poll tax or other tax.

SECTION 2. The Congress shall have power to enforce this article by appropriate legislation.

Amendment XXV. (1967)

SECTION 1. In case of the removal of the President from office or of his death or resignation, the Vice President shall become President.

SECTION 2. Whenever there is a vacancy in the office of the Vice President, the President shall nominate a Vice President who shall take office upon confirmation by a majority vote of both Houses of Congress.

SECTION 3. Whenever the President transmits to the President pro tempore of the Senate and the Speaker of the House of Representatives his written declaration that he is unable to discharge the powers and duties of his office, and until he transmits to them a written declaration to the contrary, such powers and duties shall be discharged by the Vice President as Acting President.

SECTION 4. Whenever the Vice President and a majority of either the principal officers of the executive departments or of such other body as Congress may by law provide, transmit to the President pro tempore of the Senate and the Speaker of the House of Representatives their written declaration that the President is unable to discharge the powers and duties of his office, the Vice President shall immediately assume the powers and duties of the office as Acting President.

Thereafter, when the President transmits to the President pro tempore of the Senate and the Speaker of the House of Representatives his written declaration that no inability exists, he shall resume the powers and duties of his office unless the Vice President and a majority of either the principal officers of the executive department or of such other body as Congress may by law provide, transmit within four days to the President pro tempore of the Senate and the Speaker of the House of Representatives their written declaration that the President is unable to discharge the powers and duties of his office. Thereupon Congress shall decide the issue, assembling within forty-eight hours for that purpose if not in session. If the Congress, within twenty-one days after receipt of the latter written declaration, or, if Congress is not in session, within twenty-one days after Congress is required to assemble, determines by two-thirds vote of both Houses that the President is unable to discharge the powers and duties of his office, the Vice President shall continue to discharge the same as Acting President; otherwise, the President shall resume the powers and duties of his office.

Amendment XXVI. (1971)

SECTION 1. The right of citizens of the United States, who are eighteen years of age or older, to vote shall not be denied or abridged by the United States or by any State on account of age.

SECTION 2. The Congress shall have power to enforce this article by appropriate legislation.

Amendment XXVII. (1992)

No law, varying the compensation for the services of the Senators and Representatives, shall take effect, until an election of Representatives shall have intervened.